Business and Finance

Business and Finance
for BTEC and GNVQ

Gill Clarke
and
Roger Lewis

Editor: Richard Latham

Stanley Thornes (Publishers) Ltd

First published in 1992 by:
Stanley Thornes (Publishers) Ltd.
Old Station Drive
Leckhampton
CHELTENHAM   GL53 0DN
England

A catalogue record for this book is available from the British Library.

ISBN 0–7487–1400–6

Typeset by Northern Phototypesetting Co Ltd., Bolton.
Printed and bound in Great Britain at Scotprint Ltd., Musselburgh.

Contents

How Business and Finance covers the BTEC First Modules

		Core Module 1				Core Module 2					Core Module 3				Core Module 4				
		1.1	1.2	1.3	1.4	2.1	2.2	2.3	2.4	2.5	3.1	3.2	3.3	3.4	4.1	4.2	4.3	4.4	4.5
Chapter 1	Personal organiser						•			•				•					•
Chapter 2	Starting work	•													•	•	•	•	
Chapter 3	The business world		•	•	•													•	
Chapter 4	Europe live	•		•	•		•	•		•								•	
Chapter 5	Sales and marketing				•	•	•	•		•							•	•	
Chapter 6	Communication and reception				•		•	•	•	•							•	•	
Chapter 7	Office organisation					•	•		•			•		•	•		•		
Chapter 8	Business documents	•			•		•	•	•		•		•		•		•	•	
Chapter 9	Production						•	•	•		•								
Chapter 10	Stock control					•	•	•				•		•					
Chapter 11	Financial payments									•		•		•					
Chapter 12	Keeping the books	•		•			•	•	•		•		•				•	•	
Chapter 13	Personnel					•	•	•	•				•	•	•	•	•	•	•
Chapter 14	Paying the wages					•		•					•	•	•		•	•	
Chapter 15	Meetings and travel arrangements					•	•	•	•	•		•		•			•	•	•

vi

How to use this book

We hope that this book is different from other study books. We hope you will find it easy to follow and interesting. It involves you in doing a lot of things other than sitting and reading. Doing them will help you to learn and become competent. So don't just sit and read – get active.

Each chapter, with the exception of Chapter 1, starts with an assignment. The idea is that you should do the assignment, either on your own or with school/college or work friends. The other material in the chapter is there to help you to do the assignment. This material is in the form of 'activities' for you to undertake *before* the assignment and background information and 'file facts'.

At the beginning of each chapter is a summary of what is covered (in whole or part) by the chapter and which you can use as a guide in claiming achievement of outcomes.

Summary

This chapter introduces you to the BTEC First Diploma in Business and Finance and helps you to be a better learner. You are introduced to the type of learning on a BTEC course by a series of short assignments. The following topics are covered:

▸ Introduction to the BTEC First Diploma
▸ Self assessment exercises: Personal finance
  Planning and problem solving, Communication,
  Self knowledge, Skill audit, The library

We think that it is important to do this chapter before you attempt other chapters in the book.

This chapter will help you to achieve the following outcomes:

Core Module 2   Administrative Systems and Procedures
Outcome 2.2   Identify and use different communication systems and methods of a selected organisation
Outcome 2.5   Understand the importance of maintaining and developing good business relationships with callers, customers/clients and colleagues

Core Module 3   Business Resources and Procedures
Outcome 3.4   Investigate and apply simple measures of performance

Core Module 4   People in Business
Outcome 4.5   Develop a career plan based on potential employment and training opportunities and personal career paths

The assignments can be used to cover the following performance criteria:

2.2a   oral and written messages received and acted upon
2.5a   callers greeted promptly and courteously and dealt with appropriately
3.4a   meaning of performance investigated and explained
3.4b   methods of measurement of performance investigated and described
3.4c   suitable method chosen to gauge performance in identified jobs, tasks or operations
3.4d   methods applied to job/task/operation selected and conclusions drawn from results
4.5a   own skills and experience identified

The assignments will help with the development of Common Skills, especially the following:

Applying Numeracy
Outcome 15   Applying numerical skills and techniques

Managing and Developing Self
Outcome 3   Undertakes personal and career development
Outcome 4   Transfer skills gained to new and changing situations and contexts

Communicating
Outcome 11   Participate in oral and non-verbal communication

Managing Tasks and Solving Problems
Outcome 12   Use information sources
Outcome 14   Identify and solve routine and non-routine problems

Introduction

Starting a new course is exciting but also a little frightening. Will you achieve? Will you be good enough? Will you be able to cope?

▲ *Starting out*

This chapter is designed to help you to answer 'yes' to all these questions. In this chapter you will find unfamiliar terms explained. It also tells you how to get yourself geared up and organised and tells you where you can go for information and help.

If you are taking the BTEC First Diploma you will quickly find out that this course is about being good at a job, and also about helping you to make the very best of yourself. It will help you to develop as a person, so that you can tackle tasks confidently, knowing that you have the right skills. It will help you to know yourself so that you can fulfil your potential.

If you are not taking a BTEC First Diploma this book will still help you. It will help you achieve National Vocational Qualification Levels 1 and 2 and you can also benefit from the additional help it gives you in becoming a competent person.

One of the problems of starting a course is the unfamiliar words you will come across. This is because when a group of people work together in the same 'field' they develop a kind of 'shorthand' way to communicate. This is called **jargon** and you will find it in all types of work.

If you are taking a BTEC First Diploma then it will be helpful to get to know the following terms:

- **Module** The BTEC qualification is divided into eight modules, which tell you what has to be learned. Core modules are compulsory and cover knowledge and skills vital to understanding business. Option modules allow learners to specialise in a particular subject or type of work.
- **Outcomes** Every module is made up of outcomes. Each outcome is a statement of what the learner has to achieve in order to gain the qualification.
- **Assignments** These are major pieces of work you undertake to cover a subject. Completing assignments will provide evidence that you can use to claim achievement of an outcome. In an assignment you will normally be given a rôle in a work situation in which you could realistically find yourself. You will work on the assignment by yourself or in a group and will be given a set time in which to complete it. The time limit may be up to four weeks so you will have to organise your time well in order to avoid a last minute rush.
- **Activity** An activity is a 'stand alone' exercise and not usually part of a situation. They are to help you to learn in a practical way and to provide stepping stones towards achieving an outcome.

Claiming outcomes

Claiming an outcome means that once you are sure that you can meet the performance criteria and have enough evidence then you should alert your assessor. You may be asked to perform the outcome again whilst the assessor watches you, e.g. set up a computer package, or an assignment may be used as a final assessment.

Do not forget that you can be assessed for outcomes at work, whether on work experience or in a full or part time job. Your tutor may visit you at the work place and watch you, or you may have to perform the outcome at work and ask your manager or training officer if you can submit what you have done as evidence, e.g. invoices, letters

If the outcome is dealing with customers, it may be sufficient for your manager to write a letter stating how you coped, etc. In this instance you should still be prepared to answer oral and written questions on how you dealt or would deal with certain situations.

Accreditation of Prior Learning (APL)

This means that if you feel that you have already achieved a BTEC module because you have been doing them as part of your job for a long time already, or if you have been awarded an NVQ certificate, you do not need to go through the whole process again.

If you have an NVQ certificate show it to your tutor as this will automatically exempt you from further study of two option modules or units. If you do not have a certificate but feel that you have the right experience, then you will need to collect evidence as described in the previous section.

If you wish to claim a major part of the award through APL you will almost certainly need to go through a different process from those studying the whole course. If you are at a college then alert them to this as you may well have to contact a completely different section of the college. Many colleges are setting up APL units.

Organising yourself

BTEC is not about doing a list of unrelated tasks, it is about performing those tasks in the same or a similar way to how they would be done in a business. For example, you may be able to file a pile of papers set up for you in a training office, but does this prove that you would know what needs to be filed and when to do the filing at work? To do this you would need to plan and organise your day and your work. The additional section of the BTEC course – Common Skills – allows you to answer 'yes' to the question and prove it to your prospective employer.

Your diploma will show Pass, Merit, or Distinction. Pass shows you have achieved the stated outcomes. If you achieve merit or distinction this means that your tutor has taken into account other attributes that you bring to the job. If you can not only file, but also find everything and organise your day by fitting in all the jobs that you have to do and making sure that they are done on time, then this can be reflected in the merit or distinction.

Accumulating all the evidence you will need to be assessed is not easy. Be organised. Get two folders; one for your ongoing notes and practice pieces, etc. and one for your evidence. Keep your evidence folder neatly filed away. Saying 'I did it but I lost it,' does not display your organising skills.

Each centre will have a different way of logging your achievement. If you are given a log book with all the outcomes in, it may look rather daunting. Obviously you cannot gain all the outcomes at once and a course is, therefore, very valuable in helping you to decide where to start. However, although you may be working towards an outcome or a module at school or college, it does not automatically follow that you will have achieved it by the end of a block of study/work. You may need far more practice. On the other hand, you do not want to leave all accrediting to the last week, so some organising needs to be done.

Carry out a work audit (the assignment in Chapter 2, Your New Organisation, will help you). Keep a list of the outcomes you know you can evidence at work in a section in your folder. Make your manager and tutor aware of these and concentrate hard on gaining them in the work-place.

The outcomes you know you will have little or no opportunity to carry out at work are the ones you will need to concentrate hard on at your place of study. If something is not routine or not part of your job it is always much harder to do it easily. Practice does make perfect so take every opportunity you are given to practise. Most schools and colleges have invested in a training office. You should use any time you are given in it to practise those outcomes that are most likely to give you difficulty. If you can find a holiday job in the right kind of environment, so much the better. Saturday jobs also provide a valuable learning environment.

Getting started

In order to achieve success in a BTEC First Diploma, you need to do quite a lot for yourself. Counselling and goal setting will almost certainly be part of your course but self analysis (or knowing yourself) will also play an important part. The exercises that follow are designed to:

a) Help you to be honest with yourself in knowing your own weaknesses.
b) Help you to manage and develop yourself.
c) Give you an introduction to the way you will be expected to learn and disciplin yourself while following a BTEC course.

The exercises will introduce you to some of the Common Skills and some of the words that you will meet in assignments, e.g. research, draft, etc. as well as invite you to list areas that you feel you need to concentrate on (goal setting) and areas where you need to get further help. These exercises are only intended as an introduction or induction (if you prefer) and should not take more than a week to complete.

Induction assignments

Work through the assignments as if they are a package. It is unlikely that you will be able to complete one and then go straight on to another because you will need to research them. In this respect, they are like work and you will probably need to plan your time effectively. For example, if you need to go into town, check to see if another of the assignments also requires you to do so. In this way you will only need to make one trip.

Assignment 1.1 **Personal finance** ──────────────────────────

This exercise is designed to help you to budget your money. Once you start on your course you will incur certain expenses such as travel, books, etc. If you are working this will alter your budget. If you are not working or are on a training scheme then you will need to plan your expenses carefully. Income from a Saturday job or a training allowance may seem a small sum, but good practice now will help later when you have much bigger sums to handle and a more complicated budget.

Task 1   Make your own copy of the Personal budget sheet on page 6

   a) Fill in your weekly wage or training allowance in Section 1 on your personal budget sheet.

      On the next line write any additional wages or income, e.g. Saturday job, pocket money, etc.

      Total these two.

   b) Fill in Section 2 on essential weekly expenditure.

   c) Subtract the total of Section 2 from the total of Section 1. Fill in your answer in the space provided.

      This total is available for you to spend how you choose. It is wiser to try to budget.

   d) Fill in the rest of the sheet as you choose. Do not go over the available amount to spend.

Task 2 a) Work out the proportion (%) of your total income spent on:

                    Essential   Spend now   Saving

   b) Draw a chart to show these proportions.

Task 3   You need not keep your money in your pocket or under the bed. There are many financial institutions that will take care of your money for you.

   a) Visit a selection of the following financial institutions and find out what services they offer to 16–18 year olds for looking after your money:

                    Banks   Building societies   Post Office

   b) Compare the interest rates on the savings accounts offered by the banks, building societies and Post Office. Make a table of your findings. Which do you think is the best?

Task 4   Choose one of the financial institutions you have visited to open an account with.

Which one did you choose? Why did you choose this one? What services do they offer?

Fill in the application form for the account.

Personal budget sheet

Section 1

	£	p
Weekly wage		
Other income		
TOTAL		

Section 2

		£	p
Essential weekly expenditure			
Travel expenses			
Lunch	× 5		
Board (living at home, rent if applicable)			
Instalment payments (mail order, stereo, etc.)			
TOTAL			

	£	p
Available to spend (Section 1 − Section 2)		

Section 3

	£	p
Spend now		
Entertainment		
Personal items (deodorant, shampoo, etc.)		
Save for		
Clothes		
Christmas/birthday presents		
Holidays		
Other		
TOTAL		

(This total should be the same as 'Available to spend')

How did you do?

Use the checklist to assess yourself.

		I would like help	I can do with a calculator	I can do in my head
Task 1	a)			
	b)			
	c)			
	d)			
Task 2	a)			
	b)			
Task 3	a)			
	b)			
Task 4				

I would like help with:

addition	subtraction	multiplication
division	fractions	decimals
percentages	using a calculator	other

As you are now in the world of business it is very important that you are punctual for appointments and work. In order to achieve this you need to plan your time carefully. As you will be travelling to school/college/work or both each week you will need to plan your route.

Task 1
a) Decide how you will be travelling to school/college/work.
b) You may be travelling by car, bus, bicycle, motorbike or on foot. How long should the journey take you?
c) Do you have to travel on any main roads? If you do, will you need to leave extra time to allow for the rush hour? How much extra time will you need?
d) You may find that there are some short cuts on your journey which avoid traffic congestion. Use a local road map to plan your best route.
e) If you are travelling by public transport, obtain a timetable and write down the latest bus or train you could catch. Bear in mind you will have to allow for delays, cancellations, etc. so do not choose the one that gets you there for 9.00 exactly.
f) How long will your journey take in all? Include the time it takes you to walk to or from the bus stop or station.
g) What is the latest time you can leave the house?
h) What time are you going to have to get up?

Task 2   Repeat this process for your journey to work experience or college/school.

Task 3   Using a London Underground map, give suitable directions for the following journeys:

a) Waterloo to Euston
b) Victoria to Heathrow Central
c) Oxford Circus to Wembley Park
d) Kew Gardens to Bond Street

Task 4   Mrs Walton is attending a trade fair in Cardiff on Monday 9 July. She will be staying overnight, but needs to attend a meeting in Redhill, Surrey at 11.00 a.m. on Tuesday 10 July.

a) Look at a British Rail timetable and select a suitable train for her to take from Cardiff bearing in mind the time of her appointment. Note down the departure and arrival times and work out how long the journey will take.
b) What time train will she need to catch from Victoria to Redhill? Note down the departure and arrival times and work out how long the journey will take.

Note: The journey time between Paddington and Victoria takes approximately 30 minutes. However, if Mrs Walton is travelling during the rush hour, you may be advised to allow her a little longer for this part of her journey using the underground.

How did you do?

Use the checklist to assess yourself.

	Confident	Not very confident	Needed help	Couldn't do it
Task 1				
Task 2				
Task 3				
Task 4				

I would like help with:

Map reading   Route planning
Giving directions   Time planning
Reading timetables   Other

Communication is going to be an important part of both your BTEC course and your job. One of the most important aspects of communication is the accurate taking and passing on of messages, both written and spoken.

You need to do a little preparation with a partner before you can start this assignment.

▶ *Person 1*   You work for Fitta Health Studio, a small company. There is no one to staff the telephones out of office hours so they use an answering machine. You have been asked by your manager to leave a suitable recorded message. Use a tape recorder to record your message. Make sure you give the name of the company, a suitable message and assurance that the call will receive attention.

▶ *Person 2*   You work for a company that provides drinks machines. You have been asked to phone Fitta Health Studio to arrange a meeting between your boss and Mrs Walton of Fitta Health Studio to discuss an order for a drinks machine. When you make the call you find there is an answering machine. Leave a message giving details of the name of your company, the name of your boss and why you are calling. Say your boss would like the meeting to be in the week beginning 23 September, preferably in the morning.

You will need to invent a name for your company, a name for your boss and a telephone number.

This is the end of your role in this assignment so make sure you take the role of Person 1 for the rest of the assignment.

Task 1   This task and all the following tasks apply to Person 1.

Your first job in the morning is to listen to the messages which have been left on the answer phone overnight. Listen to the tape and action the first message recorded (the message left by Person 2). Action means to carry out the instructions. You have to act on the instructions.

Fill in the message pad provided and pass it to your tutor.

Task 2   After receiving the message, Mrs Walton asks you to check in the diary and find a suitable date and time for the meeting. You will need to write the name from the recorded message in the diary in the appropriate space. You should also include brief details of the subject of the meeting.

Task 3   Write a note to Mrs Walton letting her know what you have arranged. Remember to mention who the meeting is with, what it is about and the date and time. You must also sign it. (You will find an example of a note at the end of this assignment.)

Task 4   Telephone the person wishing to arrange the meeting and confirm the date and time for which it has been arranged. Do not forget to give your name and the company's (Fitta Health Studio). In case you are asked for it, the telephone number is 0737 772611. You will need to use the telephone training equipment provided by your place of study.

Task 5   When you return from lunch you find the following message has been left for you. Action the message.

Memorandum

To : Assistant

From : Mrs Walton

I need a taxi to take me to Gatwick Airport Fri 27/9, am. Please find 2 local taxi companies. (address and telephone number needed) Thanks   Kath Walton.

How did I do?

Use the checklist to assess yourself.

	Confident	Not very confident	Needed help	Couldn't do it
Task 1				
Task 2				
Task 3				
Task 4				
Task 5				

What would you like more help with? Make a list

Self knowledge

There is one person who is present in every relationship you have: **you**.

What kind of person are you? Did you know that there is no one in the whole world quite like you? Whatever other people may think of you, you are completely unique.

If you were a postage stamp, or a coin, so rare that you were the only example in the whole wide world, people would pay millions to buy you.

Human characteristics
argumentative, beautiful, brave, caring, compassionate, co-operative, courageous, creative, cold, cruel, closed, chaotic, clean, cheerful, crazy, contented, determined, dull, dim, emotional, enthusiastic, fiery, frightened, funny, grumpy, good-looking, generous, hopeful, humorous, heartless, imaginative, intelligent, impatient, impractical, intense, intolerant, jealous, joyful, kind, a leader, loving, loyal, lively, lucky, lying, mean, meek, nervous, noisy, open, organised, patient, persistent, practical, purposeful, pessimistic, popular, proud, pretentious, playful, quiet, quick-witted, rough, strong, slow, sensuous, sincere, sunny, serious, sweet, spoilt, sulky, sad, snobbish, secretive, show-off, sociable, spiteful, stuck-up, self-important, tolerant, truthful, thick-skinned, thoughtful, timid, trustworthy, unkind, unco-operative, unlucky, unhappy, warm, witty, wild

Task 1 How do you see yourself? Choose five words which you think describe you best.

If you have difficulty thinking of words, look at the list at the start of this assignment. Try to find your own words first though.

Note: If you are choosing words from this list, first write down all the words you think apply to you, then underline the ones which apply strongly to you, and then circle the five you want.

Task 2 How do your friends see you? Pick someone who you like and who knows you quite well. Cover up the five words you have just written, then ask him or her to think of five words that he or she thinks describe you.

Task 3 How do your parents see you? Think of five words which you think they might choose (a) on a good day, and (b) on a bad day.

Task 4 How do you think other people see you, people who do not know you so well? Pick five words.

Task 5 Finally, what kind of person would you like to be? Choose five words to describe the kind of person you would like to become.

Everyone is skilled.

'Skills' doesn't just mean things like typing, or passing exams. There are thousands of different skills in life, and you already possess many of them. This assignment will show you what some of your skills are.

Step 1   Think back over your life, and think of something you have done which left you:

▸ feeling really pleased with yourself; and
▸ feeling good inside.

Write a short paragraph describing what you did.

Example   When I was 11, I took my bike to pieces and rebuilt the whole thing, cleaning all the parts. I asked for help when I got to the gears, but the rest I did myself. Then I repainted parts of it, and made the whole thing look as good as new.

Example   When I was 15, my mum and dad went away for two weeks, leaving me in charge of the family. I took charge of things, and made my two younger brothers help with the cooking, washing and cleaning. We had a great time, and I felt very proud.

Step 2   Now think of a second time when you did something which made you feel really pleased with yourself. Write about it in the same way.

Step 3   And now a third time.

Step 4   Look at the skills list below. Take your first achievement, and going slowly down the list, make a list of all the skills that you used while doing what you did.

Steps 5 and 6   Now do the same for your second and third achievements.

Step 7   Total the skills that appear in more than one list. If a skill appears in two or all three lists, this is certain evidence that you possess a 'natural' skill in this area. Develop this skill, and it will bring you a lot of fulfilment in your life.

Step 8   Make a list of your six best natural skills.

Skills List

Analysis	Human relationship	Practical
Animal handling	Humour	Problem-solving
Artistic skills	Imagination	Production
Caring	Initiative	Promotion/sales
Communication	Intuition	Repair skills
Constant hard work	Inventiveness	Research
Courage	Leadership	Responsibility
Creativity	Listening	Self-discipline
Dealing with people	Loving	Speaking
Decision making	Memory	Sport
Design skills	Money skills	Survival
Determination	Observation	Teamwork
Diplomacy	Organising	Tolerance
Driving	Patience	Trust
Efficiency	Performance	Using ideas
Energy/drive	Persistence	Working with figures
Friendship	Persuasion	Work with hands
Gardening	Planning	Writing

The library

The library is an important source of information and it is vital that you familiarise yourself with its services.

Task 1   a)   What is the Dewey Decimal System? How does it work?

b)   What subject matter would you find at:

Classification no   523
                            614–85
                            629–2

Task 2   What are the classification numbers for:

Business   Secretarial   Letter writing

Find a book on each of the above subjects. Write down the title and classification number of each book.

Task 3   Using a local directory, find the names, addresses and telephone numbers of the following:

A coach hire firm   A detective agency
A record shop   A plumber
A french polisher   An estate agency
A lingerie shop

Task 4   Find out what papers and periodicals are stocked in the library and make a list of the ones which you think could be useful on this course.

Task 5   There are many useful reference books to be found in the library. These may include the following:

▸ *Who's Who*   It tells you a bit about the life of all the people who have specially important or well known jobs in the UK.
▸ *Whitaker's Almanac*   A book full of facts and figures about the UK and the world.
▸ *Debretts Etiquette*
▸ Dictionaries   Books that give the meanings of words.
▸ Telephone directories
▸ Telephone code numbers book
▸ Encyclopedias
▸ Thesaurus   A book that lists words similar in meaning.
▸ Atlas
▸ The AA members' handbook

Use the reference books in your library to answer the following questions:

a)   What is the STD code for St Ives?

b)   What is the international dialling code for Belgium?

c)   Where is the tallest building in the world?

d)   How far is it by road from Blackpool to Coventry?

e)   In what county is Shrewsbury?

f)   How many AA recognised hotels are there in Reading?

g)   What does the word 'perambulation' mean?

h)   What word is similar to 'contempt' in meaning?

i)   What is the telephone number of your local careers office?

j) How much is the prime minister paid?

k) What is the correct way to address **i** a bishop, **ii** the mayor of your home town?

l) How many airports are there in the UK?

m) For each of the following people find out:
  i Where they were born.
  ii Where they went to school
  iii The job they are famous for

  Rt. Hon. John Major   David Attenborough
  Gary Lineker

n) Which local firm could deliver coal to your house?

o) What is the difference between 'affect' and 'effect'?

p) What currency is used in Ecuador?

q) What countries lie along the Tropic of Cancer?

r) Find a word similar in meaning to 'arid'

s) What is the history behind the word 'exchequer'? Which language does it come from?

t) Which motorways would you take to travel from Bristol to Stratford-upon-Avon?

Task 6 Use Prestel to find out:

a) Where there are problems on the M1 today.

b) If there are any delays at UK airports.

c) What the weather is like in the Lake District.

How did you do?

If you did not complete all the assignments you need to decide why. Was it that:

- You kept forgetting to do them.
- You could not be bothered.
- You found the tasks too difficult.
- You spent too long on particular parts of the assignments.

By carrying out this analysis and using the checklists you can build up a picture of the ski areas (or attitudes) you need to work at. Keep this analysis filed and use it to set your firs goals. Review this analysis every few months and update it as you think.

Useful sources of information for assignments and business are:

- Libraries and librarians
- Careers offices
- Companies (large and small)
- *Yellow Pages*
- Embassies
- Prestel (or similar services)
- Institutes (e.g. Institute of Marketing)
- Consumer groups
- Your local MP
- Pressure groups

MODULE 1

The Business World

Summary

This chapter introduces you to the world of business. The business organisation is explored through an assignment in which you have to organise an induction for a new recruit. In doing so the following topics are covered:

▸ Induction and training
▸ Employee/employer rights and responsibilities
▸ Types of organisation and purpose
▸ Organisational structure
▸ Contracts of employment
▸ Job description
▸ Disciplinary procedures
▸ Health and safety
▸ Equal opportunities at work

This chapter will help you to achieve the following outcomes

Core Module 1 Business World
 Outcome 1.1 Identify the nature and classify the purpose of business organisations

Core Module 4 People in Business
 Outcome 4.1 Investigate and analyse the nature and purpose of work
 Outcome 4.2 Identify the main rights and responsibilities of employers and employees to one another
 Outcome 4.3 Examine and compare the main job roles of different organisations

The assignment can be used to cover the following performance criteria:

 1.1c business classified by size, function and legal form
 1.1d goals of different types of business identified and compared
 4.1a reasons for working identified
 4.1b the nature of work examined and different types compared
 4.1c different organisational structures examined and compared
 4.1d different work cultures identified and their importance assessed
 4.2a basic contractual requirements identified
 4.2b financial and non-financial benefits identified and assessed
 4.2c health and safety requirements identified and followed
 4.2d commitments and mutual expectations not binding in law recognised
 4.3a functional areas within organisations identified
 4.3b job roles in different functional areas of organisations identified
 4.3c job roles compared
 4.4a relationship between organisational objectives and job role identified
 4.4b given tasks completed to agreed criteria

The assignment will help with the development of Common Skills, especially the following:

Managing Tasks and Solving Problems
 Outcome 12 Use information sources
 Outcome 13 Deal with a combination of routine and non-routine tasks
 Outcome 14 Identify and solve routine and non-routine problems

Managing and Developing Self
 Outcome 2 Manage own time in achieving objectives

Working with and Relating to Others
 Outcome 5 Treat others' values, beliefs and opinions with respect

Communicating
    Outcome 8   Receive and respond to a variety of information
    Outcome 9   Present information in a variety of visual forms

Applying Design and Creativity
    Outcome 18   Use a range of thought processes

Read the following assignment to help you to understand some of the things you should be able to do by the end of this chapter. Normally it will be best for you to read the chapter and carry out the set activities before you tackle the assignments.

Check whether you can do the assignment on your own or with one or more colleagues. Some assignments will require organising by your tutor. Seek guidance, where needed, from your tutor.

This assignment is ideally carried out through your place of employment or work placement. Use this as a resource to complement the preparation that you can do in college or school.

Assignment

Your new organisation

You are employed as a clerical assistant in the training section of your organisation. Your training officer is preparing some up-to-date information for new employees who have just left school. One morning the training officer asks you to come and see her. You have recently left school/college and are therefore fairly new to the company. It is because of this she asks you for your views on what information would be useful to young new recruits. She says, 'I know it is not easy to make the move from school to work, because there is less freedom, you work longer hours, there are deadlines to meet and there are many older people around. We need to make their first day both pleasant and helpful'.

As a result of this meeting you are asked to prepare a leaflet showing the information that would be useful to young new employees joining your organisation. You have your own ideas and will need to discuss these with your friends and colleagues in other departments in the organisation.

You will need to collect the information. Look at your own and other organisations' leaflets. Talk to section heads, perhaps the personnel officer (ask politely for an appointment, then prepare a list of questions you could ask). Talk to people who have been with the company for some time. Again be polite and tell them why you want to talk.

Once you have collected the information, written the leaflet and typed it up, you will need to arrange an induction day programme for the new employees.

The day should begin at 9.30 a.m. and end about 4.00 p.m. It will include tea, lunch and coffee. You must allow enough time for these as it provides an opportunity for the newcomers to get to know each other, to relax and to meet people already working in the organisation. You can invite experts to talk on special topics. The day must include most of the items you have looked at. The programme must be varied and interesting and should give enough time for discussion and questions. One side of A4 paper should be enough, but make copies.

As someone who remembers their own first day with the organisation, you should also give a talk yourself for, say, five minutes. You can choose any of the items you have collected information on.

Task 1   Prepare a leaflet which deals with the main items.

Task 2   Organise an induction day.

Task 3   Give a talk.

In doing this assignment you should make use of the work you have done on Chapter 1 as well as the work covered in this chapter.

Introduction

People go to work for many reasons. The most important reason is to earn money to support yourself or your family, but if you ask people why they work they will give you many different answers. For example:

- 'I enjoy meeting new people.'
- 'I enjoy being part of a team.'
- 'I like being outdoors.'
- 'I have lots of friends at work.'
- 'It's better than being stuck in the house all day.'
- 'I enjoy it – particularly the social and sports facilities.'
- 'It keeps my mind active.'

What all these people are saying is that they get a lot of satisfaction and pleasure from being at work. This 'job satisfaction' is very important and the key to being happy at work. You could spend some 85 000 hours of your life working.

This chapter contains some information which will help you to complete the assignment. You will have to collect extra information and attempt the activities which are included.

The induction process

New employees and even students feel nervous on their first day at work or college, when everything is strange and different. The induction process is the way in which the new person is shown, and learns about the organisation.

▲ *The induction process*

The induction process should happen during the first few days. There will be information about the whole organisation, its facilities and what it can offer. There will be talks on how the organisation works and general rules to be followed at work, e.g. its health and safety rules. There will be time for people to meet and make new friends. The purpose of induction is to make people feel confident and relaxed in their new surroundings. This way people will settle down more quickly and so work harder and stay with the organisation longer. During the induction people will be shown where they will work. They will be introduced to the staff and told about any special rules or regulations which affect them. There should be special attention paid to the needs of disabled workers, e.g. is there wheelchair access?

The induction process should cover the following items:

▸ History of the organisation
▸ Structure of the organisation
▸ The products made or the services provided by the organisation
▸ Company rules and regulations (hours of work, tea breaks, etc.)
▸ Disciplinary procedures and appeals
▸ Reasons for dismissal
▸ Trade unions
▸ Training and promotion
▸ Social and welfare facilities
▸ A walk or tour of the site or work place, to include: exits and entrances; fire procedures; section safety regulations; location of canteen, toilets, cloakroom and lockers, etc.
▸ Health and safety rules
▸ Key people whom the newcomer should know
▸ Organisation procedures for ensuring equal opportunity, including how to deal with sexual or racial harassment
▸ How the department or section works
▸ The contract of employment

Rights and responsibilities

All jobs, including being a student, have 'rights and responsibilities' associated with them. Generally the 'rights' are those things which you are entitled to and would be provided for by the employer or college, e.g. a safe and healthy environment. The 'responsibilities' are those things the employee must do in return, e.g. act in a safe manner, complete your assignments on time or meet daily targets of work. For example you receive a grant to attend college, in return your attendance, progress and behaviour must all be satisfactory.

All organisations exist for a purpose, which is to satisfy a real or imagined need. Shops exist to sell goods, manufacturers to make goods, religions to meet our spiritual needs. An organisation is perhaps best described as a group of people all working towards the same objectives.

Your purpose as part of an organisation is to work towards achieving the agreed objectives. These objectives could be selling the best products, providing the best service, making the biggest profit or beating the opposition. All organisations have objectives from Shell to ICI to the local builder or hairdresser. Later we will look at some of the objectives an organisation may have.

ACTIVITY

Either

Whilst on work experience find out the objectives of the organisation you are with. Compare these with the findings of other members of your group.

Or

Ask other members of your group what are the objectives of the organisation for which they work. Compare your results.

Types of businesses in the high street

Walk along any high street, or shopping area, and you will see many types of business. These are broadly divided into private sector and public sector businesses. Private sector businesses are owned by individuals, companies or institutions, i.e. they are privately owned. Public sector organisations are owned by the State.

The local greengrocer, cobbler or corner shop is likely to be a 'one-person' business, a **sole trader.** This is the simplest type of organisation. There is one owner who controls and manages the business, makes the decisions, and takes the profit as a reward for the original risk.

Estate agents, solicitors and insurance brokers are normally **partnerships**. The ownership, decision making, risk taking and profit sharing are divided between partners. The business is regulated and controlled by the Partnership Acts.

A bank or supermarket is likely to be a **public limited company** (a **PLC**), whilst a company such as 'J Green and Daughters Ltd' is a **private limited company.** 'Limited' (Ltd.) means that the liability or debt of the owners is restricted or confined to the amount they initially invested. Compare this with the sole trader, where liability is unlimited. This means that everything they possess can be taken away to pay off business debts.

Age Concern and Oxfam are voluntary organisations. Many of the people who work for them do not get paid. They are non-profit-making charities. They exist to provide specific help and support for groups of people in need.

Fast food outlets, e.g. McDonalds, and photocopying shops are likely to be **franchises**. The operator of the shop will have paid the franchiser a sum of money to use its name, product, equipment and production method. The parent company will get a share of the profits plus all the sales of material to the franchise.

The Co-op is a co-operative retail store. The customers are usually members of the co-op. A member is a shareholder or owner and receives a proportion of the profit, which is based upon the amount they spend. Every share holder or member has limited liability.

The Shell and Esso garages are examples of **multinational companies**. These companies produce, sell and operate world-wide. They produce mainly in low cost countries. They sell in countries which give the most profit. They are very large and powerful.

The DSS, the Department of Social Security is in the public sector. It is a department or branch of the central government based at Westminster in London. It is responsible for providing a wide range of benefits, e.g. income support.

Council offices are also in the public sector but are part of local government. Examples of council offices are the town hall, the education and housing departments, possibly a leisure and recreation department. Local council policies are determined by a political party. These policies are administered and implemented by permanent clerical and administrative staff.

ACTIVITY

In groups of two or three, walk along your local high street. Draw a sketch plan and identify the business units that you see. Take photographs. Classify the businesses by industry and legal form. Find out what you can about one business in each category and identify differences and similarities. Present your results to the rest of your group. Use appropriate visual aids such as the overhead projector or slide projector in your presentation.

Position in organisation structure

The structure of an organisation is the way in which it is organised. The structure is there to help the organisation achieve its purposes and objectives. Frequently this structure shown by an organisation chart, which is a map of the organisation. Like all maps depending on the scale we use, we can show either the whole organisation, or parts of e.g. divisions or departments.

When you first join an organisation as a junior employee these charts will appear extremely depressing, as you will find yourself somewhere near the bottom. Be positive and you will soon start to climb up.

The typical organisation chart which follows shows the departments or sections o manufacturing company.

The board of directors makes the policy decisions and delegates (gives the responsibility for) running the business to the managing director (or chief executive). Finance, Marketing, Production, etc. are departments, each of which could have their own head or director, e.g. finance director or chief accountant.

The chart above gives an overall view of the organisation. If we now look at one of the departments, say the finance department, it may look like this:

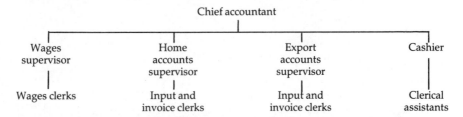

1 In this organisation the chief accountant is responsible for financial management.

2 The supervisors all report to the chief accountant who is their line manager.

3 The supervisors are responsible for the clerks and are their line managers.

4 The supervisors are all at the same managerial level.

5 The clerks are all at the same lower level

6 The chief accountant reports to the managing director.

Why do you need to know where you are on an organisation chart?

Knowing how the structure of an organisation works can be of considerable help in understanding where you fit in. It will help you identify to whom to report and of whom to ask questions. It will give you information about the management structure. Who is at the same level as you is shown by the horizontal lines and who is above and below you is shown by the vertical lines. In other words the chart shows who is responsible for you and for whom you are responsible.

Alongside the formal organisation structure there will also be informal relationships or networks and to be able to work successfully you will need to form good working relations with a range of colleagues in your own and other sections.

ACTIVITY

1 Obtain an organisation chart for your work experience or permanent employer and write notes on some of the key relationships which are shown.

2 Look at two jobs and find out what key skills are needed for them. You can use careers leaflets, or ask your careers tutor, or use your own experience.

Contract of employment

▲ *Employee–employer relations*

A contract of employment is set by the organisation and signed by the employee. A contract is a legal term meaning an agreement between parties or sides which can be enforced by law. The contract of employment is a particular type of legal agreement between the employer and the employee, and exists to give both parties a degree of protection, certainty and security. It begins when the employer makes an offer of work with the payment of money and the employee accepts the offer at that rate and agrees to work. Each side or party is giving a benefit to the other, the employer is paying the money, the employee the performance of work. This benefit is legally called 'consideration'. The offer, acceptance and consideration are the three basic parts of any contract.

Contract of employment

The contract of employment can contain the following information:

▸ Employer's name
▸ Date of starting work
▸ Pay details
▸ Hours of work and whether overtime is involved
▸ Holiday and holiday pay
▸ Length of notice required
▸ Sickness arrangements and sick pay
▸ Pension scheme details (if there is one)

▶ Job title
▶ Grievance and disciplinary procedures

In addition, both the employer and the employee have certain duties which they must carry out. These may or may not be in the written contract.

Responsibilities of employees

The employee must:

1 Personally do the job and not ask someone else to substitute for them.
2 Be honest and loyal.
3 Obey all lawful instructions.
4 Always behave correctly.
5 Be careful and efficient in carrying out work.
6 Be accountable for the employer's money, i.e. they must not cheat or steal from the company.

Responsibilities of employers

The employer must:

1 Refund expenses incurred in doing the job.
2 Pay the agreed rate.

However, the employer is not bound to provide:

▶ Work.
▶ Education or training except for health and safety and where it was originally agreed.
▶ A reference.

ACTIVITY

1 Assume that you are seeking a full-time job, what would you be looking for in terms of prospects, conditions and pay? Once you have created your list, compare it with the contract of employment. Are any items the same? Are any different? Can you say why?

2 Discuss with fellow students and your tutor a 'Course Study Contract' and then devise a contract between yourself and the centre where you are studying. Use the File Facts to give you the basic elements. State the duties placed on yourself and the centre.

Decide what might happen in the following circumstances when the contract might have been broken (i.e. breached) by one party:

a) You fail to provide assignments on time.
b) You are absent for long periods, e.g. weeks.
c) Your lecturer turns up late.
d) You fail the course.

Don't forget the 'small print' — literally small writing, where one party puts in those items which they don't want you to see when you first read it. For example, if you read the small print at the back of a holiday brochure you could find this:

The whole cost of the holiday must be paid nine weeks before you depart. If you do not, your booking will be cancelled and you will still have to pay the full amount.

Remember, don't sign anything until you have read and understood it all.

Job descriptions and job tasks

Job descriptions help employees to do their work well because they show what work is expected of them. They also protect employees from being asked to do something which is not in the job description.

It is important for employers to explain clearly the meaning of the contract of employment and the individual employee job description. They should also state the penalties that will occur if an employee's work, conduct or performance falls below the required standard.

Normally you would apply for a job in response to an advert in the paper or Job Centre, and in return you would receive an application form and job description.

ACTIVITY

Using the File Fact on job descriptions, keep a diary of your work experience or permanent work activities and draw up a job description of your tasks which could then be given to the next person to join that organisation.

Job description

A good job description should contain the following information:

1 Basic details, e.g. job title, department or section, to whom you are responsible, a job or code number.

2 Brief details on the purpose of the job with some indication of how it fits into the department or section.

3 Main duties involved, e.g. typing, filing, some telephone work.

4 Details of previous experience (if any), education and training with qualifications, skills and personal qualities required. These items are sometimes called the person specification.

5 An equal opportunities statement.

A typical job description

Department: Marketing

Job title: Secretary

Job purpose: To provide a word processing service with administrative assistance.

Responsible to: (Marketing manager)

Duties:
1 Processing a variety of marketing documents including specifications.
2 Filing – maintaining a client file.
3 Reception/telephone – dealing with calls and enquiries from clients.
4 Arranging travel and business meetings.

Previous experience: None – full training will be given.

Qualifications: BTEC First Diploma in Business and Finance.

Skills: Social and interpersonal skills are necessary for this busy, sometimes hectic office.

Disciplinary procedures

▲ *Breaking the rules*

Within any organisation, whether as a student or an employee, you will have to follow rules and regulations. These may be either for your own benefit and for that of your colleagues, or for the benefit of the company. They may be simple rules, relating to the type of dress or style of behaviour which is expected, e.g. rings cannot be worn when dealing with food, or complex procedures involving the Health and Safety at Work Act. When you join an organisation, you are agreeing to follow these rules. The consequences of failing to do so are given in the File Fact on disciplinary procedures.

All organisations should have a clearly defined disciplinary procedure which is readily available to all employees. It is usually in the staff handbook. The procedure given in the Fact File below is typical of many companies and a similar process ought to apply to you as a student. In this latter case your tutor might give the first warning and the final warning will probably be given by the head of department.

Disciplinary procedures are rarely used and then only for serious cases. Most of the time everything runs very smoothly, with everyone doing the job they are supposed to. Hopefully you will never require them, but know them just in case.

Disciplinary procedures

Suspension

When a serious alleged offence has taken place and it would be unwise for the organisation or the employee for the employee to stay at work, then the employee may be suspended from work. For instance if you are involved in a fight at work it would be unwise of the company to allow you to stay at work and probably unwise of you – the fight might erupt again. You would be suspended from work until the cause of the fight had been investigated.

Oral warning (first warning)

This is given when an employee fails to meet the organisation's required standards of work or behaviour. A note would be made in the employee's file and the immediate line manager would probably be informed.

Formal warning

This may be oral, but is more likely to be an oral and written warning. It should contain targets which the offender must achieve and point out the consequences of failing to meet these. It would be confirmed in writing with copies for the employee's file and for management.

Final warning

This would be an oral and written warning issued for a persistent offence when the employee has ignored or failed to achieve the required standards. It would state that the employee will be suspended or dismissed if specific targets are not met within an agreed time. There would be confirmation in writing with copies as for a formal warning.

Dismissal

For a serious offence or when all forms of warning have failed, the employee may be dismissed. The period of notice to leave is given as required by the contract of employment with that organisation. After the period of notice has been worked, the employee no longer works for the organisation.

Summary dismissal

When the contract of employment has been seriously broken, e.g. in the case of theft, there would be an investigation with the employee and a 'friend' present (the friend could be a lawyer or union representative). If found guilty, the worker could be dismissed immediately with no notice.

Other reasons for summary dismissal are:

▶ Assaulting other employees.
▶ Deliberately breaking company rules.
▶ Destroying company property or premises.
▶ Repeated insubordination (not obeying instructions).

Wherever there is a disciplinary procedure there is an appeals procedure. Normally an appeal must be made in writing within three working days of the warning being given.

ACTIVITY

Obtain the disciplinary and appeals procedure for your organisation. Does it follow the outline given in the File Fact? Is anything missing or is anything extra added?

Health and safety legislation

NO SMOKING

RECEPTION ▷
◁ CASUALTY
PHYSIOTHERAPHY ▷
OUTPATIENTS ▷
◁ DISPENSARY

R.B.JACKSON

▲ *Health and safety*

The aim of health and safety legislation is to improve the health and safety of people at work. Every organisation must have a health and safety policy. An excellent source of information is the Health and Safety Executive – the HSE. It publishes some very good leaflets which you can obtain.

Some 'do's' and 'dont's' for using office equipment:

- **Do** make sure that the safety guards on machines are working.
- **Do** switch off machinery after use.
- **Do** tidy away flex and cables.
- **Do** take care when using staplers or guillotines (paper cutting machines).
- **Do** keep your workplace neat and tidy.
- **Do** report all accidents.
- **Do** take care.
- **Don't** use a machine which is faulty.
- **Don't** try to repair a machine.
- **Don't** touch anything electrical with wet hands.
- **Don't** fool around in your workplace.
- **Don't** overfill filing cabinets or drawers.

> **Memorandum**
>
> This is a good opportunity to show your design skills. Can you and your colleagues get together and draw pictures of each of the do's and don'ts for using office equipment. They must be dramatic and make an immediate impact.

Safety signs

There are four types of safety sign. All signs must conform to these rules:

1 Warning signs, e.g. risk of electric shock. These are on a yellow triangle with a black border.

2 Prohibition signs or 'don't do' signs – on a red circle with a red diagonal band, e.g. no smoking.

3 Mandatory or 'must do' signs – solid blue circle with a white symbol, e.g. a pair of white gloves on a blue background for 'wear hand protection'.

4 Safe condition or 'safe way' signs – green square with a white symbol, e.g. a direction arrow

Health and Safety at Work Act (HASAWA) 1974

This Act gives rights and responsibilities to employers and employees.

Employers must provide:

▸ A safe and healthy workplace.
▸ Proper safety procedures – including fire drills, fire notices and exits.
▸ Safe machinery and equipment, which is properly guarded.
▸ Trained safety staff.
▸ A written local health and safety policy which is available to all employees.

Employees must:

▸ Act so as to protect themselves and others.
▸ Follow health and safety procedures.
▸ Not misuse health and safety material and equipment, e.g. it is a criminal offence to pla with a fire extinguisher, cause a false alarm, or write on/change safety signs.

The Act applies to all workplaces. Both employees and students have a responsibility to obe the Act.

In Chapter 7, Office Organisation there is a health and safety checklist for you to use as pa of an assignment.

Control of Substances Hazardous to Health Regulation 1988 (COSHH)

These regulations lay down the ways in which hazardous substances (e.g. cleaning a decorating materials) can be controlled. They also say how people can be protected fro them. All employees have the right to be told about the risks in their workplace, and wh precautious should be taken.

Hazard and Risk Explained

Control of Substances Hazardous to Health Regulations 1988 (COSHH)

HSE
Health & Safety Executive

Words

'LOOK OUT - those stairs are a real **hazard**!'
'It's a bit of a **risk** leaving your door unlocked at night!'

We all know what we mean when we use these words at home. But do they mean the same thing at work? What about when the law says you have got to assess the risk from using a chemical or a label tells you a substance is hazardous?

What does the risk from something mean? Is the hazard of a chemical the same as the risk from it?

In ordinary speech we may use these two words interchangeably but at work each has a special meaning. This leaflet helps explain how the Health and Safety Executive uses these words in talking about substances at work.

Hazard

The **hazard** presented by a substance is its potential to cause harm. It may be able to make you cough, damage your liver or even kill you! Some substances can harm you in several different ways; eg, if you breathe them in, swallow them or get them on your skin.

Risk

The **risk** from a substance is the likelihood that it will harm you in the actual circumstances of use. This will depend on:

* the hazard presented by the substance,
* how it is used,
* how it is controlled,

* who is exposed ... to how much ... for how long,
* what they are doing, and so on.

Poor control can create a substantial risk even from a substance with low hazard. But with proper precautions the risk of being harmed by even the most hazardous substance can be adequately controlled.

Labels

Drums and containers of dangerous substances have to be labelled under the Classification, Packaging and Labelling of Dangerous Substances Regulations 1984 (CPL)* The labels have hazard warning symbols and two types of guidance phrases.

R-phrases identify the **hazards**, eg:

* toxic by inhalation,
* irritating to the eyes.

S-phrases give advice on how to minimise the **risk**, eg:

* keep away from heat or
* avoid contact with skin.

* See sources of further information at end of leaflet.

COSHH

The Control of Substances Hazardous to Health Regulations (COSHH) require employers to assess the **risks** created by work in which a hazardous substance is used.* One starting point to help with this assessment will be the information on the label if the substance is

subject to CPL. For all substances information should be provided by the supplier to enable the substance to be used with safety. (This is required by Section 6 of the Health and Safety at Work etc Act 1974.*)

* See sources of further information at end of leaflet.

Action under COSHH

Employers

First you must determine the hazard of a substance. Then you have got to:

* assess the risks to people's health from the way that substance is used in **your** workplace,
* see if you can prevent anyone being exposed to the substance; if not
* decide how you are going to control exposure to reduce that risk,
* establish effective controls,
* train and inform your workforce;
* you may also need to monitor your employees' exposure and provide health surveillance.

Workers

You need to know more than just the hazard presented by a substance before you use it. You should be trained to understand:

* what the risks are from using it at your workplace,
* how those risks are controlled,
* the precautions you have to take,

then you can use most chemicals with little risk of harm.

▲ *Extract from a COSHH leaflet produced by the HSE*

ACTIVITY

Look at the local health and safety policy for your organisation. For the induction leaflet you will need to say:

▸ Who is responsible for health and safety.
▸ What the duties of an employee are.
▸ How to exit the building if the alarm sounds.
▸ Whether there are special health and safety rules when you work with computers, VDUs (visual display units) or other office equipment.

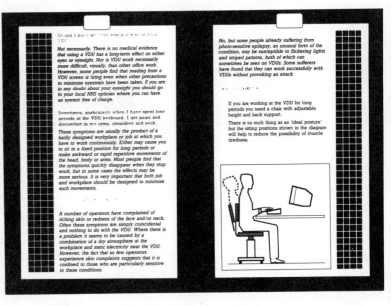

▲ *Extract from an HSE leaflet on the health and safety issues arising from working with VDUs*

Equal opportunity for all

Equal opportunity laws

The legal acts described below apply to job advertisements, interviews, appointme
pay and promotion.

Equal Pay Act 1970

The purpose of the Equal Pay Act is to give women the same pay as men for similar or
work. In other words, men and women should get equal pay for equal work. Emplo
must not discriminate (deal unfairly with a person, racial group or minority thrc
prejudice) between men and women.

Sex Discrimination Act 1975

At the workplace men and women must be treated equally and fairly. Employers mus
discriminate between men and women. They should be recruited on the same conditi
given the same contract of employment and the same opportunities for promotion
training. Likewise, the reasons for dismissal should be similar.

Race Relations Act 1976

The Race Relations Act makes it illegal to discriminate on the grounds of colour, rac
ethnic origin.

The following is an extract from the Southwark College Student Handbook 199
reproduced with kind permission of Southwark College.

ANTI RACIST CODE OF PRACTICE

The College is totally opposed to racism in all its
forms. Racist behaviour, language and activities
discriminate against and disadvantage black péople
and other ethnic minorities. Racism is also hurtful and
damaging to individuals ,the College and the
community.

Racism may be obvious or more disguised. **Obvious
(overt) racist acts** include assaults, threats, comments,
"jokes", name-calling, graffiti, wearing racist badges,
bringing racist material into college and attempts to
recruit students to racist groups.

**Any such offences against the Code may lead to
suspension and exclusion from the College under the
Disciplinary Procedures.**

ACTIVITY

Obtain the equal opportunities policy for your organisation. Then in the induction leaflet

▸ The key features of the policy or what the policy should be.
▸ How someone should report racial or sexual harassment within your organisation.

Discrimination

Discrimination comes about because of peoples' attitudes and prejudices. These develop over many years. They are not helped by what we see, hear or read from an early age. In many childrens' books, boys help their fathers dig the garden, girls arrange the flowers. These often repeated images are called stereotypes. Equal opportunities policies and laws are supposed to correct the problems caused by discrimination. You can judge for yourself how successful they are.

---/ **ACTIVITY** /————————————————————————

For this activity you should work in groups of five or six. Discuss each of the issues in the list and come to a positive conclusion about what you would do. Compare your conclusions with those of other groups.

a) One of your colleagues is always telling racist jokes.
b) The males in your group always get to the computers first.
c) A girl in your group is constantly being harassed by a senior male colleague.
d) You find racist graffiti in the toilets.
e) One of your colleagues is very slow and quiet and is always being laughed at.
f) Do you see discrimination around you? Where – on television, in films or in newspapers and books?

Trade unions

A trade union is an organisation of employees working together to achieve specific aims. These could include:

- Good, safe working conditions.
- Higher wages.
- Better job satisfaction.
- Shorter working hours.
- Some say in the running of the business.

Employers would probably have a different set of aims, such as:

- Restrict wage costs.
- Greater production and productivity.
- Workers willing to do a variety of jobs.
- Longer hours.

It can be very difficult for trade unions and employers to agree, however there are laws which try to help them get together. If they fail to agree and the talks break down, there is an organisation called ACAS, the Arbitration, Conciliation and Advisory Service, which tries to help. ACAS will talk to the employees (or trade unions) and employers separately and try to find out where they agree. Talks can then take place to find a solution to the original problem.

Many companies have agreements with trade unions. This means that a trade union can negotiate or bargain for the workforce, with the company. Such agreements normally set out procedures to be followed by management and trade unions in handling disputes.

Find out which trade unions are recognised by your employer. Find out whether or not you have to belong to a trade union when you start work. Find out how you could join a trade union. Then write this information in the induction leaflet.

Personal effectiveness

ACTIVITY

1   At work one day you notice your supervisor taking company property and putting it into his/her bag. He/she comments to you, 'It's one of the perks of the job. You'll soon learn!' You find this very wide spread, but at your interview you were warned in very strong terms that the company has a policy of prosecuting and dismissing anybody found doing this. As one of your duties is filling in stock records you are really worried that it may be **you** who is implicated.

    What do you do?

2   At work a young male trainee wears an earring. He has been told to remove it. In the canteen he bemoans the fact that the boss is just a fuddy duddy and old-fashioned and that it is perfectly acceptable for men to wear earrings these days. As he serves members of the public as part of his job, try to put the other side of the argument.

Summary

This chapter looks outward from the business organisation to see how it influences and is influenced by the world around it. The assignment and activities in this chapter use the example of a wood furniture manufacturing company to do this and to show how business organisations change over time. The following topics are covered:

▸ The external environment
▸ Economic influences and change: interest rates, prices and unemployment
▸ Social influences, including population and social class
▸ Technological changes including production methods, information technology and new products.

This chapter will help you to achieve the following outcomes:

Core Module 1   The Business World
  Outcome 1.2   Illustrate the effects of business organisations on the local and national communities
  Outcome 1.3   Examine how and why the community may seek to influence the conduct of business organisations
  Outcome 1.4   Examine the relationships between an organisation and its customers

The assignment can be used to cover the following performance criteria:
  1.2a   roles in local and national economy identified
  1.2b   main social and environmental effects distinguished and evaluated
  1.2c   main political impact of business organisations identified
  1.3a   reasons for community influence over business explained
  1.4c   changes in customer needs and business response identified
  4.4a   relationship between organisational objectives and job role identified
  4.4b   given tasks completed to agreed criteria

The assignment will help with the development of Common Skills, especially the following:

Communicating
  Outcome 8   Receive and respond to a variety of information

Managing Tasks and Solving Problems
  Outcome 12   Use information sources
  Outcome 13   Deal with a combination of routine and non-routine tasks

Applying Numeracy
  Outcome 15   Apply numerical skills and techniques

Read the following assignment to help you to understand some of the things you should be able to do by the end of this chapter. Normally it will be best for you to read the chapter and carry out the set activities before you tackle the assignment.

Check whether you can do the assignment on your own or with one or more colleagues. Some assignments will require organising by your tutor. Seek guidance, where needed, from your tutor.

This assignment is ideally carried out through your place of employment or work placement. Use this as a resource to complement the preparation that you can do in college or school.

Profit from facts

You have just got a job working in the office of the Worldwide Furniture Company (WFC). It has factories in Brazil and the United Kindom. The UK factory is situated close to where you live. It employs a large number of production workers, but few salespeople. You work in the general office which overlooks the 'shop floor' where the furniture is made. Your job is to collect statistics about items which might affect the sales of furniture.

The company makes 'cottage-style' old fashioned furniture such as chairs, tables, cupboards and bookcases. These are all made by hand. The company uses traditional methods of working with hardwoods such as teak and mahogany. The company is in financial trouble. The managing director, Jim Pearce, was quoted in a recent newspaper article as saying, 'Nobody buys our furniture any more. The public don't want rare wood from South America, they prefer chip board from Houston Homecare'.

To try to solve their problems, WFC have employed a marketing manager, Jane Everdene. She has come up with a number of ideas to improve their profits. One of these is that the company should make and sell furniture for schools and colleges. To do this, it must change its methods of making furniture. It must buy (invest in) new equipment and machinery. You have been employed because of your BTEC background and your ability to 'contribute to change and development in the organisation'.

Your job description says you have to gather information, data and statistics which could affect the sale of furniture by using newspapers and official government publications.

The company has not previously collected data on a regular basis. However, Jane Everdene has identified a number of key, or important statistics she believes would help to improve sales and profits. She has already spoken to you about this particular project. You arrive the next day to find the following memo on your desk.

Memorandum

To: Assistant   *Re:* New statistics
From: J Everdene   Today's date

Sorry about this, but I will be away for the next three weeks. Could you please make a start on collecting the information we talked about. Can you bring the data and graphs up to date please for the following:
* Interest rates – remember we want to borrow money, perhaps you could ask or call in to a local bank, they usually have lots of information about borrowing money and helping businesses. Midland and Nat West are always advertising. You might find that the rate of interest hasn't changed much recently, so you will have to find out if interest rates have been rising or falling over the past year.
* Prices – I want to know what has been happening to the prices of goods in shops – in other words retail prices. You can get this data from the publication 'Monthly Digest of Statistics'.
* Unemployment – here I want local figures. How many males and females are unemployed? You will have to look in the local reference library.
* Population – we are only interested in those people under 20. The data are usually in age groups, e.g. 0–4 yrs, 5–9 yrs, 10–14 yrs, 15–19 yrs. Remember, the figures will be in millions.
Just try to get all the figures ready by the time I come back. Make sure they are accurate and well presented. Try to say something about how the company might be affected by, for example, high or low interest rates, high or low prices. Don't worry if you can't, I will write the final report. I also want you to keep your figures up to date over the next three months.

                                                   J Everdene

Task 1 Collect up-to-date information on prices, interest rates, unemployment and population.

Task 2 Prepare a presentation for the rest of your group on one of the topics.

Task 3 Maintain a file on this information putting in new monthly figures – you will need to update Ms Everdene continually.

The economic system

Organisations form part of the economy of a country. Most countries do not have enough resources to produce all they want. People, therefore, have to choose between different alternatives. The economic system has to solve the following problems:

▸ What to produce, e.g. bread, cars or caviar?
▸ How much to produce – 20 million cars and/or one thousand loaves of bread?
▸ For whom to produce – only those who can afford to pay?
▸ Where to produce – should all heavy industry be located in East Anglia?

Each country has its own way of addressing these problems.

Economies can be divided roughly under three headings, depending upon who makes the decisions.

1 Centrally planned   Every economic decision is made by the government. Prices are fixed and the supply of goods and services is controlled. Decisions about what, where and how much to produce are all made centrally. There are no market processes involved.

2 Free enterprise or market economy   The government is not involved in economic activity. Prices are determined by the market forces of supply and demand. All decisions are made by companies and consumers.

3 Mixed economy   The decisions about 'what', 'how much', 'for whom' and 'where' to produce are split between the government and the private sector. The UK is a mixed economy. Companies decide 'what' and 'how much' to produce, consumers decide what to buy. The government gets involved by setting targets for the economy such as low inflation. The government may intervene when it believes the market system has failed to operate. For example, it gives benefits to people who are unemployed.

External environment

The external environment is everything that exists outside the business organisation. All organisations are part of the environment. The decisions made by organisations can affect or change what happens around them, whilst events outside the organisation will affect what they do. This is a two-way process:

● Organisations can change the environment.
● The environment can change organisations.

The environment we are talking about includes everything, not just the land, trees, water or air. The external environment can include the:

● **Legal environment**, e.g. what new and existing laws and legislation do organisations have to follow?

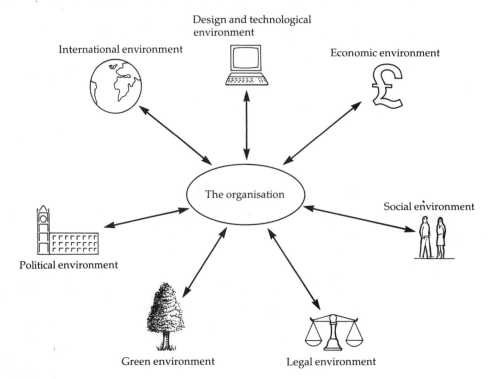

Design and technological environment

International environment

Economic environment

The organisation

Social environment

Political environment

Green environment

Legal environment

▲ *The external environment*

- **Economic environment**, e.g. how are organisations affected by interest rates, prices or taxation?
- **Social environment**, e.g. how do changes in consumers' habits and life styles affect the way organisations behave? How do population changes affect the company?
- **Design and technological environment**, e.g. how do production methods change as a result of the introduction of computers? What do the words 'new' and 'improved' mean when you see them on a packet? When do you use new materials?
- **International environment**, e.g. how will the organisation be affected by the momentous changes taking place in Europe, Asia and the Middle East?
- **Political environment**, e.g. if there is a change in the political party which runs central or local government will this affect the decisions the organisation makes?
- **Green environment**, e.g. is your deodorant 'environment friendly'? Are you buying 'recycled' products?

ACTIVITY

Working in groups of at least three identify a local issue concerning an organisation or business in general. Examples could be:

a) A plan by the local council to redevelop the town centre or build a shopping centre using a major food retailer as the main investor.

b) A planning proposal by a large company to extend its mining earthworks activity closer a nearby village or build a new access road.

c) Rumours that a large multinational company is about to close (or severely cut back c the operation of its local company which is a major employer in the local community that it is about to relocate its HQ in your town.

Having chosen a suitable issue:

1 Investigate and research the issue from a variety of viewpoints.
2 Distinguish and evaluate the impact of the proposed action on the community.

3 Identify and explain how the local community has attempted to influence the decision of the organisation.

4 Present your findings to the rest of your class/course group.

Legal environment

All organisations have to operate legally. Individuals have to behave and act legally. Laws and rules are made by Parliament, Government departments and judges. This is the legal environment.

Table 3.1 How companies are affected by the law

Company activity	Laws which have to be followed
Setting up a company	Company law on the type of business and method of trading. Copyright and trade marks
Obtaining raw materials and dealing with suppliers	Contract law which deals with how agreements are made/broken
Obtaining finance	Banking law covering cheques and how to obtain finance
Employing workers	Employment law which covers the contract of employment and laws against discrimination on the basis of sex, race, colour or disability
Finding premises	Land and property laws about how to own or rent a property. Planning permission from the local council
Starting production	Health and safety legislation covering safe production methods and ways of working
Making goods	Laws on pollution (e.g. noise, waste disposal, etc.) Trade union laws, industrial relations and contract of employment
Selling goods	Consumer law – are the goods fit for sale, are they of the right weight and quality?
After sales service	Consumer law covering the changing of goods and the refunding of money to customers
Closing down a company	Employment law dealing with making workers redundant Finance law on how to deal with creditors

Possible effects of changes in the law

Changes in the law are taking place all the time. Parliament can make changes. Judges can make changes by giving different explanations or definitions of existing laws. Many of these changes will have social and economic outcomes. Examples 1–3 show how a company might respond to a change in the law.

Example 1
A decision to allow shops to open on Sundays could have many effects:

- Shops would pay out more in wages.
- Workers could be paid more.
- Workers could work longer hours.
- Shops could sell more.
- Town centres could be crowded on Sundays.
- Churches could be empty.
- Costs and prices could increase.
- Town centres could be 'more fun' on Sundays.

You may decide that these effects are good or bad. It depends on what you think and what you do. People who own shops will have different views from people who work in them.

Example 2
A decision that companies must put more information on food labels could:

- Help the customer to know more about the product.
- Confuse the customer because of the specialised words.
- Increase the cost of producing the product.
- Increase the price.
- Change the customers' shopping habits.

Example 3
A decision to make all workplaces 'no smoking' areas could:

- Stop some people from applying for jobs.
- Force some smokers to leave the company.
- Force trade unions to say that the contract of employment has changed.
- Improve working conditions.
- Increase stress for smokers.
- Increase absenteeism for smokers.

What is the best decision – cost benefit analysis
In each of the three examples above different groups have been affected in various ways by the initial decision. Some groups have gained, some have lost. An organisation needs to be able to identify the groups involved and look at the advantages and disadvantages brought about by the decisions.

An organisation needs to answer the questions: should we open shops on Sundays? should more information be put on food labels? should workplaces be made no smoking areas? Cost-benefit analysis helps an organisation to do this.

Look at the effects of allowing shops to open on Sundays. Some of them are costs (disadvantages), e.g. shops pay out more in wages and workers work longer hours. Some are benefits (advantages), e.g. workers could be paid more and shops could sell more. These costs and benefits only affect the individual shops and shopworkers. They are called **private costs and benefits.** However, there are other costs and benefits if shops open on Sundays. These affect the local areas. Town centres could become crowded on Sundays and there would be traffic jams and car fumes: these are called **social costs**. Making town centres more fun on Sundays would be a **social benefit** for some age groups.

An organisation must be able to make the best decisions. It does this by looking at both the private costs and benefits and the social costs and benefits of a decision. If there are more benefits than costs then the decision is the right one to make. This is especially true when looking at how a decision affects the local area.

/ **ACTIVITY** /

Use a chart like the one below to look at the costs and benefits of the following decisions:

a) Giving up smoking cigarettes.
b) Doing more assignments.
c) Building a new supermarket in your local area.
d) The Worldwide Furniture Company increasing production.

	Private	Social
Costs		
Benefits		

Memorandum

To: Assistant
From: J Everdene

Can you please work out the private and social costs and benefits of introducing the new range of furniture. If you can type or WP it, so much the better.

The economic environment

An organisation needs to answer the question: how are we affected by economic events such as a rise in unemployment or a fall in interest rates?

We will use three sets of economic statistics to tell us how well or how badly the economy is doing. These statistics are sometimes called economic indicators. There are several activities for you to complete in this section on the economic environment. You have to collect up to date information to finish the tables and draw graphs and charts of the information. The statistics we will look at are:

- Interest rates
- Prices
- Unemployment

Interest rates

The rate of interest is very important for organisations. Companies could be borrowers or lenders of money. Companies that borrow money must pay interest to the institution that lends it. The borrowers are paying for the use of money they would not otherwise have. Companies have to repay the original amount of money borrowed plus any interest which is due. With high interest rates companies:

- Will have to pay back a lot more than they borrowed.
- May be less willing to borrow money.
- May not be able to afford to pay back the interest.
- Could take longer to pay back the original loan.
- Could be unable to do other things that they might have wished, e.g. introducing new packaging. This is called the opportunity cost, or what you have to give up to do something else.

INTEREST RATE CUT

HOME LOAN RATES DOWN

Home owners were surprised and delighted yesterday by the 1% cut in the mortgage rate. Four million borrowers will now be better off. First time house buyers . . .

Consumers are also affected by high interest rates, particularly if they are borrowers. People who have a large mortgage (money borrowed to buy a house or other property) will have to pay back more to clear (pay off) the loan. They will have less money to spend on other goods and services. This will mean that organisations which sell these products will have lower sales. Should this fall in sales continue, the company may be forced to lay off workers or even close down. During 1990 some 23 000 businesses failed, largely as a result of high interest rates.

Presenting data

Graphs

Graphs are useful for showing post trends in data. They can be confusing if too many lines are shown on the same graph.

How to draw graphs

1 Find the lowest and highest number represented in your data.
2 Put 'time' (weeks, months or years, etc. over which the data was taken) on the horizontal axis (the x-axis).
3 Put interest rates, or prices or unemployment (or any other statistic you want to plot) on the vertical axis (the y-axis).
4 Label each axis and choose a title for the graph.
5 Choose a simple scale, e.g. 1 cm = 1% of interest rate or 1 cm = 5% of prices or 100 000 unemployed.
6 Make sure that your graph with all the figures on will fit the page.
7 Put in the figures, using dots and join them up.
   To describe the information shown on the graph make comments like:

   ▸ Between August and December prices went up/down by . . .
   ▸ Between 1980 and 1985 prices rose/fell by . . .
   ▸ Between 1985 and 1990 prices remained the same.

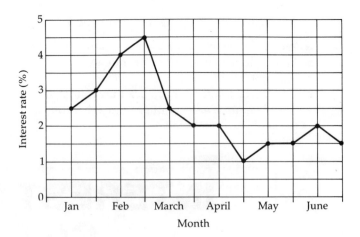

▲ *Example of a graph – interest rates over a six month period*

Bar charts

Bar charts attract people's attention. They can show totals and/or parts of a total easily. The are quickly interpreted and can be drawn to a high level of accuracy.

Instead of using dots a rectangle or bar that extends to the height of the statistic on t vertical axis can be used to show the figures. This makes a bar chart.

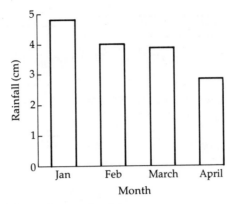

▲ *Example of a bar chart – rainfall over a four month period*

Pie charts

Pie charts are ideal for showing how a total is broken down or split into its parts. They are used to give an overall impression with reasonable accuracy. They do not give a good idea of the total figure.

A circle can be divided up in the same proportion as the data to form a pie chart. For example if 75% of the driving population of the UK drive British cars then 75% of the circle would be used to show this.

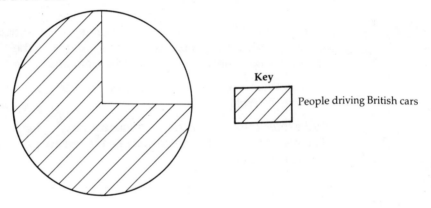

▲ *Example of a pie chart – the percentage of the population driving British cars*

Pictograms

Pictograms are best used to give a quick impression and to draw attention. They are not very accurate.

Pictograms are pictures or drawings which are used to show data. The size of each pictogram is used to give an idea of the size of the data, e.g. cars could be used to show car production or, as in the pictogram below, coins could be used to show the average weekly wage.

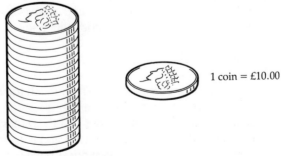

1 coin = £10.00

▲ *Example of a pictogram – the average weekly wage*

Study the following data on interest rates.

Monthly Digest of Statistics, April 1991 (from Table 17.5). Based upon selected retail banks' base rate.

1990		
	Mar	15%
	April	15%
	May	15%
	June	15%
	July	15%
	Aug	15%
	Sept	15%
	Oct	14%
	Nov	14%
	Dec	14%
1991	Jan	14%
	Feb	13%
	Mar	12.5%

Plot the data on a graph. Put the interest rate on the vertical axis and the dates/time on the horizontal axis. Leave enough space on the axis to plot the most recent data available, and to be able to show the data for the next three months.

Find the most recent information available and plot it on your graph. You can use this in the assignment 'Profit from facts'.

Write three comments/sentences about the data saying how it could affect the Worldwide Furniture Company. (Hint, you will need to redraw this graph in steps as the interest rate moves in jumps.)

Prices

All organisations are concerned about prices. Rising prices can affect them in many ways:

- Consumers will have to pay more.
- Consumers may buy less.
- Employees may demand higher wages.
- Supplies of raw materials cost more.
- Profits may fall.
- Consumers have less money to spend.
- Consumers may buy cheaper products elsewhere.
- The cost of making the goods will rise.

FILE FACT

The retail price index shows by how much the prices of goods and services we buy change. The changes in the prices of certain goods (most of which would be found in an average shopping basket) are measured month by month. The change in prices is measured from base year; this is the starting point and is given the arbitrary number 100. So if today the number is 120 we can say that prices have gone up by 20% since the base year.

1   Complete the table below showing the general index of retail prices with up-to-date figures. (Use the latest edition of *Monthly Digest of Statistics* published by HMSO.)

Make your own copy of the graph below and add your up-to-date figures to it. Write three comments that describe the graph.

Prepare the information for the assignment and say how the Worldwide Furniture Company could be affected.

General index of retail prices. All items 13 January 1987 = 100.
(*Monthly Digest of Statistics*, April 1991 – from Table 18.1)

1990	Jan	119.5
	Feb	122.0
	Mar	121.4
	April	125.1
	May	126.2
	June	126.7
	July	126.8
	Aug	128.1
	Sept	129.3
	Oct	130.3
	Nov	130.0
	Dec	129.9
1991	Jan	130.2
	Feb	130.9
	Mar	131.4

Notes: Since Jan 1987 retail prices have gone up by 31.4%. Between Mar 1990 and Mar 1991 prices have gone up by 10%

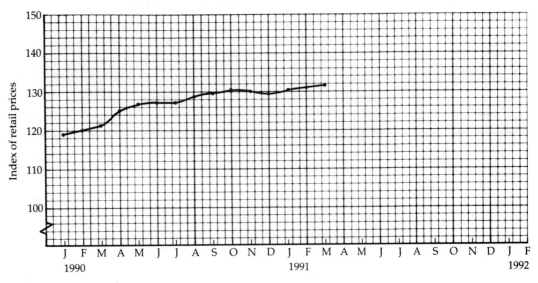

▲ *General index of retail prices*

2   Make your own index of retail prices.

   a)   Choose a small number of items that you buy regularly from your local supermarket or shop and note down the prices.

b) Note the price of your local cinema or disco.
c) Note the price of your bus or train ticket.
d) Note the price of your local hairdresser.
e) Note the date of your first observation, this is the start or base date.
f) Keep a record of how the prices change each week.
g) Over a period of six months calculate the percentage change.

Types of occupation

Primary (extractive)

Agriculture, forestry, fishing and mining are primary industries. Workers in these industries provide raw materials or resources for other industry.

Secondary

The manufacturing and construction industries are secondary industries. They include metalworking, car manufacturing, shipbuilding, chemical, engineering and building industries.

Tertiary

Distribution, insurance, banking and finance, transport, docks and ports are all tertiary industries. Professional services such as doctors, dentists, teachers, solicitors are also tertiary industry.

The UK economy

The best way to keep up to date with information about the UK and the UK economy is to know what statistical publications are available.

The *Annual Abstract of Statistics* is the major reference book for economic data. It is published every year by the central Statistics Office (CSO). The *Monthly Digest of Statistics* provides monthly data. *Economic Trends* and the *Department of Employment Gazette* are published monthly. They provide excellent information on prices, wages and employment.

The *Business Monitor* series is an excellent source of information for individual industries whilst the *National Food Survey* and *Family Expenditure Survey* are good for consumer information, particularly regional differences.

You should find all these publications in your library. Many of the activities in this book require you to keep an up-to-date statistical record of how the UK economy is behaving.

Unemployment

The amount of unemployment in the UK is a very good pointer to how well it is doing. Unemployment means there are more people looking for work than there are jobs for them. The figures on unemployment are usually written in thousands of people. The amount of unemployment is different from one town to the next. It also varies between different parts of the UK. Particular areas will be affected differently. In small towns with a high level of unemployment the effects will be severe and seen everywhere in the town. Most organisations will be affected:

- People will be unable to afford to pay their bills.
- Small shopkeepers may be owed hundreds of pounds.
- Businesses may close due to the fall in sales.
- Businesses may need to make workers redundant.
- More people may use libraries – why?
- More people will need unemployment benefit.
- People will buy less.
- People will take their money out of banks and/or building societies.
- People will postpone or delay buying new goods.

Table 3.2 *Employment News*, January 1991. There were one million, eight hundred and fifty thousand people unemployed at the end of 1990. (Figures are in thousands.)

Date	Unemployment (UK) Total seasonally adjusted			Vacancies (UK) Unfilled vacancies notified to Job Centres seasonally adjusted	
	Total (unadjusted)	Number	Change since previous month	Number	Change since previous month
Aug 1989	1741	1745	−42	220	−1
Sept	1703	1694	−51	221	+1
Oct	1636	1675	−19	213	−8
Nov	1612	1652	−23	208	−5
Dec	1639	1635	−17	198	−10
Jan 1990	1687	1612	−23	201	+3
Feb	1676	1610	−2	200	−1
Mar	1647	1604	−6	198	−2
April	1626	1607	+3	200	+2
May	1579	1612	+5	195	−5
June	1556	1618	+6	185	−10
July	1624	1632	+14	172	−13
Aug	1658	1655	+23	168	−4
Sept	1674	1671	+16	159	−11
Oct	1671	1704	+33	143	−16
Nov	1728	1763	+59	132	−11
Dec	1850	1844	+81	129	−3

Table 3.3 *Monthly Digest of Statistics*, April 1991. Unemployment. (Figures are in thousands.)

		UK total unemployment	Percentage rate of unemployment	No. of unemployed in the South-East*
1990	Jan	1687.0	5.9	339.4
	Feb	1675.7	5.9	339.5
	Mar	1646.6	5.8	339.3
	April	1626.3	5.7	345.8
	May	1578.5	5.5	349.4
	June	1555.6	5.5	354.4
	July	1623.6	5.7	359.7
	Aug	1657.8	5.8	372.3
	Sept	1673.9	5.9	383.8
	Oct	1670.6	5.9	399.1
	Nov	1728.1	6.1	422.6
	Dec	1850.4	6.5	456.7
1991	Jan	1959.7	6.9	478.3
	Feb	2045.4	7.2	514.8
	Mar	2142.1	7.5	562.8

*Statistics for other regions are shown in Table 3.11 of the *Monthly Digest of Statistics*.

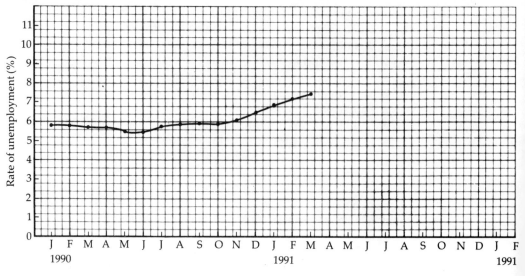

▲ *Unemplopyment rate*

/ **ACTIVITY** /

Collect up-to-date information on unemployment in your local area (use the *Employment Gazette* which you will find in your local library).

Show the number of males and females unemployed on a bar chart.

Write a short set of notes describing the main points illustrated by the data, e.g. has the level of unemployment gone up or down?

Explain briefly how the Worldwide Furniture Company could be affected by the amount of unemployment.

Copy Table 3.3 and the graph above and continue them with up-to-date information. Add the unemployment figures for your area in the last column of Table 3.3. Draw a graph to show the figures for your area.

Say what would happen if the main employer in your area was to close down.

Social environment

The term social environment covers the events which go on in society. We are a consumers of goods and services. The way we behave, act or think will affect organisations. There have been many changes in consumer tastes and behaviour in recent year The fashion in clothes is changing all the time; hem lines go up or down; trouser leg become wider or narrower; shorts may be more or less colourful. It is interesting wonder whether it is consumers who lead the fashion trends and influence the supplie of clothes, or whether the clothes manufacturers decide what the next fashion will be. Is the social environment (society) which influences the organisation or is it the organisation which affects society? We leave you to decide.

Eating and drinking

Drinks

An interesting example of the way tastes and fashions change is the demand for beer a lager. The figures in the table opposite show how the demand for beer and lager changed over the last few years. Can you suggest why this might have happened?

Table 3.4 Percentage of the market held by beer and lager

Year	Beer (% of market)	Lager (% of market)
1985	59.1	40.9
1986	56.6	43.4
1987	53.4	46.6
1988	51.2	48.8
1989	48.3	51.7

ACTIVITY

Either

Draw the information on demand for beer and lager as pictograms using bottles or glasses. Give your pictograms a title.

Or

Draw the same information in the form of pie charts. You can use a computer to do this for you.

Food

Fashions in food also seem to be changing, e.g. high fibre diets, low salt diets, etc. The current fashion seems to be for whole or natural foods with 'no artificial colours, additives or preservatives'. Instant desserts are 'virtually sugar-free'; jam has 'more fruit'.

ACTIVITY

Look at the ingredients of an instant dessert – the type to which you 'just add milk'. Can you find out what each ingredient does, and what it is?. Can you say why 'instant foods' have been developed by companies?

Population

Statistics about the current and future population are important for a wide variety of organisations. Companies making baby products will want to know about the birth rate. Government departments which provide benefits or education will also be concerned. Undertakers will want to know the death rate, as will the local authorities which run cemeteries or crematoria.

With accurate and up-to-date statistics about expected population changes companies can plan ahead. Figures which give the size of the population by age group and sex are also useful. Any change in the structure of the population will affect the demand for goods and services. This will be important for the Worldwide Furniture Company. If there are more young people in the country then the demand for educational furniture will rise. If there is a rise in the number of births then the effect of this will be felt in primary schools in five years' time. In eleven years' time the effect will be felt in secondary schools. In sixteen years' time the labour market will feel its effects through a rise in the number of school leavers.

47

This information is needed for the assignment. Some figures have been provided from the *Monthly Digest of Statistics*, April 1991. You should find more in the current issue.

1 Get the current statistics on population and the expected population for the next five years. Plot these on a graph.
2 Get the statistics on the number of school pupils in each age group, e.g. between 0–4 years, 5–9 years, etc. (Look in *Social Trends*, No. 19 may have them.)
3 Very briefly say how this information could affect the Worldwide Furniture Company.
4 How would population data help or affect your organisation?

Age distribution of the estimated resident population as at 30 June 1989. Figures are in thousands. (*Monthly Digest of Statistics*, April 1991 – from Table 2.2.)

Age range	Males	Females
0–4 years	1713.8	1632.4
5–9 years	1629.4	1548.4
10–14 years	1517.1	1434.1
15–19 years	1830.1	1739.0

FILE FACT

Population forecasting

Population forecasting works on the basis that the population now is the population one year previous plus the number of births, minus the number of deaths, including any movement of people into or out of the country.

An example will show how this works.

Population last year = 60 million
Number of births this year = 800 000
Number of deaths this year = 700 000
Inflow of people into the country (immigration) = 100 000
Outflow of people from the country (emigration) = 80 000

▶ Births are greater than deaths by 100 000, so population rises by 100 000.
▶ The number of people entering the country is greater than the number of people leaving, s▪ population rises by 20 000.
▶ Therefore total increase in population = 100 000 + 20 000 = 120 000.
▶ So the population now is 60 million plus 120 000 = 60 120 000

Forecasts of the school population also use figures produced by the government. F▪ example, a forecast about how many pupils are likely to stay on at school after the age of 1▪ will enable education planners to make decisions about further education and tertia▪ colleges. The whole population is counted very accurately once every ten years. This is th▪ census of population, last taken in 1991.

FILE FACT

Where to get more information on social issues

These are the contents of *Social Trends* published yearly by Her Majesty's Stationery Off▪ (HMSO):

Population	Housing
Households and Families	Transport and Communication
Social Groups	Environment
Education	Leisure
Employment	Public Safety
Income and Wealth	Law Enforcement
Resources and Expenditure	Participation
Health	

Design and technological environment

Technological change affects all organisations, there are:

- New machines, e.g. automatic ticket machines.
- New products, e.g. cordless telephones.
- New materials, e.g. non stick coatings.
- New types of job, e.g. software designers.
- New production methods, e.g. robot welding.

We see the changes everywhere. Shops now use bar code readers at the check-out point, these itemise your bill and inform the head office of what is being sold. In offices there are fax machines, computers and word processors. In factories there are automatic robots used for painting and welding. In the home there are microwave ovens, dishwashers and cordless phones.

In the organisation the computer has probably had the most impact. The storage and retrieval of information has totally changed. Massive amounts of data can be stored on disk.

Introducing computers into an office can be a difficult process. The benefits or advantages include:

- Easier storage of information.
- Easier and quicker access to data.
- Better communications.
- Better administration systems.

The costs or disadvantages can be:

- Fear of working with machines which can cause stress and strain.
- Need for training.
- Changed working conditions requiring a new office design.
- Visual display unit (VDU) health hazards. (New directives have just been published by the European Community. Check that your library has them.)

Production methods

Production methods have changed dramatically. New technology has altered the types of raw material that can be used in production. Plastics have been made which can do jobs which used to be done by metals. They can, for example, be used to make nuts and bolts.

New automatic methods of production have been introduced, these:

- Reduce the amount of labour needed.
- Increase efficiency and productivity.
- Reduce costs.
- Make production quicker.
- Increase the amount produced.
- Produce a standard quality.

A good example of automatic production is the manufacture of biscuits. Biscuits are made continuously. The ingredients are weighed and measured automatically. The quantities are controlled with a computer program. The ingredients are then mixed and the mixture is rolled out to the required thickness. The pastry cutter is a giant machine which turns continuously. The uncooked biscuits are put on a conveyor belt and pass into ovens (some 60 metres long). They keep moving, and stay in the oven for the required cooking time. For example if this is seven minutes the conveyor belt will move slowly through the oven taking exactly seven minutes. The hot cooked biscuits remain on the moving conveyor belt until they cool. Up until this point very few workers are needed. At the final stage the biscuits are weighed and wrapped, then placed in boxes. Finally they will be sent to warehouses and shops. This process clearly shows how automation (controlling production by electronic equipment) can be used to make goods.

When products are made by using a large amount of capital equipment and machinery and a small number of people, the industry is called **capital intensive**. However, if a large amount of labour is used and very little machinery, the industry is called **labour intensive**.

Location of industry

Why are organisations located or situated where they are? Use the list below to help you to identify some reasons. Assign each reason listed a level of importance from 1 to 5 for the organisation you are studying (1 represents 'not important at all', 5 represents 'extremely important').

Name of organisation...
Name of Product...
Location address
....
....
....

Reasons

Transport costs
Road
Rail
Canal
Airports
Other

Type of product
Bulk, volume, weight
Value

Premises costs
Land, rents, business rates
Water and sewerage
Waste disposal
Power and fuel
Gas, oil, electricity, coal
Nearness to markets
Closeness to raw materials
Density of population

Access to finance
Computer and IT facilities

Government policy – inducements
Grants
Special loans rates
Cheap lease or factory

Government policy – deterrents
Planning permission
Planning and physical controls

Environment
Attractive, green

Personal
Hobbies, countryside

Labour
Age, type, quantity, quality, training

ACTIVITY

Complete the checklist in the File Fact 'Location of industry' for your organisation. Indic the level of importance of each item on a scale of 1 to 5 with 5 = very important and unimportant.

DESKS OUT THE DOOR

A new concept for workplaces could revolutionise our daily lives

Jane Bird writes

Later this year 750 staff of the customer services division of a computer company will move into smart refurbished headquarters in Basingstoke, Hampshire.

They will occupy a space that housed 500 people before it was burnt down in March last year. But the 50 per cent increase in capacity does not mean more desks crammed together. In fact, the new building is more spacious.

The gains have been made by abolishing the idea that everyone has a desk. Nigel Dowler, the intelligent building services marketing manager for Digital Equipment, says: "The previous building was half-occupied most of the time because the majority of staff spent a lot of time away from the office visiting customers."

Instead of personal desks, the £30 million showpiece office comprises working modules for different types of activity. Staff book the modules for the days they work. They might choose a compact workstation checking electronic mail, or an area with desk space for writing reports, while conference rooms can be reserved for meetings. The building is being wired with a computer network to monitor who is at a particular desk so that telephone calls can be correctly routed. "A single network will handle data, voice, security, access, heating, ventilation and air-conditioning – processes traditionally managed separately, each with its own control system," Mr Dowler says.

Every desk will have a computer point into which equipment from different suppliers can be linked. Space sharing is the key feature of the office of the future, says Mr Dowler, who has just launched the company's consultancy service, which advises on building design.

Environmental control is also essential. The spread of desktop PC's and terminals, especially those with colour screens, requires buildings to have better ventilation.

"In the old days, computers were hidden in air-conditioned rooms in the bowels of a building. But now vastly more heat-dissipating units are being spread around offices and entire buildings have to be environmentally controlled," Mr Dowler says.

Increased mobility is another feature of the modern workforce. Radio telephones are beginning to offer services such as telepoint, which enable staff to carry cordless handsets. But how will staff feel about no longer having their own desks?

Mr Dowler believes they will accept the change if their company involves them in the analysis of how much time they need to spend in the office.

To encourage acceptance of the new office, Digital Equipment has installed leisure areas, comfortable chairs, and showers for lunchtime joggers.

"The current collapse in the commercial property market presents a great opportunity for companies to acquire premises for bargain prices and fit them up for long-term use," Mr Dowler says.

▲ The Times, *Thursday 30 May 1991*

Information technology has a major affect on where companies are located or based. Many buildings built before 1980 are not suitable for modern technology. They do not have:

● Enough space for new machinery in offices.
● Air conditioning, which is needed to take away the heat produced by computers, printers, disk drives, etc.
● Enough room to put in computer and telecommunications cables.

Paper revolution frays at edges

Offices face new challenges if they are to cope with the demands of information

Matthew May writes

Whatever happened to the paperless office? During the Eighties it became a fashionable term, conjuring up an image of a future in which filing cabinets would become obsolete and employees would enjoy a lighter workload as new office equipment became integrated and handled huge amounts of information automatically.

While business equipment has proliferated, the use of paper by most offices is still increasing, and, recessions apart, increased business has resulted in staff being as busy as ever.

Today, it is the management of information throughout a company that has become most important when investing in business technology. With it comes the idea that the successful use of such technology can provide an important advantage over rivals. For many companies, however, new technology is a necessity if the organisation is to stand a chance of competing effectively.

The personal computer was a mixed blessing for some organisations because it provided a new piece of technology that could be bought off the shelf, installed in an office, and run independently. Although performing work previously carried out by much larger and well-planned computer rooms, many departments in the early days of personal computers often bought their own equipment for specific tasks and gave little thought to a central strategy.

When networking technologies arrived and began to offer companies the ability to connect large numbers of personal computers and share information, the problems of companies with incompatible and needlessly duplicated equipment soon became apparent.

In the Nineties, purchasers realise that care is needed. Recent surveys show that a significant minority still do not get it right and end up being less than satisfied with the technology they have bought.

A survey by Touche Ross last month concluded that almost a third of directors and senior managers from 500 organisations questioned believed money they had spent on office automation systems had been of no real value.

The advice culled from organisations that considered their money well spent included using business managers rather than technical experts to lead projects, concentrating on automating a business process rather than the work of an individual, and making sure that senior management actively supported the plans.

Suppliers of business technology are trying to make their products easier to use. This is particularly true in the use of computers, where the office user wants to become the equivalent of a car driver and has little desire to become what all too often he or she has to – the equivalent of a car mechanic needing to understand how the machine works.

The giant US software firm Microsoft this month announced a programming system, Visual Basic, for its Windows package that uses small pictures and symbols to help the user.

Among the list of expected customers cited are casual programmers and consultants solving business problems in the hope they will be able to develop applications.

The business technology industry is having a difficult time; customers have less to spend and the number of suppliers continues to expand.

The boom in facsimile machines, for example, may not be over, but is certainly static. According to *What to Buy for Business* magazine, there are now more than 250 machines available from 38 suppliers in a field in which, with 750,000 businesses already online, sales are largely expected to be replacements.

Suppliers have an advantage over some other industries because developments usually mean that each year products can be made both cheaper and more powerful. With budget facsimile machines now starting at £300, suppliers are hoping that new markets will develop outside that of the standard company fax machine.

The recession and fierce competition have led to hefty price-cutting. Analysts say customers are becoming more "technically secure" and are willing to buy cheaper products. This forces manufacturers of better-known brands to compete far more on price.

▲ The Times

Many companies that had old buildings in central London have moved out, e.g. Pearl Assurance. They have specially built offices in places such as Peterborough, Bristol and Coventry. Modern telecommunications has allowed companies such as the TSB, the company which likes to 'say yes', to move the administration function out of its branches to cheaper locations. Buildings can now be linked electronically. Documents can be 'sent' by electronic mail. Video conferencing has meant that staff can be based wherever it is most cost-effective (cheapest). All these changes have helped places outside London to attract business because costs in central London are three to four times higher than elsewhere. Today there are two items that companies look at when deciding where to set up a business. The first is the cost, quality and quantity of suitably trained staff. The second is the property: how cheap it is to run? can it take modern technology?

New jobs
Look in any newspaper under the 'recruitment' section and you will see jobs which use new technology. The following examples are taken from a local newspaper.

Administrative Assistant

We are a well known national company. We require a young person with a good understanding of word processors. You will be working in the foreign travel section of . . .

Electronic Service Trainee

To work on the installation of weighing systems linked to electronic printers and computers. If you feel you have the ability to . . .

Design Trainee Required

To help with the reproduction of artwork in the form of leaflets, documents, posters and drawings. You will use an Apple Macintosh DTP system. If you . . .

These jobs need new:

- Skills
- Training methods
- Education courses, e.g. the BTEC First Diploma in Information Technology.
- Health and safety regulations.
- Working methods.
- Pay structures.
- Job descriptions.
- Attitudes.

1   In a memo to Ms Everdene explain how your job at the WFC might be affected by:
    a) The introduction of a computer into its office. (At the moment you calculate and
       present all statistics manually.)
    b) Some automation of its production methods.

2   If you are not already doing so, present the statistical information asked for in the
    assignment and activities using a computer package.

4   *Europe live*

Summary

This chapter encourages you to look at the wider world in which business organisations exist and how organisations are influenced by European and world issues. The following topics are covered:

- Advertising and promotion
- The European Community
- Green environment and business
- Political environment of business
- Pressure groups
- Impact of national government policies
- Communicating
- Interpersonal skills

This chapter will help you to achieve the following outcomes:

Core Module 1   Business World
Outcome 1.3   Examine how and why the community may seek to influence the conduct of business organisations

Core Module 2   Administrative Systems and Procedures
Outcome 2.2   Identify and use different communication systems and methods of a selected organisation
Outcome 2.3   Produce documents and material and process data
Outcome 2.5   Understand the importance of maintaining and developing good business relationships with callers, customers/clients and colleagues

Core Module 4   People in Business
Outcome 4.4   Contribute to achievement of organisational goals by fulfilling job role

The assignment can be used to cover the following performance criteria:

1.1e   the need for businesses to be dynamic in order to survive recognised
1.3a   reasons for community influence over business explained
1.3b   main forms of influence noted and outlined
1.3c   effectiveness of influence evaluated
1.4a   importance of customers recognised
2.2a   oral and written messages received and acted upon
2.2b   information obtained from appropriate sources
2.2c   routine business communications produced
2.2d   channels of communication identified and used
2.2f   electronic telecommunications used to receive and send information
2.3a   business documents produced using a word processing package
2.3b   information processing equipment used to run standard applications
2.3c   data examined and analysed using a spreadsheet package
2.3d   copies of original documents produced using reprographic equipment
2.5c   liaison and communication with peers and senior colleagues conducted effectively
2.5d   rapport and mutual respect between colleagues and customers/clients established
4.4a   relationship between organisational objectives and job role identified
4.4b   given tasks completed to agreed criteria

4.4c contribution made both as an individual and as a member of a team to the achievement of agreed targets and goals

The assignment will help with the development of Common Skills, especially the following:

Managing and Developing Self
Outcome 1 Manage own roles and responsibilities
Outcome 2 Manage own time in achieving objectives
Outcome 4 Transfer skills gained to new and changing situations and contexts

Working with and Relating to Others
Outcome 5 Treat others' values, beliefs and opinions with respect
Outcome 6 Relate to and interact effectively with individuals and groups
Outcome 7 Work effectively as a member of a team

Communicating
Outcome 9 Present information in a variety of visual forms .
Outcome 10 Communicate in writing
Outcome 11 Participate in oral and non-verbal communication

Managing Tasks and Solving Problems
Outcome 13 Deal with a combination of routine and non-routine tasks
Outcome 14 Identify and solve routine and non-routine problems

Applying Technology
Outcome 16 Use a range of technological equipment and systems

Applying Design and Creativity
Outcome 17 Apply a range of skills and techniques to develop a variety of ideas in the creation of new/modified products, services or situations

Read the following assignment to help you to understand some of the things you should be able to do by the end of this chapter. Normally it will be best for you to read the chapter and carry out the set activities before you tackle the assignment.

Check whether you can do the assignment on your own or with one or more colleagues. Some assignments will require organising by your tutor. Seek guidance, where needed, from your tutor.

Assignment

Organising an event

You work as a clerical assistant in the publicity department of the Worldwide Furniture Company, who specialise in environmentally friendly furniture.

Their address is:

Business Unit 4
Stamford Street
Brighton BR1 9LS   Telephone: 0273 439770

One of your newest ranges of products is called The MENSA Range which is a new range of 'educational furniture for intelligent people'. The main advantages of this range are:

▸ All the materials used can be recycled, i.e. used again to make new furniture. The company is environment friendly. When an existing customer requires a new design, they will be given 20% discount off their new order if they return their old furniture to be recycled.
▸ The furniture is safe. It is fire resistant and conforms to British and European standards.

To maximise publicity for the new range of furniture, Worldwide Furniture Company have decided to hold an official launch.

Task 1   You have been sent the following memo:

Memorandum

To: Clerical Assistant – Publicity   *Ref:* PS/GC

From: Publicity Manager   *Date:* 20 February 19—

Subject: MENSA Range – publicity launch

Please note the following information concerning the publicity launch in connection with the above:

A large room is needed for displaying the full range of new furniture, complete with catalogues, product information and price lists. Another room will also be needed in which to serve refreshments for the specially invited guests on the opening day. We have contacted The New European Exhibition Centre about hiring one of the Conference Suites called The Gallery and also their refreshment room.

The rates for these facilities are:

£246.00 per day
plus 10% service charge on the total for stewarding
plus 17.5% VAT on the *service charge only*

Exhibition opens   1900 hours Friday   5 May
       closes   1600 hours Friday 12 May

Hours of opening: 1000 hours – 2000 hours every day.

Admission free

The exhibition will need to be set up 5 May and removed 12 May so we will need all day bookings on these days.

As this is information which is often forgotten when setting up these exhibitions, etc., I think it would be a good idea for you to design a standard form which collates all relevant information. This could then be used on this and future occasions.

When you have designed this form please send me a blank and then complete one with the details of the above launch.

Task 2   An outline plan of the furniture to be displayed at the exhibition has been prepared. You realise, however, that no insurance has yet been arranged. You mention this is to your boss, who is so pleased with the initiative that you have shown that he rewards you by asking you to phone a local insurance broker to arrange cover.

Your boss explains that they will charge a premium based on the total value of the furniture to the nearest £100. There will be ten chairs, two in each colour available, and two tables from every design. Using the press release and price list at the end of the assignment, work out the value of the furniture that needs to be insured.

Your boss also reminds you that you will need to cover the period they will be in transit from your office to the exhibition and back, so to give the insurance broker both addresses.

Being organised, you make telephone notes first – so write these out.

You will need to obtain a suitable broker from *Yellow Pages*.

Task 3   It has been decided that 200 people will be invited to the opening of the launch. After that, the display will be left for five days for the general public to view.

As we are now a member of the European Community and environmental issues are a major concern, the Worldwide Furniture Company believe that Europe will be a good market. It has been agreed, therefore, that the launch will be opened by a prominent environmentalist in the presence of your local MEP. Find out the names of these two people.

Prepare the invitation, mentioning the above piece of information. The invitation will be sent from MD of Worldwide Furniture Company and should give full details of time, date and place. Replies should be sent to the Publicity Department, Worldwide Furniture Company.

You will need to find out an acceptable layout for the invitation – *Debretts* will help you.

Task 4   Once your invitations are prepared you will need to compile a guest list. This should include anyone who could possibly help to endorse the product and therefore maximise sales, plus people who are likely to buy the products. Find the names and addresses of some of the guests who could be invited. You must include the following:

▸ Minister for Trade and Industry.
▸ Local MP.
▸ Mayor.
▸ Local councillors.
▸ Representatives from 'green' groups.
▸ People from schools and colleges.
▸ The local paper.
▸ A suitable national paper.
▸ Local radio.
▸ Possible distributors.
▸ Possible buyers.

Once you have compiled a list, enter the names and addresses on to a database and, if possible, use the mail merge computer package to help you with the mailing list for the invitations.

The company will be represented at the launch by the MD, five directors, four department heads and six area sales supervisors.

Task 5   Obviously refreshment will have to be served at the opening of the launch. Look at the N European Menus at the end of the assignment and choose an appetising menu. Remember however, you have a budget of £2,750 which you must not exceed.

Task 6   Write a memo summarising your actions to date giving costs where applicable.

Worldwide Furniture Company

Press Release

Contact: BTEC Trainee
May 1991

New from the Worldwide Furniture Company
The MENSA Range – Educational furniture for intelligent people
5 new designs of environment friendly furniture!

1. The **Mont Blanc** a high chair ideally suited to the needs of very small chilren, made of high-tech moulded plastic which can be totally recycled. Once the child has grown too big for the Mont Blanc, trade it in for the **Continental**.
2. The **Continental** – a hard wearing chair and table specially designed for general classroom use. It will suit children up to seven years old.
3. The **European** is an ergonomically designed chair and table for children of today. Perfect for children aged 7–10 years old. This chair is made completely from materials which can be recycled. Keep Europe green, buy this chair.
4. The **21st Century** – chairs and tables of the future available today. Perfect for 10–15 year olds who care for their environment. Every part can be re-used. Perfect styling, modern appearance – yet totally functional.
5. Reach for the sky with the **Alpine**. Climb to the top with this young executive chair and desk set. The Alpine will appeal immediately to the 15+ age range. Good looks with plenty of green appeal.

All items in the MENSA Range are available in five environment friendly colours. Only natural products are used in our dyes. Choose from:

- Ice blue
- Sunset red
- Forest green
- Deep space
- Sunripe yellow

PRICE LIST

		No. of chairs/tables bought			
		1–5 £	6–20 £	21–99 £	100 + £
	Mont Blanc				
Chair	Ref. MB 200	10.80	10.70	9.40	9.00
	Continental				
Chair	Ref. C 3000	13.20	13.00	12.10	11.90
Table	Ref. T 300 1	17.10	16.20	15.60	15.10
	European				
Chair	Ref. E 4000	13.90	13.60	13.10	12.20
Table	Ref. F 400 1	18.00	17.60	17.00	16.05
	21st Century				
Chair	Ref. C 5000	11.90	11.40	10.70	10.10
Table	Ref. CA 500 1	17.90	17.40	16.60	15.90
	Alpine				
Chair	Ref. A 600	18.60	18.10	17.50	15.20
Table	Ref. T 60 1	20.30	20.00	19.40	18.90

NEW EUROPEAN MENU

An informal reception, drinks at the end of a conference, a drinks party with friends or a reception pre-concert or theatre, the *New European Menu* can take many different forms.

These prices are exclusive of 10% service charge and 17.5% VAT.

Menus 1 ands 2 are not designed as a substitute for a meal, purely for a short reception, whilst menus 3 and 4 are more substantial.

Menu 1
£4.00 per head

Savoury Biscuits, assorted Salted Nuts and Marinated Olives

Cold
A Selection of trayed Canapes including:
Palm Hearts and Parma Ham
Smoked Salmon
Pastrami
Chicken Liver
Danish Caviar
Bouchees of Scallops in Curry Mayonnaise
Blue Cheese and Bacon Dip with Corn Chips and Crisp Vegetables

Hot
Chipolatas with Sour Cream and Mustard Sauce

Menu 2
£5.85 per head

Savoury Biscuits, assorted Salted Nuts and Marinated Olives

Cold
A Selection of trayed Canapes to include:
Palm Hearts and Parma Ham
Smoked Salmon
Pastrami
Tartlets of Salmon and Brill Pate
Tartlets of Chicken Liver

Open Sandwiches of:
Smoked Salmon
Beef and Turkey

Blue Cheese and Bacon Dip with Corn Chips and Crisp Vegetables

Hot
Fantail Shrimps
Cheese Profiteroles
Baby Hamburgers in Sour Cream

MENU 3
£9.05 per head

Savoury Biscuits, assorted Salted Nuts and Marinated Olives

Cold
A Selection of trayed Canapes including:
Grissini Sticks with Parma Ham
Salmon Pate "En Croute"
Galatine of Duck with Pistachio
Gravadlax of Salmon on Pumpernickle
Bouchees of Crab in Asparagus Mayonnaise

Advertising and promotion

This is a major part of the marketing function, so much so in fact that very often the advertising will not be handled 'in-house' that is by the company, but by an advertising agency which is a company specialising in media advertising. An advertising agency has personnel qualified in graphics, media scheduling, etc.

However, promoting and advertising are still likely to be part of any job. There are many ways of promoting and advertising your product, e.g. leaflets and competitions. Open days and stands at exhibitions are popular as they can attract a wide range of people from committed buyers to casual observers. Having attracted the audience it is then up to the representatives of a company to convert them to customers.

From the actual event (e.g. open day, trade fair) stems more publicity which is often free. Local press will almost certainly attend and write about the event. If it is unusual or eyecatching enough so too may local radio or television. To encourage coverage your company may well send out a press release. This is written by the promoting company but given to the press who use it to fill spaces in their magazines or newspapers. There is an example of a press release in the assignment. This would most likely be sent to a trade magazine but a press release of the event would be available to visiting media at the launch. When organising such an event it is common to give a 'hook' or offer. Examples may be a prize draw, cookery demonstration with free drinks and a recipe book, free trials on the sunbeds.

ACTIVITY

Scan your local paper for events and note the different inducements to attend. You can include non-profit making concerns such as charities as well as social clubs.

In any event you will have to notify the public and potential customers. For one-off events posters and newspaper advertisements can be placed.

Essential information to include on your poster or advertisement is:

1 Who is holding the event.
2 What form the event will take.
3 When and at what time the event is happening.
4 Where it is to be held.
5 Attractions.

These items are in order of priority and should be presented in this way. It is up to the designer to present the information in an eye-catching and interesting way. If you are a good artist or designer you may find this easy, but even if you cannot draw you can still produce effective posters. The key is to use simple designs. Much can be achieved through using stencils for lettering or computer packages.

ACTIVITY

Collect or notice posters advertising events. Note what you like or do not like about the posters. Give reasons for your comments and discuss them in class.

If you make a check list of all the points raised by the class you may find subjective reasons for not liking the posters being given, e.g. 'I don't like the colour green', 'I hate tennis'. Although these comments are not strictly concerned with good design they are a good indication of the prejudices designers have to overcome. Another key to designing posters, therefore, is to consider your audience. The more wide ranging and less specialist your audience is, the less controversial your design needs to be. If you are aiming at a particular group of people, your design can reflect their tastes or knowledge.

ACTIVITY

Design a poster for one of the following:

▶ An open day at a company's sports and social club.
▶ A fund raising event for charity.
▶ The Worldwide Furniture Company launch.

Discuss the finished posters in your class or group and pick out the good design points and where improvements could be made. Make the improvements.

The event

To organise a successful event it is necessary to have planned and organised well in advance not only administrative systems but publicity material. However, the e would be spoiled if attention is not given to the design and layout of the actual site, be it a stand or a whole building. The site should be made as visually attractive and interesting as possible and should also guide your public around, pointing out features and relevant details you want them to notice.

In order to ensure that the public are picking up the points that the company wishes to make, these features and details are usually presented on publicity leaflets and hand-outs as well as on posters dotted around the stand or exhibition. If a company has carried out their market research well, then they will know what their customers want and which features of their products to emphasise.

In the assignment the Worldwide Furniture Company have arranged their launch to target several markets and therefore maximise their chances of success. The decisions of this company, and any other company wishing to be successful will not rest on willy-nilly decisions and local research but will also take into account factors which govern the economy, the environment, and economic issues. Lets look in turn at the areas they are targeting and some of the background information which helped them to make their decisions.

The European angle

Worldwide Furniture Company have used names with a European feel for the products in their new range. They have also invited their member of the European Parliament to be present at the launch. The following section helps to explain why they have done this.

The European Community (EC) has been evolving since 1957 and now has 12 countries as members. These are France, Belgium, Germany, Luxembourg, Italy, The Netherlands, Denmark, United Kingdom, Eire, Greece, Spain and Portugal. It is most likely that others will join.

▲ *Member countries of the European Community*

Aim of the European Community

By 1993 there should be a Europe where:

- There are no frontiers or borders between member countries.
- People can move freely and live and work wherever they want within the EC.
- Goods can be bought and sold in any country within the EC.
- There should be common or single European decisions on:

Social affairs	Monetary systems	Competition
The environment	Foreign policy	Health and safety
Economic issues	Agriculture	Taxation, etc.

Almost every part of our lives will be affected.

How the European Community works

The aim of the EC is to have a common market. All the countries should co-operate or work together. Companies should be able to buy and sell goods in any of the member countries. They should not have to pay any duties or taxes when their goods cross a frontier or border (duty free shops could disappear). To help the European Community achieve its aims there are various European institutions. Some of these are mentioned below.

The European Commission

This organisation is based in Brussels, the capital city of Belgium. It has 17 members or commissioners chosen from different countries. They are supposed to act and think as Europeans. They should not represent the country from which they come.

The European Commission has four main aims. These are:

1 To make policies and decisions which cover all community activities.
2 To get the governments of member countries to agree on policies.
3 To make sure that the laws of the community are obeyed.
4 To manage and direct community business.

All EC documents are translated into nine official languages (the United Nations only has six). This is very expensive. Many translators have to be employed.

The Council of Ministers

All important EC decisions are taken by the Council of Ministers. Each country sends a government minister to the meetings. Membership is not constant and it depends upon what is to be discussed as to who will go, for example, if the discussion is to do with finance then the UK would send the Chancellor of the Exchequer. Each minister will act in the interest of their own country, unlike the European Commission members.

European Parliament

The European Parliament has 518 members or MEP's (Members of the European Parliament). They represent approximately 329 million people. As these MEP's are voted locally there are many political parties represented. They do not sit, therefore, by country but in political groups. The European Parliament meets in three centres – Strasbourg, Brussels and Luxembourg. MEP's are elected every five years.

The European Parliament can:

- Be consulted by the Commission on new plans.
- Decide how the community is to spend its money (the budget).
- Criticise and question the Commission.
- Advise the Council of Ministers.

The Court of Justice

The judges who are members of the Court of Justice are free to make decisions in the best interests of the community. They are independent. All laws made by the Council of Ministers must be obeyed in all the member countries and if anyone breaks them they can be taken to the Court of Justice, regardless of any decision which might have been made by a country's own judicial system.

Making Community laws

1 The Commission drafts or writes its proposed legislation

↓

2 The draft is sent to the European Parliament for discussion

↓

3 It is then passed to the Economic and Social Committee which has a membership of employers, consumers and trade unions

↓

4 It passes next to the Council of Ministers. If they accept it, the proposal becomes law

Effects of the new Europe

Language

When the Channel Tunnel is completed you will be able to travel to Paris or Brussels in three hours. Many Europeans already speak English, for example in Holland 65% of the population do. However, very few British people speak any foreign language so many Europeans will be in a position to trade over here, but we may have difficulty trading over there. This will affect business.

Passports

Have you applied for a new passport recently? Did you receive the new maroon coloured passport? Air travellers between France, Germany, Belgium, Luxembourg and The Netherlands do not even need a passport. The UK, however, will continue to issue passports with the words 'European Community' stamped on the front.

Try to get hold of an old British passport and a new style European Community passport and list any differences you can see. Why do you think these changes have been made?

Cheques and financial services

If you have a Eurocheque Card and Eurocheques you can use them on the Continent to buy goods or get cash from the bank or cash machines. As stated by *Europe without Frontiers – Completing the Internal Market* published by Official Publications of the European Community 1987 you should also be able to arrange insurance, buy unit trusts or have access to the full range of banking and mortgage facilities in any member state. This means that a Spanish householder, for example, could take out a mortgage from a German finance house, buy shares on the London stock market and take out an insurance policy from an Italian company.

As can be seen, the European community opens up a large market to businesses and *Europe without Frontiers* helps businesses to trade easily. (No wonder the Worldwide Furniture Company want to make sure they appeal to Europe.) However, it must also be noted that there are laws as to the standard of goods sold and all goods must match these standards. These standards are concerned largely with the safety of goods and ensure that goods are comparable in every member country. Once goods have passed the test and are found to match the required standards then they are given the EC mark.

───/ **ACTIVITY** /───────────────────────

Europe facts and figures

	Surface area (1000 km^2)	Population (millions)
France	544	55.2
Spain	505	38.6
Germany	356	78.1
Italy	301	57.1
UK	244	56.6
Greece	132	9.9
Portugal	92	10.2
Ireland	70	3.5
Denmark	43	14.5
The Netherlands	41	14.5
Belgium	31	9.9
Luxembourg	3	0.4

- Display these data on two bar charts.
- Which country has the largest population per 1000 km^2?
- Which country has the smallest population per 1000 km^2?
- All the countries are potentially important markets – but which would you choose as t one in which you would gain most sales most easily. Give reasons for your answers a listen to other people's viewpoints. Look carefully at your answers on the density population, that is the number of people per 1000 km^2.

The green environment

Worldwide Furniture Company have invited a prominent environmentalist to open the launch. The environment is a concern of the European Community, but there are also other reasons why the environmentalist has been invited. Nowadays people are very concerned about the way in which organisations affect the environment (yes, we are now talking about the physical environment – the air, water, land and trees).

What are the environmental problems?

- Destruction of the rain forests.
- Pollution of the air by smoke, fumes and gases (including CFCs).
- Pollution of land and rivers by industrial waste materials, sewage, etc.
- The increased 'greenhouse effect'.
- Destruction of the ozone layer.
- Acid rain.
- Changing weather patterns.
- Litter.

Let us look in more detail at some of these problems and concerns and see how they are caused.

Destruction of the forests

Many thousands of square miles of forest in tropical areas such as Brazil are being destroyed every year. The forests contain hardwoods such as teak and mahogony. They are cut down and burned to make the land available for agriculture. Some of the wood is exported to Europe and North America but much of it is burned. When the trees are

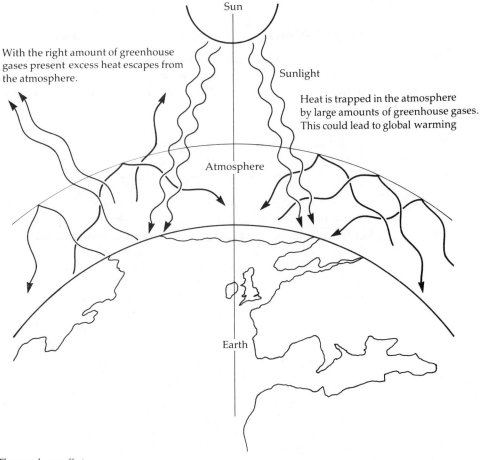

▲ *The greenhouse effect*

burned large amounts of 'greenhouse gases' (e.g. carbon dioxide) rise up into the atmosphere. 'Greenhouse gases' trap heat in the atmosphere and warm the Earth up. This is called the greenhouse effect. Burning a lot of trees makes the greenhouse effect worse.

As the rain forest is destroyed many plants and animals become extinct. Many of our modern medicines contain substances which were first found in rain forest plants. By destroying the forests we may have already have destroyed plants which could have provided cures and treatments for some of the many diseases that afflict us.

CFCs

CFCs (chlorofluorohydrocarbons) are gases found in some refrigerators and aerosol cans. When the aerosol cans are used or refrigerators disposed of, CFCs are released into the atmosphere. It is now realised that CFCs in the atmosphere are dangerous because they destroy the ozone layer. The ozone layer is a layer of gas in the Earth's upper atmosphere. The layer of ozone stops harmful radiation from the Sun reaching us. One of the effects of reducing the ozone layer would be an increase in the incidence of skin cancers due to more of the harmful radiation from the Sun reaching us.

Acid rain

We burn fossil fuels (which have taken millions of years to form) such as coal, oil and natural gas to heat our homes and fuel our power stations. The gases produced from burning these fuels dissolve in water droplets in the atmosphere to form a weak acidic solution. When this 'acid rain' falls, it damages and destroys trees, plants and buildings and makes the soil and water acidic. Acid rain has already done considerable damage over large areas of Europe.

Why should we worry about the environment?

The Earth's natural resources are limited but our demands are unlimited. Everytime we use these resources there are less available for present and future generations. It must be remembered that these resources evolved over millions of years so it is not just a case of waiting for them to replenish themselves.

Pollution is another problem associated with our demands. The more of the environment we pollute with smoke, litter, exhaust fumes, chemicals, etc. the fewer clean resources are available to us. This can affect our health, for example an increase in asthma and allergy cases has been linked to an increase in air pollution.

Unless we address environmental problems, we could find our health affected, our living standards reduced and eventually our planet dying. It has been the work of many organisations and pressure groups to bring environmental issues to our attention in order that we too can put pressure on governments and businesses to help us to take action. You will almost certainly have noticed recycling schemes in your area, e.g. bottle banks, paper banks, can deposits, etc. Recycling schemes are good and many products are now made from recycled paper, but do these measures go far enough? We leave you to answer the question.

───/ **ACTIVITY** /────────────────────────────────

Look around the room you are in and notice all the things in it. How many have been recycled or are environmentally friendly? Do you know if alternatives are available for those which are not environmentally friendly? Try to find out.

Much as the public can do to help protect the environment by careful buying and recycling, it is in fact manufacturers and companies who really need to address environmental issues as many are the major polluters of the world. The public can bring pressure to bear on these organisations by boycotting their goods and this is why many companies are now presenting a 'green' image – if they do not then they could sell less and lose profit.

ACTIVITY

There are many ways in which companies try to present an image of caring for the environment. As a group brainstorm as many examples as you can. You can include adverts (be specific as to advert and company), labels on packaging, etc.

In what ways is the Worldwide Furniture Company presenting an environment friendly image?

In groups carry out a survey of your place of study to see what policies they have adopted to become more environmentally friendly.

Construct a questionnaire and carry out research to discover how aware of environmental issues the other people in your building are.

Write a report for your teachers or article for the college/school magazine on your findings and try to suggest areas for improvement.

The political environment and local community

MPs, councillors, schools and colleges were invited to the Worldwide Furniture Company launch as well as the exhibition being open to the public. Why were these people invited? The MENSA furniture range is particularly developed for educational establishments, so why should anyone else be invited? The following section should help to answer this question.

The political environment

The political environment is the society formed by our government. Different political parties will create different political environments. Politicians are people who are interested in or active in politics. They may be paid or unpaid and usually belong to a political party. People in the same party will share similar views and vote together to beat a rival party. Every politician wants to achieve power so that their party's policies can be put into action. The words 'left' and 'right' are sometimes used to describe political parties.

Left   Right

Communist Party   Labour party   Liberal Democrats   Conservative party   National Front

▲ *The political spectrum*

Each party produces a manifesto. This document shows what ideas and policies they have. Each party has different ideas about what society should be like. For example, different parties have different views on:

- The education and health systems.
- Housing and welfare policies.
- Benefits.
- Defence.
- How companies should behave.

- The amount of government intervention.
- Economic objectives on inflation, unemployment, etc.
- Social policies.

People vote on the basis of the policies and premises of political parties. Organisations are also affected by the political process. The level of central and local government intervention depends upon which party is in power (i.e. which party has formed the government).

The international political environment is also important and can affect the way organisations act. Civil wars, unrest, revolutions all affect the decisions that organisations make.

In the United Kingdom the politicians who represent us in parliament are elected by the general public – the voters. Anyone over the age of 18 years can vote. The politician who gets the most votes in an election becomes a Member of Parliament (MP). The party which gains the most members wins the election and gets to form the Government.

To be able to vote you must be registered, that is your name must be on the electoral role. Once you have done this you are allowed to vote in elections for:

1 A Member of Parliament (MP) who will be your representative in the House of Commons.
2 A local councillor who will represent you on the local council.
3 A member of the European Parliament (MEP).

There are two Houses of Parliament:

- The House of Lords or the Upper House, whose members are not elected.
- The House of Commons, whose members (the MPs) are elected.

Results of the general election held on 9 April 1992.

Political party	Number of seats in House of Commons	Percentage of total votes
Conservative	336	41.9
Labour	271	34.5
Liberal Democrat	20	17.9
Scottish National Party	3	1.9
Plaid Cymru	4	0.5
Other parties	17	3.3

Conservative majority 21 seats.

ACTIVITY

Find out:

- The name of your local MP.
- The political party to which your MP belongs.
- The name of your parliamentary constituency (the area or place represented by your MP
- The name of your local councillor.
- The political party to which your councillor belongs.

By now you should be asking why you need to collect all this information. The answer because you want your views to be known. For example, if a local company is polluting t environment, a good method of complaining is to write to your local councillor and/or lo

MP. You could get a group of people to form a committee and start a campaign to save the environment in your town. These groups of people are called pressure groups – they are trying to force (put pressure on) other people to do what they want. This is why the Worldwide Furniture Company wants local people to attend their launch – they want local people to put pressure on the schools and colleges to buy environment friendly products.

Central government

The policies of central government affect us all. This is because of the way **it spends money** (e.g. on defence, health services, etc.) and **collects money** through taxation (e.g. income tax, VAT, etc.).

Among the things the Government spends money on are:

- Defence.
- Industry, trade and employment.
- Agriculture.
- Transport.
- Housing.
- Environmental services – parks, etc.
- Law and order.
- Education and science and arts funding.
- Health and social services.
- Social security.

The sources through which the government gets its income or revenue include:
- Income tax – the tax on a person's income.
- National insurance (NI) contributions.
- North Sea oil royalties – the money paid by oil companies for exploration and extraction.
- Government borrowing, e.g. National Savings Certificates.
- Value-added tax (VAT) – this is a tax on a person's spending.
- Corporation tax – tax paid by companies on the profits they make.
- Duties on tobacco and drinks.
- Car tax.

Central government spending can have very important effects on local communities. In the aerospace industry, 60 per cent of all the work done is for the Government (defence spending). Some towns, such as Barrow-in-Furness where Trident submarines are made, would be badly affected if the Government decided to cut defence spending by cancelling its order for Trident submarines.

Local government

Local government comprises of county and district councils (occasionally parish councils are involved too). Local policies are determined by elected councillors. Sources of income for local government include business rates and community charge (poll tax). Central government grants and payments for services are also available to fund local government.

Local government spending can also have important effects on local communities. A decision by local government to build a local road or school will have a positive effect on a community. To start with the builders will benefit, then the building suppliers, then the companies which provide services such as lighting and telecommunications. Once the project is under way the local shops and cafes will gain from the extra spending of employees, visitors, etc. This is called the **ripple effect.**

However, the opposite could also be true if local government decides to close a school. In this case many people will lose their jobs, and the shops, cafes, etc. where they spent their money will also get into difficulty.

A similar ripple effect can be caused by private industry. If an organisation decides to set up business in a town, then the town can prosper. If an organisation moves away from a town, the reverse situation is equally true.

---/ **ACTIVITY** /---

Because local government collects a percentage of its money through the community charge, they have to publish where they spend that money. A leaflet containing this information is sent out every year with community charge bills. If you don't have one of these leaflets in your home, collect one from your library or local government office and see where their (or your) money was spent.

Recently the Government has decided that responsibility for expensive items of their budget should be given to the spenders. An example of this is in education. 'Spenders' of the education budget are schools and colleges.

Under the new arrangements schools and colleges will be given a fixed sum to spend as they see fit (previously local government was responsible). This is known as local management of schools (LMS) or Local Management of Colleges (LMC). As both schools and colleges need furniture, the Worldwide Furniture Company wishes to capitalise on this market with their MENSA range of educational furniture. They offer a good financial incentive to this market with their discount on further orders and bulk discounts. They believe their environment friendly image will appeal to parents and students and hope that these groups will put pressure on the schools and colleges to make a good environmental choice.

Thus it can be seen that manufacturers have many environments and markets to consider before they launch a new product. It follows that if they have 'read' their market correctly, then they need to inform all interested parties through advertising.

Administration

The assignment 'Organising an event' concerns the launch of a product and deals with issues of marketing and promotional activities. There are, however, a variety of skills and competences attached to the administration of such a business event which would be applicable in many other business related activities regardless of the company or type of work you are involved in.

Accurate handling of information is vital and you will be required to display your ability and skills in a variety of ways.

Collating information

A common method of collating necessary information is on a form. A form may be designed specifically for one occasion, e.g. a survey, questionnaire, or a standard form may be devised if the same type of information is required regularly, e.g. job application form, booking form, accident report form.

The reason for having a form is to ensure that information is not missed and that it is easy to pick out at a glance. A good form will, therefore, be logically set out, group certain types of information together (maybe by using subtitles), and be easy to fill in.

---/ **ACTIVITY** /---

Collect some forms together and discuss these in a group or with your teacher. Notice what information is given first and try to give possible reasons for this. What devices are used help the person who fills in the form make as few errors as possible?

You should arrive with a checklist of good design points which will help you with Task 1 of the assignment.

Once the information has been collected and acted upon the form will most likely be filed, at least until the task is closed. This may be in a manual system, but if several cross-references are needed or other departments need access to the file, then a computer may be more appropriate.

—/ **ACTIVITY** /————————————————————

Make a chart of the different types of filing system used in offices. Give examples of where each would be most appropriate and why.

List as many advantages as you can (at least four) of using a centralised computer system.

(For more information on filing systems, see Chapter 7, Office Organisation.)

Telephone notes

Many telephone calls require you to handle information orally. When you make a personal call you probably do not think about writing down what you want to say, but you have almost certainly planned it in your head. In business however you may need to make many calls and there is no guarantee that the person you wish to speak to will be available to take your call at the time you phone. There is always a danger that, with other interruptions and demands on your time, information will be forgotten. It is therefore necessary that you plan your call first and make notes for yourself.

Telephone Notes

Name of company

Tel. number

Name of contact (*If known, otherwise write it in as soon as you are connected to the right person*)

1 Give my name, company *Port Talbot College*

2 State reason for the call *Wish to order from new range of chairs and tables*

3 *MENSA range — recently advertised*

4 Details *55 Alpine chairs ref A600, 55 Alpine tables ref T601*

5 *Colour — forest green*
   Please send quote to Port Talbot College, Station Road, Port Talbot

Thank receiver of call *West Glam., SW13 4JN*

Telephone notes follow the same principles as a good form – a logical order which is easy to follow.

A suggested format for telephone notes is shown on p. 73. (Note that you are **not** writing a script to follow.)

⎯⎧ ACTIVITY ⎫⎯

Make telephone notes and role play the call for the following situations:

- Hairdresser's appointment.
- Booking a restaurant for a business lunch.
- Booking a dog/cat into kennels.

When you are confident try to make some more complex calls.

After any successful promotion the work does not of course stop but starts. Below are a few of the requests the Worldwide Furniture Company received for quotations.

A quotation is a list of current prices or costs given by a seller of goods to possible buyers. It can also show whether the seller is willing to give a discount for:

- Payment by cash.
- Prompt payment.
- Large purchases.

⎯⎧ ACTIVITY ⎫⎯

Use the press release and price list from the assignment to reply to the requests for quotations received by the Worldwide Furniture Company.

1

> Port Talbot College
> Station Road
> Port Talbot
> West Glam
> SW13 4JN
>
> The Worldwide Furniture Co
>
> Dear Sir/Madam
>
> We are very interested in your new range of MENSA furniture which can be recycled. Could you please send a quote for 55 Alpine chairs and 11 tables in ice blue and for 18 chairs and 4 tables in sunset red.
>
> Yours faithfully
>
> *M Paul*
>
> M Paul

2

St Martins Junior School
Bromley
Kent
BR1 5ZY

Worldwide Furniture Co

Dear Ms Everdene
We were very impressed with your new chairs, which we saw advertised recently. Could you please give us a quote for 10 Mont Blanc in forest green, and 80 Continental in sunrise yellow.

Yours sincerely

A Burton

A Burton

3

Abbey Local Education Authority
The Green Borough
County Hall, Abbey

Worldwide Furniture Co
Managing Director

Dear Mr Oak
We are attempting to refurnish many of our secondary schools in an attempt to stop them from opting out.

Could you please provide us with a quote for your new **MENSA** range of furniture.

We are looking for a special discount given the size of the order.

We would require:

800 21st Century chairs in Deep Space
400 21st Century tables in Deep Space
350 21st Century tables in Ice Blue
425 21st Century tables in Sunset Red
200 Alpine tables in Forest Green
240 Alpine tables in Sunripe Yellow
700 21st Century chairs in Ice Blue
850 21st Century chairs in Sunset Red
400 Alpine chairs in Forest Green
475 Alpine chairs in Sunripe Yellow

Yours sincerely

J Thomas

J Thomas
Chief Executive

Sales and marketing

Summary

This chapter looks in depth at how the business organisation deals with customers – as individuals as well as a group. It does this by introducing you to customer care with an assignment set in the insurance industry and then takes you into the work of sales and marketing departments. The following topics are covered:

▸ Aspects of the insurance industry
▸ Dealing with customers
▸ Telephoning
▸ Market research
▸ Questionnaires
▸ Advertising and promotion
▸ Marketing department
▸ Presentation of sales/marketing information
▸ Consumer law
▸ Customer relations and after sales care
▸ Interpersonal skills

This chapter will help you to achieve the following outcomes:

Core Module 1 **Business World**
 Outcome 1.4 Examine the relationships between an organisation and its customers

Core Module 2 **Administrative Systems and Procedures**
 Outcome 2.3 Produce documents and material and process data
 Outcome 2.5 Understand the importance of maintaining and developing good business relationships with callers, customers/clients and colleagues

Core Module 4 **People in Business**
 Outcome 4.3 Examine and compare the main job roles in different organisations
 Outcome 4.4 Contribute to the achievement of organisational goals by fulfilling job role

The assignments can be used to cover the following performance criteria:

 1.4a importance of customers recognised
 1.4b types of customers identified
 1.4c changes in customers needs and business response identified
 1.4d need for employees to present positive image of the organisation fully understood
 2.1a documents filed in correct location and sequence
 2.1d business records managed using a simple database
 2.2a oral and written messages received and acted upon
 2.2b information obtained from appropriate sources
 2.2c routine business communications produced
 2.3a business documents produced using a word processing package
 2.3b information processing equipment used to run standard applications
 2.3c data examined and analysed using a spreadsheet package
 2.3d copies of original documents produced using reprographic equipment
 2.5b polite and effective responses made to a range of customer/client situations
 2.5d rapport and mutual respect between colleagues and customers/clients established
 4.3a functional areas within organisations identified
 4.3b job roles in different functional areas of organisation identified
 4.3c job roles compared

4.4a relationship between organisational objectives and job role identified

4.4b given tasks completed to agreed criteria

4.4c Contribution made both as an individual and as a member of a team to the achievement of agreed targets and goals

The assignment will help with the development of Common Skills, especially the following:

Managing and Developing Self

Outcome 1 Manage own roles and responsibilities

Outcome 2 Manage own time in achieving objectives

Working with and Relating to Others

Outcome 6 Relate to and interact effectively with individuals and groups

Outcome 7 Work effectively as a member of a team

Communicating

Outcome 8 Receive and respond to a variety of information

Outcome 9 Present information in a variety of visual forms

Outcome 10 Communicate in writing

Outcome 11 Participate in oral and non-verbal communication

Managing Tasks and Solving Problems

Outcome 12 Use information sources

Outcome 13 Deal with a combination of routine and non-routine tasks

Outcome 14 Identify and solve routine and non-routine problems

Applying Numeracy

Outcome 15 Apply numerical skills and techniques

Applying Technology

Outcome 16 Use a range of technological equipment and systems

Read the following assignment to help you to understand some of the things you should be able to do by the end of this chapter. Normally it will be best for you to read the chapter and carry out the set activities before you tackle the assignment.

Check whether you can do the assignment on your own or with one or more colleagues. Some assignments will require organising by your tutor. Seek guidance, where needed, from your tutor.

Assignment

A risky business

You work as a junior clerk in an insurance brokers called Crisease, 99 Nine Elms Road, Birmingham BR1 2EE, Tel No. 0232 44454.

As a registered broker you are not confined to using one insurance company but may choose the best deal for each individual customer. This is an extremely competitive business and so sales and marketing are important functions needed to keep the edge on competitors. Emphasis is given to a personal service where clients are made to feel like valued individual customers rather than just another customer number among thousands.

Task 1 To ensure that the business is giving the right service a 'snapshot' survey of the market is carried out at intervals.

Draw up a questionnaire to use in face to face interviews. The questionnaire should be suitable to find out the type of insurance most commonly used for each age group, who people insure through, how they apply, why they chose that insurance company, and what, if anything, would persuade them to change company.

Carry out a market research survey on 20 people using the questionnaire. You could work in pairs and halve the workload, or better still make this a class or group effort. The more responses you get the more accurate a reflection of the market your results will give.

Task 2 Analyse the survey results and set them down in a form of report. Give your conclusions on which insurance is needed most by which age group. Try to say where there may be a gap in the market and then recommend how you could capitalise on this.

Task 3 Insurance brokers can use various computer networks for their information on policies, prices and quotations, but they also have some companies they have tried and tested. Research as many different insurance companies as you can as a group to find out what they are offering, plus any special deals, and put them on a data base for your use in helping with enquiries.

You will need several fields, e.g. type of insurance, name of company, special deals, file number (or location in your filing system). Add any further fields you may consider necessary.

Task 4 Organise all the prospectuses and proposal forms you have collected in a physical file so that you can pull out the details for clients when you need them.

Task 5 People need to be made aware of your company and told of the advantages of dealing through you and the services you offer. Customers also need to know what they may need to be insured for and whether there are any pitfalls.

Draft a leaflet which your boss may use. When you have finished and had it approved you could desk-top publish it.

Task 6 During the course of a busy morning you have several customers who ring or call in person. Role play or state how you would handle the following:

a) A young couple buying their first home want advice on contents insurance. How much should they insure for? How can they estimate this? What should their cover include? Their house is a small two bedroom terrace. They own the usual stereo, television, etc. but nothing of outstanding value.

b) A middle-aged woman needs cover for her new Ford Escort 1.2 car. She has not had to make an insurance claim in the last 15 years.

c) A family consisting of two adults and two children (ages seven and nine years) are travelling independently by air to a hotel in Greece. They leave immediately, will be away for three weeks and need cover for the holiday.

d) A telephone call from an angry man who has not received cover for his daughter as a named driver on his insurance policy. She has a driving lesson this afternoon.

e) A letter from a fine arts and antiques dealer angry that a stolen picture is not covered.

f) A telephone call from a person who has just moved to the area and wants to know what services you offer. You would need to find out their details during the course of the call.

g) A client who has had a car accident involving another vehicle.

Where you believe you have relevant information you should work out the cost of the various policies.

You can use some of these solutions: apologise, consult the data base, get your boss, arrange phone back, give/send prospectus, arrange instantly.

Task 8 Your boss wants to advertise locally. He suggests:

▸ Asking car showrooms and driving schools to allow him to leave leaflets there.
▸ Post Office media graphics.
▸ *Yellow Pages.*
▸ Local radio.

He wants to know the cost of each and the advantages or disadvantages. Research information and draw up a memo report for him giving the information.

Task 9 Design a simple advert for a leaflet, Post Office media graphics, *Yellow Pages* or local radio. Do not forget to mention the name of your company, what you do, your address and your telephone number.

Simulation Set up an area at your college or place of study for an 'Insurance – who needs it?' information week.

    a) Promote the event around the college. Give times, dates and venue.
    b) Set up the enquiry desk using leaflets, posters, etc.
    c) Staff the desk.

Introduction

The following sections explain in more detail what you need to know for the assignment and give you some practice activities. Either read through them in conjunction with the assignment or before you start.

The assignment is about the sales and marketing function of a company. In a large company there will almost certainly be a marketing department and a sales department, sometimes these are put together. The marketing department is responsible for finding out what product is needed and what price can be charged. It then needs to find out whether the company can provide the goods or service and distribute them at a profit. The marketing department is also responsible for devising the necessary promotion or advertising to allow customers to know of their products.

There are many things to consider and the marketing department is often, therefore, quite large, and has several sections. Here is a typical structure:

If you work for a small company then you may find there is no special department but, nevertheless, the functions would still have to be carried out by someone

Market research

Before a company can put a new product or service on the market it needs to find out peoples' buying habits or opinions. There are various ways a company can research the market and all have a part to play.

Desk research is one method that nearly all companies will use. This involves looking through sales reports, reports from professional bodies and consumer reports such as *Which?* reports.

---/ **ACTIVITY** /--

What do you think is happening to the sales of the two different products judging from the graphs on p. 80?

Can you say any more about the sales of the products, i.e. why do you think one chart shows a falling-off and then a pick-up?

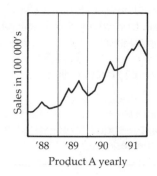

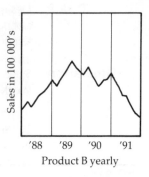

1st ¼ 2nd ¼ 3rd ¼ 4th ¼	'88 '89 '90 '91	'88 '89 '90 '91
Product A monthly	Product A yearly	Product B yearly

Sales in 10 000's (Product A monthly)
Sales in 100 000's (Product A yearly)
Sales in 100 000's (Product B yearly)

With which product do you think the marketing director would continue and which do you think he might drop?

Questionnaires are another popular method used to find out peoples' buying habits or opinions. They are used in many contexts, from finding out political views to what shampoos are used. Sometimes questionnaires are given to people to fill in and return. This is especially helpful if you need responses over a timed period, e.g. a week, or if the subject needs plenty of thought. However, the drawback of this method is that you must allow for people forgetting to fill the questionnaire in or not bothering to return them. This method is often used when you need an extremely large sample of people or when you have a wide geographical area to cover, e.g. a magazine readership.

▲ *Door-to-door interviews*

▲ *Face-to-face interviews in the street*

▲ *Telephone interviews*

▲ *Group interviews*

The most effective way to get instant feedback is by interviewing people face to face. You will almost certainly have seen people in shopping centres with clip boards asking shoppers questions. Some more popular interview methods are illustrated opposite.

In the assignment you are asked to use face-to-face interviewing based on a questionnaire. If you want people to co-operate, remember that you are intruding on their time for no reward so:

Do
- Say good morning/afternoon.
- Introduce yourself and state why you are researching and on what.
- Ask if they would mind answering a few questions.
- Accept 'No' for an answer.
- Thank them for their time when you have finished.

Do not
- Ask people who are obviously in a hurry.
- Mothers coping with toddlers and young children.
- Young, unaccompanied children. (This is for safety reasons – they should not be speaking to strangers for any reason.)

Having established a few rules for interviewing, we now need to concentrate on the construction of the questionnaire.

Construction of the questionnaire

Firstly, you need to establish what you want to know.

Marketing managers have to consider:

1 The **product** or service they are marketing. Is it a consumer product, e.g. shampoo; a service, e.g. insurance; industrial equipment, e.g. blast furnace?
2 The **price** they need to sell the product at in order to make a profit. The company needs to consider the market, e.g. do they wish to sell a basic product cheaper than competitors or a more expensive, high-quality product. The competition would influence this choice and the 'gap' in the market that has been identified.
3 The **place**, or where the product is to be sold, e.g. High Street chain stores, party plan, supermarkets, etc.
4 The **promotion**, i.e. what will make people buy the product, e.g. a special offer, a competition offering the chance of winning an exotic holiday, etc. Advertising also comes into this area.

The considerations above are known in marketing circles as the **marketing mix** or the 4 Ps.

The questionnaire would need to supply answers or data to give information on what the marketing mix should be, so questions may be arranged as follows:

- **Product** Do they have any insurance? What is it for? When else may they have taken out insurance? Do they know of any other situations when insurance may be needed? Do they think any of the following could be insured? Would they have them insured? etc.
- **Price** Are they able to pay in instalments? Would they pay slightly more for a better service if they could pay in instalments? etc.
- **Place** How do they apply for insurance? Do they get the same company to handle all their insurance needs? etc.
- **Promotion** Where did they see their insurance company advertised? Where would they look if they needed another policy?

You do not need to use these headings on your questionnaire, they are only for you to use as a guide, just number your questions.

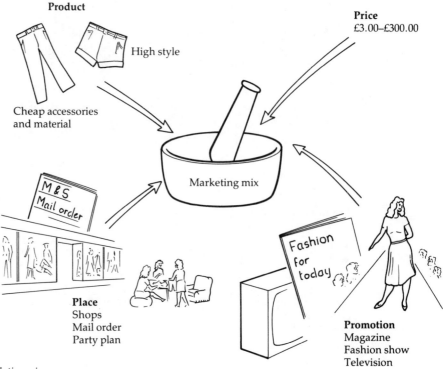

▲ *Marketing mix*

Market research will show where there are gaps in the market, e.g.:

- Young people want a cheaper product which they can buy in their High Street.
- Working people prefer to shop from the comfort of their homes.
- Housewives enjoy shopping in the evening when they are more relaxed and can combine shopping with meeting friends – so party plan might be preferred.

When you construct questions for a questionnaire try to make them 'closed', that is questions with 'yes' or 'no' answers, or a list of options from which one (or some) must be picked. Closed questionnaires save the interviewer time (no long answers to write down) and are much easier to code when analysing the answers.

You should use a different question sheet for every respondent, and do not forget to mark whether they are male or female and the age bracket they fall within, e.g. 18–29, 30–45, 46–60, over 60.

Market Research on Insurance

(*Tick boxes as appropriate*)

Male ☐   Female ☐
Age: 18–29 ☐   30–45 ☐   46–60 ☐   Over 60 ☐

1 Do you have any insurance?   Yes ☐   No ☐

2 If you do have insurance, what is it for?
   Car ☐   Boat ☐   Bicycle ☐
   House ☐   Stamps ☐   Jewellery ☐
   Other (please specify)..

3 When do you think insurance may be needed?
   Travel ☐   Driving ☐
   Work ☐   Other ☐

4 If you do have insurance, do you pay in instalments?
         Yes ☐   No ☐

In pairs draw up a questionnaire of ten questions to discover who does and who does not use the canteen at your place of study. If you find out the respondents' reasons for using it or not you should be able to conclude what the canteen does well and then recommend what improvements they could make to attract more custom. As this is a practice activity you need not interview a large sample of people, your group may do.

Once you have completed your survey you will need to analyse the results, draw conclusions and possibly recommend a course of action. As a rule results are given as percentages of total sample. For example; to the question, 'Do you think there is enough choice of insurance policies for single items such as bicycles, walkmans, etc.?' 45% said 'Yes', 40% said 'No', 5% said 'Don't know'. When this was further analysed it was discovered that half of the respondents who said 'No' were in the 16–21 year-old age bracket.

A conclusion to be drawn from this could be that insurance companies do not target students and that this could be a gap in the market. It is often helpful to draw graphs to illustrate results.

Professional companies would use a computer program to analyse results. You may have access to a program. If you have, use it to analyse your results for the main assignment.

Publicity

Once your product is on the market the marketing function does not stop. Companies need to keep the user aware of the product and also respond to any moves the competition may be making. Ways of doing this may include advertising, consumer competitions, money-off coupons, gifts, etc.

Supermarkets Wage War

Supermarkets are involved in an out-and-out price war writes our correspondent Julie Salmon.

Tescop has been cutting prices to attract huge numbers of customers from their nearest competitors Sainsways. A representative from Sainsways commented that, 'Even their new lower prices are no lower than ours always have been.'

It is not only on the price front that lines have been drawn up. More and more supermarkets are using celebrities to advertise their stores. Goody Wallen has signed a £100,000.00 contract with Tescop to appear in a series of adverts. He is not alone – Sainsways are to use ever-popular soap star Nina Reel in their advertisements.

Save-it stores have chosen not to compete in the escalating supermarket wars. 'We prefer to pass on the benefits of our profits to the customer through competitive pricing. When you offer the best deals in town, you do not need expensive advertising.'

Take a product or service and chart the campaigns used by several different companies offering them. It may be useful to follow progress over a couple of months or a season, noting dates, to get a full picture of companies' campaigns and responses to each other.

If you are working, use your own company's product. Note their campaign (if they have one) and the competition's. Try to find out the effect on sales in your own company.

Publicity leaflets

▲ *Publicity leaflets*

Publicity leaflets are a good and fairly inexpensive means of keeping your existing customers and potential new customers aware of your products. The advantage of leaflets is that there is space to give fairly detailed information and people can keep them, unlike an advert on the radio or a newspaper advertisement which will be thrown away.

▲ *Persil advertisement*

This company has chosen to appeal to people's sympathies. They promote themselves as 'caring' and imply that the consumer isn't caring if they do not buy their product.

Other promotion ploys are 'caring for the environment' and 'no animal testing'.

ACTIVITY

Collect as many leaflets as you can, individually or as a group.

1 What is each leaflet trying to do – sell, inform (e.g. government leaflets), offer advice, etc.?

2 What features are the same, e.g. how is the paper folded, are pictures included, are layouts similar, etc.?

Here are some general points about leaflets for you to note:

● Leaflets are in general made from folded paper with 'front' and 'back' pages and 'inside' pages.
● The title of the leaflet and the name of the company/organisation that produced it appear on the front page.

- Bold subtitles often in the form of questions appear on the inside pages.
- Information about the product/service appears on the inside pages as answers to the subtitle questions.
- Pictures and graphics often are in full colour.
- A summary of the leaflet's contents and what you should do next appears inside or on the back page.
- Form to fill in on the back page.
- An address for where to send or write for further information on the back page.

Leaflets will quite often be made available at the point of sale, i.e. in the sales room, on the counter, etc., but they are also useful to mail to customers and potential customers.

ACTIVITY

Collect all the leaflets that are sent to you over a two week period. If you are not the main householder or live with your parents ask if they would pass on to you any leaflets they have received. These leaflets will most likely fall into groups:

- Those which are unsolicited, i.e. nobody contacted that company and the householders were not thinking of necessarily buying that type of product at the present, e.g. double glazing, home insurance, life assurance.
- Those which came with a letter from an organisation with which you deal but offering unrelated services or goods.
- Those which are directly related to the service or goods you use from an organisation.
- Those which you have specifically requested.

Sometimes these leaflets and adverts are referred to as 'junk mail' because people often throw them away without even opening them.

Discuss with your group why you think companies still continue to send these letters and leaflets? Do you think they could be quite helpful or interesting or are they a nuisance.

ACTIVITY

Compare the information given on a leaflet with that given in *Yellow Pages*, on the radio and in newspapers. What information is always given? What information varies – why?

▲ *Yellow Pages*

You may wonder where the organisations that send you leaflets get your name and address from. In today's society there are, in fact, many sources. Some of these sources are mentioned in Chapter 13 'Personnel'. Names can be taken from information sources open to the public, e.g. telephone books, electoral rolls, etc. If you send in a coupon then you are likely to be entered on a data base as a potential customer.

Service and building customer relations

In order to do well in a competitive market, emphasis must be put on offering a good service. What is a good service and how do we achieve it?

Part of a good service is offering the right product at the right price and making sure it is available to those who want it, but even given these things, more is needed in a competitive market to retain customers and gain customer loyalty.

After-sales care

Even with the most careful attention to detail there will inevitably be a few problems that arise once goods are sold. Guarantees are one way of dealing with customer complaints on quality. However, often it is not a fault to be corrected that people need, so much as advice on the proper care or how to get the best out of the product or service. Giving after-sales advice fosters good public relations, customers are satisfied and the manufacturer's reputation is protected. To provide after-sales care the customer must know how to contact you and should receive a friendly, helpful service when they do.

ACTIVITY

Find out how manufacturers encourage customers to get the best out of a product by collecting examples of their literature. Look on bottles, packets, leaflets, etc. given with the product. What form does this advice take? For example:

● 'For more ideas and recipes . . .'
● 'For further advice on your knitting pattern . . .'
● 'Caution: do not exceed given quantities.'
● 'Instructions: Apply sparingly then rinse off and repeat.'

What is the advantage to the manufacturer of getting people to write to them?

MULTI SURFACE CLEANER
HANDCARE:
As with any household cleaner, after each cleaning job, rinse your hands and then dry them thoroughly. Avoid prolonged contact with the product.

NOTE:•
In case of contact with eyes, rinse immediately with plenty of water. This product is not recommended for use on rugs or upholstery. Accidental spillage of neat product should be rinsed off immediately. Avoid prolonge' · ··

▲ *Product advice realia*

Consumer Law

The Sale of Goods Act 1979 was passed to protect the consumer. Under this act any person selling goods should promise:

1 That they actually own the goods.
2 That the goods fit their description.
3 That the goods are 'of merchantable quality' or of a good standard.
4 That the goods are fit for the purpose for which they are sold.

You may have come across many excuses given by sellers when you have tried to return goods to a shop such as: 'Sorry it's down to the manufacturer', 'There are no guarantees with these goods', 'We cannot replace 'sale' items'. Provided the goods you are trying to exchange or get a refund for are genuinely faulty (not that you just do not like them or have changed your mind) these excuses will not hold up in a court of law.

Companies have different policies on compensating customers. It is important to foster good relations with customers, but at the same time it may not make economic sense to repair or replace broken or worn out goods, so alternative appropriate action needs to be taken. One way of dealing with this problem is to offer trade-in terms on a new model.

ACTIVITY

Find out from your company or work placement what their policy is on after sales care Compare these as a group.

Personal service

Although much can be done by manufacturers or companies to improve their product and implement policies that improve service, it is the personnel of a compny who hav contact with the public who actually control the impression a customer receives.

ACTIVITY

Write down the things that annoy you most when you are buying a product. Write down t things that please you most. Try to think of the point of buying as well as the actual produ Now see if you can categorise these things into product, price, availability and person service, e.g.:

● The jeans have good styling and fit well. (Product)
● The last ones you bought from that manufacturer lasted well. (Product)
● They were expensive, but worth it. (Price)
● They did not have your size for two weeks. (Availability)
● You had to go to another town to get what you wanted. (Availability)
● The first shop assistant tried to sell you a pair that were too large. (Poor service)
● The shop assistant did not try to find out which branch did have them in stock. (P service)
● The assistant went off to chat with her friend when you didn't offer to buy them. (F service)
● The second assistant sympathised and searched the stock room. (Good service)
● The assistant asked her manageress if you could have a slight discount as the button come off. (Good service)

- The assistant hoped that you had a good time on your holiday and that you would come back to see them when you got back as they would have some exciting new-season styles that would suit you. (Good service)

To give a good service you need to:

- Make the customer feel valued and important.
- Pay attention to detail – little things count.
- Be reliable – if you say you are going to do something, do it.
- Be aware of presentation from neatly presented letters through to personal appearance.
- Possess good interpersonal skills.

Interpersonal skills

Interpersonal skills are those we refer to when we describe somebody as 'nice', 'friendly', 'helpful'. Although most people know that these are the correct attitudes to project it is not always as easy in practice.

▲ *Body language*

Body language is a powerful way of projecting the right attitude, as is tone of voice. 'It's not what you say, it's how you say it,' is an expression you most probably have heard.

One of the most important elements needed to achieve good interpersonal skills is confidence. 'Be confident' is easy enough to say but more difficult to achieve, however there are positive steps you can take to boost your confidence.

─/ **ACTIVITY** /───────────────────────────

Describe a person you believe to be confident. You may find that it is their physical make up you are describing or their knowledge.

Try to copy some of the techniques they use to see if they help you feel more confident.

Confidence comes from many sources. If you are relaxed then very often you will exude an air of confidence. Try relaxation techniques and breathing exercises, e.g.:

● Breath deeply from the stomach – hold your breath for a moment – and then breath out slowly.
● Tense your muscles and then consciously relax them – start at your toes and work up.

Smile   It is not really possible to frown or look cross or tense if you really are smiling. Smiling at a customer is not only going to make you look more friendly, it will actually help you to relax. Smiling also helps when speaking to people on the telephone, they cannot see you smiling but they will sense you smiling – try an experiment.

Think positive   'I can deal with this – I'll get help.'

Look good   You will not feel confident if you think your hair is a mess or if you have got a button missing and your shoes are down at heel.

Feel comfortable   Decide what you are comfortable with and stick to it. (You may find that there is a conflict here if your company issues uniforms. Why do you think some companies like their staff to wear uniforms? What type of industry are they usually in? How do you think you can develop a more positive attitude towards the uniform you have to wear?)

Be honest   If you don't know an answer to a customer's question don't fudge – say that you don't know and that you will try to find out.

Know your facts and products   This may sound obvious but you will find it difficult to deal with customers unless you really do know what your company has to offer. Study the products or service they offer, take an interest in them, consider what you personally like about them.

If you are selling washing machine spares it may be difficult to feel anything about the products but study the literature and compare with the competitors and find the good points, e.g. better quality, easier to fit, etc. When dealing with customers, remember these points and concentrate on them. This enthusiasm will bubble through to your customer and is one of the reasons why companies often offer staff discounts on their goods or services. If you use, know and like the product this will be passed on to customers and they will feel your confidence.

Armed with all the above you should feel more confident in dealing with people already but how do you send them away saying, 'What a nice person, I will come back here'?

─/ **ACTIVITY** /───────────────────────────

● Write down a list of what you consider to be your good points (include physical attributes as well as personality).
● Why do you think other people like you?
● Now ask someone who knows you to write down your goods points.
● Compare their list with your list. Add anything you have missed off your list to it.

Now that you have a long list of all your good points you should feel better about yourself. Remember these points when in any situation which involves interacting with people use them.

Dealing with interruptions

When you are dealing with customers face to face then interruptions are most likely to be caused by the telephone. If you break off immediately from your customer and get involved with a long telephone conversation, then quite rightly they are likely to become annoyed. If, on the other hand, you ignore the phone you may lose a customer. One way to deal with this is to give the person you are dealing with something to do: 'Would you like to read through this while I answer the phone?', 'Could you just fill this out, I won't be a moment'.

Answer the phone and then give your customer undivided attention. You may have to offer to phone back so get details of name, telephone number and nature of enquiry. It is better to give a time limit if you are calling someone back, but make sure it is realistic, e.g. 'I will call you back this afternoon,' is better than 'I'll be straight back to you,' if you know that you have not realistically got much of a chance.

ACTIVITY

Look at your list of what annoys you about personal service. Try to suggest some solutions that you would find more acceptable.

Dealing with difficult customers

Always listen to customers. Often annoyed customers are not angry with you but with something else. It is a natural enough defence to be angry back, especially if you feel you are coming under unfair attack. However the golden rule is: **Never become angry with a customer**. This is easy enough to say, but more difficult to put into practice. You could try some of these suggestions to help you cope:

- Hurried customers often appear brusque and rude, but you may have sympathy if you discover why they are hurried, e.g. they are about to get a parking ticket, they couldn't park, etc. then you can sympathise and try to be as quick as possible.
- If the customer has a complaint, listen carefully to exactly what the problem is, and if necessary, call a superior.
- Again, try to put yourself in their shoes, many people have difficulty complaining because they lack confidence. This often means that they come out with a torrent of speech they have prepared beforehand in case you will not listen to them. If you smile, listen and are sympathetic they will often calm down and then you can deal with the complaint in the appropriate way.

ACTIVITY

Can you think of some more 'coping' devices? Use your personal experiences to help you with this activity. It may also be helpful to examine some of your prejudices. Are you more intolerant to certain accents, ages, ethnic groups? If you are, try to find out a little more about these people and their backgrounds as this often helps in overcoming prejudices.

Why not collect suggestions from all your group and make a 'How to deal with difficult customers' chart or poster?

MODULE 2

Administrative Systems and Procedures

Summary

This chapter helps you to improve your communication skills and to practise them in a reception area. This is done through an assignment in which you have to set up and run a reception area. This is an important chapter in helping you to be efficient in a work setting. The following topics are covered:

▸ Dealing with customers and callers
▸ Methods of communication
▸ Written communication
▸ Message handling
▸ Telephone
▸ Electronic communications
▸ The reception area

This chapter will help you to achieve the following outcomes:

Core Module 2   Administrative Systems and Procedures

Outcome 2.2   Identify and use different communication systems and methods of a selected organisation

Outcome 2.3   Produce documents and material and process data

Outcome 2.4   Understand and follow health and safety procedures

Outcome 2.5   Understand the importance of maintaining and developing good business relationships with callers, customers/clients and colleagues

Core Module 4   People in Business

Outcome 4.3   Examine and compare the main job roles in different organisations

Outcome 4.4   Contribute to achievement of organisational goals by fulfilling job role

The assignment can be used to cover the following performance criteria:

1.4d   need for employees to present positive image of the organisation fully understood

2.2a   oral and written messages received and acted upon

2.2b   information obtained from appropriate sources

2.2c   routine business communications produced

2.2d   channels of communication identified and used

2.2e   incoming and outgoing mail processed

2.2f   electronic telecommunications used to receive and send information

2.3a   business documents produced using a word processing package

2.3b   information processing equipment used to run standard applications

2.3d   copies of original documents produced using reprographic equipment

2.4a   potential hazards to the well-being of self and others recognised and reported

2.4b   equipment used in accordance with operating instructions and procedures

2.4c   work area kept free from hazards

2.5a   callers greeted promptly and courteously and dealt with appropriately

2.5b   polite and effective responses made to a range of customer/client situations

2.5c   liaison and communication with peers and senior colleagues conducted effectively

2.5d   rapport and mutual respect between colleagues and customers/clients established

4.3a   functional areas within organisations identified

4.3b   job roles in different functional areas of organisations identified

4.3c   job roles compared

4.4a   relationship between organisational objectives and job role identified

4.4b   given tasks completed to agreed criteria

4.4c   contribution made both as an individual and as a member of a team to the achievement of agreed targets and goals

The assignment will help with the development of Common Skills, especially the following:

Working with and Relating to Others
Outcome 5   Treat others' values, beliefs and opinions with respect.

Outcome 6   Relate to and interact effectively with individuals and groups

Outcome 7   Work effectively as a member of a team

Communicating
Outcome 8   Receive and respond to a variety of information

Outcome 9   Present information in a variety of visual forms

Managing Tasks and Solving Problems
Outcome 13   Deal with a combination of routine and non-routine tasks

Outcome 14   Identify and solve routine and non-routine problems

Applying Technology
Outcome 16   Use a range of technological equipment and systems

Applying Design and Creativity
Outcome 17   Apply a range of skills and techniques to develop a variety of ideas in the creation of new/modified products, services or situations

Outcome 18   Use a range of thought processes

Read the following assignment to help you to understand some of the things you should be able to do by the end of this chapter. Normally it will be best for you to read the chapter and carry out the set activities before you tackle the assignment.

Check whether you can do the assignment on your own or with one or more colleagues. Some assignments will require organising by your tutor. Seek guidance, where needed, from your tutor.

Assignment   ## Service as normal

You work for The Fitness Machine a small supplier of sporting equipment.

The company has been doing well recently and has decided to refurbish its offices.

Being a small team, you have offered to staff a temporary reception area until their refurbishe one is ready and the receptionist vacancy is filled. Your job will be to receive visitors, answer th switchboard and help out with some of the word processing.

For this assignment you will need to make a video showing how you would handle a typic morning's work.

Task 1   Setting the scene

You have been given a fairly free hand as to how you set out the temporary reception area. Y have some of the furniture and fittings from the old area, e.g. a coffee table, chairs, leaflets. Fin suitable space at your place of study and set up a temporary reception area.

Task 2   Produce a scale drawing of the area with a key to the fittings you consider to be essential. If feel it would be necessary to spend some money, cost out how much this would be o separate sheet. Remember not to go over board as this is only a temporary area so any mo you spend should be able to come out of petty cash. If necessary fill in a petty cash slip example is shown on p. 184.

Task 3 The scene

Role play the following situation:

You are busy word processing or typing several letters and memos. Use any handwritten scripts from *other* people in your group. The scripts can be from other assignments if necessary. The following visitors will call during the morning. (Note: your video need not be continuous and your group can use their role playing skills to the full.)

a) Mr Amaldi arrives for his appointment with the accounts department.
b) A sales rep calls for Mrs Brunshaw of office services, with no appointment.
c) A nervous young man arrives for an interview. He is rather early.
d) The postman with a pile of letters and parcels.
    i One of the letters is Recorded Delivery.
    ii One of the parcels looks suspicious.
e) An extremely angry customer with no appointment.

You also receive the following telephone calls:

a) Request for a new catalogue.
b) Enquiry as to why a delivery is over a week late.
c) A message from the window cleaners to say that they have not received their cheque yet.
d) One of your sales reps wanting to know if there are any messages for him/her.
e) The sales manager, Mr Patel, to inform you that he is expecting a visitor, Mr Robinson, from Challenge Co Ltd at 4.30 today.

Communicating

Humans, being social creatures, have devised many ways of communicating with each other. These ways of communicating can be divided into five main categories:

1 **Verbal** – talking face to face, interviews, telephone conversation.
2 **Written word** – letters, memorandums.
3 **Number** – receipts, invoices.
4 **Graphic** – maps, pictures, charts.
5 **Non-verbal communication** – gesturing, facial expressions, clothes.

Think of some more examples of each method of communicating and add them to the appropriate list.

In business, much of our success depends upon good communication skills. This means, not only knowing which form of communication to choose, but also how to send it. For instance, if you have an urgent message there is little use sending it by post, a fax would be quicker. If you also need a reply quickly, you may prefer to speak to the person on the telephone.

Choosing the most effective method of communication

In your everyday life you probably have little problem choosing how to communicate with the people around you. From birth you have been learning the best ways and the acceptable ways (the conventions) of communicating in our society. Business also has conventions, but these you will probably need to learn, just as you would have to start from scratch if you were to move to a new country or society.

In business you need to consider:

● Who you are communicating with.
● What you are trying to achieve.

The tone and language you use will be affected by who you are communicating with and the situation.

Consider the differences between the use of tone and language with the following people:

a) Your close colleague.
b) Your immediate supervisor.
c) Someone from a different department, but on your level.
d) The departmental manager.
e) A potential customer.
f) A well known customer.

How might you start a conversation with these people if you met them?

Imagine you are in the middle of a long complicated task which you need to finish and one of the above interrupts with a request. Consider your response. If you find it easier, role play these situations. When you have finished discuss how your response to these people may affect your future working relationship with them.

It would be better if you could repeat this exercise over a number of weeks because if you are not really working hard, it will not seem so frustrating when somebody interrupts you. Note your reactions when your teacher, workmates or college/school friends interrupt you.

You should have noticed from the activity that even with the same person, in some situations it is acceptable to be informal but still business-like, whilst in other situations you may need to adjust to a more formal method of communication.

We call this tone and language.

Which medium of communication should you use?

Table 6.1 Advantages and disadvantages of communication media

Medium	Advantages	Disadvantages
Written	You have proof of what was said or agreed.	It takes time to produce and reproduce.
	You have evidence of when it was sent.	It takes time to receive a reply.
	The receiver can keep it for future reference	
Verbal	It is quick.	Does not allow you time to think.
	You can receive an immediate reply.	Can lead to misunderstandings of what has been agreed.
		There is no record of the conversation
Graphic and non-verbal	Can simplify numerical information.	May not be sufficient on its own.
	Can add to verbal description.	May be misinterpreted.
	Can be more interesting	

The media for communication are the routes or way you have chosen to send a message e.g. you may have chosen to write something down, but should it be a note or a letter? There will be many considerations for choosing which medium to use: cost, time, accuracy and legal requirements are a few.

Cost in business is relative. Although at home you may consider writing a letter abroad much cheaper than telephoning, in business you need to take other factors into consideration. For instance, if you write a letter you should consider the cost of the time to compose it, the typist's time to type it, the letterheaded paper which has to be printed, etc. Similarly, a long telephone call abroad may be expensive but if you have 'conference facilities, think about which is cheaper in this situation: linking up several people by telephone to the same conversation or organising for them to travel to the meeting from abroad, hence incurring travel and hotel expenses?

A verbal message to a customer may be quite acceptable, but if your customer forgets what you have said or later disputes your message, what proof have you got? This can just as easily happen internally, between departments.

There are, therefore, certain advantages and disadvantages to all the different types of media and a wise businessman or businesswoman mixes them to the best advantage.

Table 6.1 lists some of the main advantages and disadvantages of the different media. Try to add to the table.

Try to think of some actual examples of each medium and state the advantages, e.g. verbal – public address system – can speak to many people at once.

Effectiveness

No matter what form of communication you choose, it will not be effective unless it is clear. There are some general rules that can be applied to all forms of communication be they interviews or invoices.

1 Make it clear to whom the message is directed. This may require you to merely look at the person or actually address them by name.

2 Introduce the subject matter and put the communication into context, e.g.:

- I should like to apply for the post of clerical assistant as advertised in *The Daily Journal*.
- Thank you for your letter dated 21 June requesting further information on our new range of photocopiers.
- I had better tell you what was said at the sales meeting last Thursday.

3 Give any further details that are required or action you intend to take.

4 Finish with any action your recipient should take unless this is implied by the form of communication, e.g. an invoice.

5 State who the communication is from. This may need to be given at the beginning and/or the end, e.g.:
- Telephone call – beginning.
- Invoice – beginning.
- Letter – beginning (headed note paper), – end (author's name and position).
- Report – beginning (terms of reference), – end (signature of author).

Formats for communication

When you are working in business you will notice that each company has a house style. This is particularly important when sending communications outside the company so that even though the recipient may receive communication from different departments they still have the impression that they are dealing with one identity. A great deal of money is spent by companies on their image and logos to ensure their customers are receiving the right impression.

/ ACTIVITY /

Collect several logos from large and small companies. What do you think they are trying to convey? What impression do they convey? How important do you think colour is?

Choose a suitable name and design some logos for the following:

- A small travel company offering tailor-made holidays and personal attention.
- A paper supplier who can offer large discounts for bulk buying.
- An insurance broker.
- A family-run florist.
- A small shop offering photocopying and fax services.
- A large company offering consultancy on communication technology.
- A small partnership offering gardening services.

Formats for internal communication

Although you may find that the company you work for has its own style, the examples given follow a generally accepted format.

Note/message
This is an informal type of communication.

Telephone message pad
Very often these will be pre-printed. There are certain details that must, however, be included whether they are printed or not. These are:

- Message for . . .
- Message from (name and company).
- Details of message.
- Action required, e.g. call back, they will contact you, etc.
- Name of person who took the message.
- Date and time message was received. This is particularly important if you are taking messages for people who are often out of the office and spend a great deal of their time 'on the road' as they may have already contacted them or actioned the message.

▲ *Example of a pre-printed message pad*

MESSAGE FOR

M S HANLEY

WHILE YOU WERE OUT

M R ANGELOU

OF Q – TEX

PHONE NO. 071 – 35310

TELEPHONED	✓	PLEASE RING	✓
CALLED TO SEE YOU		WILL CALL AGAIN	
WANTS TO SEE YOU		URGENT	✓

MESSAGE:

Requires urgent confirmation of order details if deadline is to be met

DATE 3.1.92 TIME 9.15
RECEIVED BY Roger

Memorandum

This is a more formal type of internal communication. It may be filed and is therefore often typed. Note the form of address may be to a person's title rather than their name. If a manager wishes to inform all his staff of a matter it is acceptable to address the memo 'To all staff'.

Memorandum

To: R Jones, Sales Manager   *Ref:* GC/RJ

From: H Wood, Production Manager   *Date:* 25 June 199–

Subject: Production Run for New Chairs – Style 00567

Further to our meeting on Friday 21 June, I should like to confirm that we have planned the following production runs:

1/7	6000 black trim
14/7	5000 navy
21/7	3500 white/blue
28/7	3500 white/red

The first chairs will be ready for delivery from the factory 12/8. I trust this is in order.

If you were the sales manager would you keep this memo? Can you think of anyone else in his department who may need this information? How could you make the information available to them?

Report

There are several different types of report. Routine reports are often forms. Occasional reports may be formal or informal but generally have the following sections and layout:

REPORT WRITING

1.0   TERMS OF REFERENCE
      This section should state who requested the report to be written, who was to write it or investigate the matter, what the report was to cover and when it was to be completed.

2.0   PROCEDURE
      If the report is a formal report then you would have a section explaining how the information was obtained. This may include interviews, desk research or visits.

3.0   FINDINGS

      3.1   *Main subtitle*
            When writing a report you group your subjects into headings. If, for instance, you were writing a report on a residential course your first heading may be 'The Accommodation'.

      3.2   *Main subtitle*
            Your second main sub-title may be 'Day Activities'. If you then wished to break this section down further you would use more subtitles, e.g.:

3.2.1   Rock climbing
You could now write a section or paragraph on this subject.

3.2.2   Caving
Note how the numbering system works. As these are only sub-titles of Day Activities you use the main sub-title number (3.2) followed by another point, in this case point 2 (3.2.2). The reason for a numbering system is to ensure that it can be easily rearranged in sequence should it be split up. It also enables readers of the report to find specific sections of the report easily.

3.3   *Main subtitle*
When you wish to start another main sub-title you follow the number of the main subtitle above it. This section may deal with Evening Activities.

4.0   CONCLUSION
This is a summing up of what was found. For the report on a residential course you may end with something like, 'It was a most enjoyable and useful experience. The instructors were very professional and helpful, etc.' Note, that there are no sub-sections in the conclusion although you would use paragraphs if necessary.

5.0   RECOMMENDATIONS
These are not always requested but if they are they should be numbered, e.g.:

5.1   The residential course is offered to next year's students.

5.2   The week is brought forward to nearer the beginning of the term.

SIGNED

DATE

ACTIVITY

Write a report on one of the following using the format given above:

- A residential you have attended.
- Work experience.
- College course.
- Car parking facilities at college or work.
- Sixth form facilities at school.

Formats for external communication

Letter

It is usual in Business to use the fully blocked style of layout. This means that everything starts on the left hand side of the page. This format was originally adopted to save typist time. Now, so many letters are set out on word processors that you may find companies adopting other styles.

Try not to use meaningless cliches such as 'waiting in anticipation', try to use plain English but avoid colloquialisms. There are phrases or words generally accepted in day to day speech but not for writing, e.g. OK.

If you follow the master rules of putting a communication into context and introducing the subject in the first paragraph you can avoid the over used and rather inaccurate phrase 'I am writing'.

IMPRESSIONS PHOTOCOPIERS LTD
301 Acacia Road
Taunton
Tel 234567

25 October 199–

Ms Jones
Administration Manager
Naturewatch
14 New Road
New Forest

Dear Ms Jones

<u>XLJ 300 Series Photocopier</u>

Thank you for your telephone call of today requesting a brochure of our new photocopier series.

Please find enclosed our brochure which gives full details of all the models in the new XLJ 300 series. As you will notice, it is a most comprehensive range and offers a model to suit most budgets and needs. A demonstration of the photocopiers can be arranged.

I should just like to remind you that on delivery of the photocopier a representative will install it and give full training should this be required.

An order form is attached to the last page but if you would prefer to order by telephone, or require any further information, please do not hesitate to call me on the above number.

Yours sincerely

Peter Watson

Peter Watson
Customer Service

▲ *A letter using fully blocked layout*

The telephone
For many people, one of the most nerve-racking things to do when they first start a new job is to answer the telephone: Who will be on the other end? Will I be able to help them? Will I know who to ask for help or put them through to?

Even if you have had some experience before, this is not necessarily helpful or reassuring because you do not tend to remember all those occasions when you dealt with people successfully. You remember 'difficult customers': the ones who launched straight into the problem, 'barked' at you, expected you to know the answer straight away; those who did not speak clearly so that you had to keep asking them to repeat themselves, whilst despite the bad line, they progressively treated you as an idiot. It is hard to remember in these moments of panic that it is they, the caller, who is using poor telephone technique.

What is good telephone technique? The clues, as is so often the case when dealing with people, lie in what you, personally, find irritating.

ACTIVITY

Discuss in a group the things you find most irritating when you are on the phone. Use your personal calls to friends as well as any calls you have made to companies.

The problem with the telephone is that as the person cannot see you there is a temptation to allow intrusions that you probably would not allow if you were face to face. For instance, how often have you fallen into the trap of carrying on a communication with somebody else in the room by sign language, or how often do you eat or type whilst on the telephone? Although you may think the other person on the telephone cannot tell, there are, in fact, many ways you can be betrayed and give the caller the impression you are not listening to them: your voice may go 'distant', you may have to ask them to repeat a simple message because you have let your attention wander and not heard what they have said, they may hear you eating or tapping on the keyboard.

The golden rules of using the telephone are:

1 Give one hundred per cent of your attention.
2 Smile – people will sense this in your voice.
3 Speak slowly and clearly – despite technology you are still talking down a 'line' with all the distortions and interferences this can bring.

How you answer a telephone will depend on what point in the call you become involved and on in-house style.

If you are on the main switchboard or are first line of contact then it is usual to announce the company name, e.g.: 'Fitness Machine. Good Morning. How can I help you?'.

'How can I help you?' has become more popular than 'Can I help you?' as it is a more positive response. The telephonist then switches the call to the appropriate person or department. This sounds simple enough but there are still likely to be some problems encountered and the telephonist will have to use initiative and problem-solving skills. For instance, what would you do if the line to the person the caller wished to speak to was busy or they did not answer it? You may well have written down being left to 'hold' on telephone as one of the things that annoys you most; being transferred from department to department to find 'somebody there who might be able to help you' can be equally annoying.

ACTIVITY

What do you think companies do, or could do, to minimise the problems mentioned above

Here are a few solutions. State what you consider to be the advantages and drawbacks each:

1 An organisational chart for the telephonist defining departments' responsibilities.
2 Music while the caller waits to receive attention.
3 If the line is busy, switching to another extension within that department.

Example An enquiry department: all unspecified calls sent here.

Advantage – Customer is attended to without jamming the switchboard for incoming calls.

Drawback – May not get an immediate answer, someone may still need to phone the customer back causing an aggravating delay.

If you are working, try to find out what your company policy is for dealing with incoming calls.

If you are not the first line of contact, but receive calls after they have come through a switchboard, then the rules for answering the telephone will differ:

1 When you answer the call you should give your name and department and ask 'How can I help you?'
2 Listen to the nature of the call and decide whether you can help or not.
3 Take the caller's name and telephone number. Ask for the company name and extension number if appropriate. It is essential to get this information right at the beginning of the call in case you get cut-off or forget later.
4 If you cannot deal with the call and no-one else is available, offer to take a message.
5 Reassure the caller by letting him/her know that you are listening – give encouraging feedback such as 'Yes', 'No' or 'I see' in appropriate places.
6 Always repeat the gist of the message back to the caller.
7 Always ask for spellings of names, roads and companies. Use the police alphabet (alpha, bravo, charlie, etc.), or obvious spellings such as 'A as in apple'.
8 Always repeat numbers back to the caller to ensure that you heard them correctly.
9 Give an action statement or tell the caller what will happen next, e.g. 'I will pass your message on and get someone to call you back', 'I will send you the catalogue and price list', 'Please would you confirm those details in writing'.
10 End with a courteous close such as, 'Thank you for your call, goodbye'.

Always remember that your customer need not be from outside your company or a member of the general public. These rules apply equally to those contacting you from inside the company.

Electronic communication
With today's modern technology the office worker has a whole range of equipment that simplifies or speeds up communication.

/ **ACTIVITY** /

In your group brainstorm as many pieces of equipment which speed up communication as you can.

Write them on a board or flipchart. When your list is complete ask each member of the group to pick one piece of equipment. You should then research, prepare and deliver a short talk about it. You could include what it looks like, how it works, advantages and disadvantages in terms of speed, cost, etc.

Here are a few of the more common pieces of equipment that you are likely to come across:

Telex The telex uses the written word, but as the message is sent through telephone lines it has the advantage over a letter of being delivered immediately. Telex operators can communicate with each other 'live' so you also have the advantage of immediate feedback (provided of course that the operator can supply the required information). The advantage of the telex over the telephone is that you get a printed copy of the message and so a record of the message. It is, however, quite expensive to use a telex and messages should, therefore, be kept short and concise. To keep messages concise many standard abbreviations are used, e.g. u = you, bi bi = finish live transmission, rms = rooms, qty = quantity.

The other problem with a telex is that the party you wish to contact must also have a telex and this is not always so.

Old telex machines used punched tape but nowadays a telex facility can be linked to an electronic typewriter or word processor. Once the message has been keyed in, the sender will dial the required number and transmit the message.

One obvious use for the telex is to reserve hotel rooms. Can you think of some other occasions when it would be useful to send a telex? Write a message you would like telexed. Swap your message with a partner. See how short you can make the message without losing the meaning.

Facsimile (fax) This increasingly popular method of sending a communication has many of the advantages of the telex and works on a similar principle of sending a written message electronically over a telephone line. The great advantage of a fax is that it can also send pictures and diagrams as well as the written word. A fax 'scans' the message from the piece of paper on which it is written and converts it to digital signals. The message is then transmitted to a screen, or printer for hard copy, at its destination. Thus a letter can be typed on headed notepaper and transmitted. Below is a diagram of the facsimile with the main features labelled.

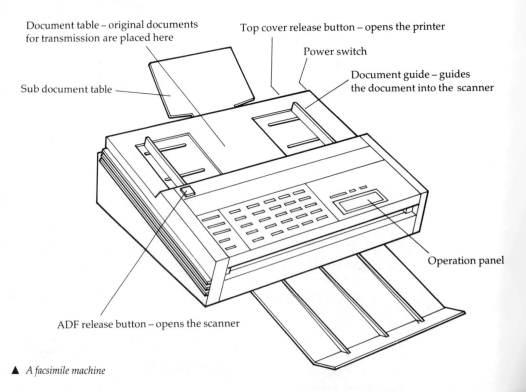

Document table – original documents for transmission are placed here

Top cover release button – opens the printer

Power switch

Sub document table

Document guide – guides the document into the scanner

Operation panel

ADF release button – opens the scanner

▲ *A facsimile machine*

Prestel Prestel is a viewdata service provided by British Telecom. It stores informati~~on~~ on electronic pages, which can be selected by users to give a vast range of informati~~on~~

(*Ceefax* uses the same principle but uses television signals.) *Prestel* can be linked up to a computer so that information can be responded to. For instance, it is possible to send an order for goods to a company advertising on *Prestel.*

Teletext is an additional service offered by British Telecom which offers other benefits such as electronic mailing. This means that a message can be fed into *Teletext* along with a list of customers and addresses and each will receive a copy of the message. Again, however, it does depend on your customer being linked to the system too.

/ **ACTIVITY** /

Go to your library and find out what information services are available on *Prestel*. List a few and try to give examples of how they may be useful to people in business.

Reception

There are many ways in which your customers and clients will gain an impression of your company, but the first physical impression will usually be gained from reception. Despite your company's location and building (over which a company can exercise little control), reception will make the first real impact on your customers of the 'living company'.

▲ *First impressions count*

▲ *First impressions count*

You may enter modest buildings but feel comfortable, or you may enter plush su[r]roundings but feel uncomfortable and overwhelmed. All of the following will help [to] make a customer feel comfortable:

- Plants
- Comfortable chairs
- Coffee machine
- Leaflets about the company and its product
- Carpets
- A friendly face

Reception is not only about creating an impression, there are other considerations for [the] company such as:

- Security
- Health and safety laws
- Efficiency
- Practicality

Most companies will ask you to fill in a visitors book. An example of the details requ[ired] are given opposite. How are some of the company requirements listed above satisfie[d by] filling in a visitors book?

Visitors Book				
Date/Time	Name	Company Address	Visiting	Out

What else do you think may be given to a visitor on entering a reception area? Can you give reasons for this?

Summary

In this chapter you will learn about how an office works. The assignment involves you in researching and designing a better and more efficient office layout/environment. A variety of related activities will involve you in carrying out some office routines. The following topics are covered:

▸ Office functions and organisation
▸ Office roles and routines
▸ Office design and layout
▸ Office resources and technology
▸ Information processing including filing
▸ Health and safety in the office

This chapter will help you to achieve the following outcomes:

Core Module 2   Administrative Systems and Procedures
   Outcome 2.1   Understand and be able to use established information storage and retrieval systems
   Outcome 2.2   Identify and use different communication systems and methods of selected organisation
   Outcome 2.4   Understand and follow health and safety procedures

Core Module 3   Business Resources and Procedures
   Outcome 3.2   Contribute to the effective use of physical resources
   Outcome 3.4   Investigate and apply simple measures of performance

Core Module 4   People in Business
   Outcome 4.1   Investigate and analyse the nature and purpose of work
   Outcome 4.3   Examine and compare the main job roles in different organisations

The assignment can be used to cover the following performance criteria:

2.1a	documents filed in correct location and sequence
2.1b	different methods for filing and storage compared and contrasted
2.1c	explanation of importance of effective storage, control and retrieval of information given
2.1d	business records managed using a simple database
2.2a	oral and written messages received and acted upon
2.2b	information obtained from appropriate sources
2.2c	routine business communications produced
2.2d	channels of communication identified and used
2.2f	electronic telecommunications used to receive and send information
2.4a	potential hazards to the well-being of self and others recognised and reported
2.4b	equipment used in accordance with operating instructions and procedures
2.4c	work area kept free from hazards
3.2a	audit of physical resources carried out
3.2d	suggestions made or implemented to improve the use of physical resources
3.4a	meaning of performance investigated and explained
3.4b	methods of measurement of performance investigated and described

3.4c	suitable method chosen to gauge performance in identified jobs, tasks of operations
3.4d	methods applied to job/task/operation selected and conclusions drawn from results
4.1b	the nature of work examined and different types compared
4.1c	different organisational structure examined and compared
4.1d	different work cultures identified and their importance assessed
4.3a	functional areas within organisations identified
4.3b	job roles in different functional areas of organisations identified

The assignment will help with the development of Common Skills, especially the following:

Managing and Developing Self
Outcome 1   Manage own roles and responsibilities
Outcome 2   Manage own time in achieving objectives
Outcome 3   Undertakes personal and career development

Working with and Relating to Others
Outcome 5   Treat others' values, beliefs and opinions with respect
Outcome 6   Relate to and interact effectively with individuals and groups
Outcome 7   Work effectively as a member of a team

Communicating
Outcome 8   Receive and respond to a variety of information
Outcome 9   Present information in a variety of visual forms
Outcome 10   Communicate in writing
Outcome 11   Participate in oral and non-verbal communication

Managing Tasks and Solving Problems
Outcome 12   Use information sources
Outcome 13   Deal with a combination of routine and non-routine tasks
Outcome 14   Identify and solve routine and non-routine problems

Applying Design and Creativity
Outcome 17   Applying a range of skills and techniques to develop a variety of ideas in the creation of new/modified products, services or situations
Outcome 18   Use a range of thought processes

Read the following assignment to help you to understand some of the things you should be able to do by the end of the chapter. Normally it will be best to read the chapter and carry out the set activities before you tackle the assignment.

Check whether you can do the assignment on your own or with one or more colleagues. Some assignments will require organising by your tutor. Seek guidance, where needed, from your tutor.

Organising the office

The layout of the workplace is important. It affects:

▸ **The people who work in it** A pleasant, attractive environment leads to better morale and motivation. People will often say that there is a nice atmosphere in their office and that they enjoy working there.
▸ **The amount of work done** A well planned office will help efficiency.
▸ **The quality of the work** A well laid out workplace leads to less wastage and consistent quality.

There are many different styles of office. In a large organisation, everyone in one office may be doing the same job, e.g. dealing with export orders. In a small organisation many jobs could be done in the same office, e.g. all the jobs from dealing with enquiries to completing the final invoice. The actual office space could be divided into a series of small offices or could be a large open-plan office where the work areas are separated by dividers, potted plants or filing cabinets. Whatever the style of the office, they all have the same purpose – they give a service. In the course of providing the service they may:

▸ Receive information by fax, telephone, letters of enquiry, quotations, invoices,.etc.
▸ Store information either on computer disk, on file or in account books.
▸ Analyse information, e.g. in accounts, sales figures, costings, personnel data.
▸ Supply information to enquiries, customers, suppliers, distributors and management.

The Office

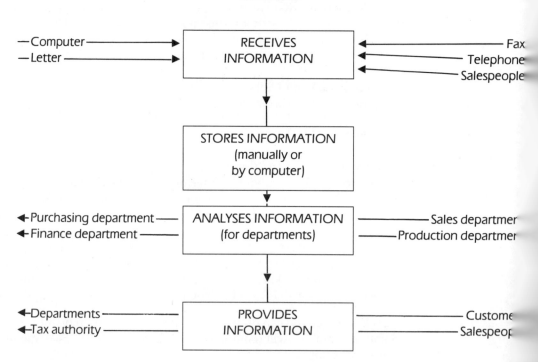

Tasks For this assignment you will have to work in groups. Your objective is to find a better and mo efficient layout of your workplace.

Group 1

a) Measure the workplace and draw a scale plan of it. You must work out the floor area of workplace. This is measured by multiplying the length by the width. The answer will be area in square metres,

e.g. 9 m × 6 m = 54 square metres or 54 m²
The best way of drawing a plan to scale is to use graph paper.

b) Draw the present layout of the furniture and equipment to the same scale.

c) Work out the floor area taken up by the furniture and equipment. Also find the area left for the movement of the people.

d) Find out by asking your health and safety representative how much room people should have to work in. Is there enough room in your workplace?

e) Draw a new plan showing how you think the space should be set out (you will have to talk to the other groups to do this). Show the windows and doors, and the equipment and furniture on your plan.

Group 2

a) What activities take place in the room, e.g. typing, word processing, administration, filing, etc.? Each of these activities needs a different type of space. Different work surfaces and seating are needed for specific jobs. Make a list of these activities in order of importance.

b) How often do these activities take place? You will have to measure the time taken on the different activities, e.g. for how many hours out of the working day is it used for typing? Draw a pie chart to show your results.

c) What facilities do these activities need? Do they need power points? Does the furniture get moved around? Have they got the right type of desk or chair for particular activities?

d) Make suggestions as to how the space could best be used for particular activities.

Group 3

a) Make a list of the resources that are used in the room. Is there space for computer paper, reference books, files, etc.?

b) Are all the resources you need available in the room? Do you have to go to another room? How long does this take? Find out.

c) Find out if there is enough storage space or if there is too little. Are some of the cupboards empty?

d) Make suggestions for the best type of storage for the resources used in the room.

Group 4

a) Count the number of times people move around to get more paper or to get to their folders, etc. in an 'average' day.

b) Find out where people walk to in the room and how much time they take up doing this.

c) Draw a bar chart which shows how often people get up and move around and how long it takes.

d) Talk to Group 3 and suggest what improvements can be made in the storage system for resources.

Group 5

You need to find out what the health and safety requirements of the area are.

a) Use the safety checklist at the end of this chapter to compile a list of questions you could ask.

b) Does the present layout of the workplace meet health and safety needs? Can people get out in an emergency? Is the fire equipment easy to reach? Is the fire equipment of the right type? Can you see the fire notices?

c) Will the suggested new layout be safe? This is your group's key task, you will have to check with the other group to find out.

All five groups will need to work together to produce a new layout for the room. This must be presented as a written report to the head of section.

Individual groups must give an oral presentation which describes what they have found, what is right about the workplace and what is wrong. Finally, they must give their ideas for improvements.

Summary of main tasks
- Produce a written report which covers the present layout of the workplace.
- Find out what is right and what is wrong about the present layout of the workplace.
- Suggest improvements which could be made to the workplace.
- Give an oral presentation on the proposed new layout of the workplace.

Working in an office

The administrative section of an organisation helps to make the business or institution run smoothly. There are many types of administrative office job, e.g. an invoice clerk completes and checks invoices, a clerk/typist does general office work and some typing.

In some offices many activities take place at the same time – a telephonist could be working on the switchboard, someone could be word processing, several people could be completing forms, one person may be dealing with enquiries from the public.

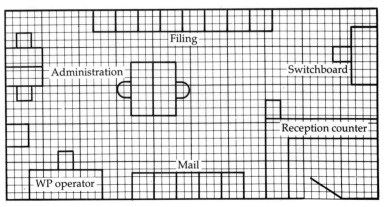

Scale: 1 cm = 1 m

Area of office = 10 m × 5 m = 50 m^2

▲ *Typical office layout*

A typical office layout is shown above. The counter is needed to prevent people from walking directly into the office. This is important when money is handled or if documents are confidential or secret. In an emergency the people in the office will have to get out very quickly so there must be a flap in the counter to allow people through.

Health and safety in the office

The main problems

Falling and slipping
▸ Always use steps to reach the top shelf/cupboard.
▸ Always clear away spilt drinks, etc. immediately.

Storage
▸ Never store material in high places from where it is likely to fall.
▸ Always bend your legs and not your back when lifting heavy objects.

Fire hazards
▸ Know the fire drill.
▸ Keep fire equipment accessible and fire exists clear.
▸ Store dangerous materials carefully.

Electricity
▸ Ask for electric points and plugs to be checked regularly.

Study the picture and find out how many times the Health and Safety at Work Act has been broken. List everything that is wrong.

Receiving information

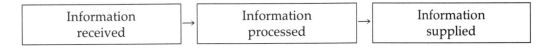

Information received	→	Information processed	→	Information supplied

The purpose of the office is to process the information that an organisation needs. The information is kept either because the government or tax authority says it must be kept, or because the organisation requires it. The organisation may require information:

- To help the management make decisions.
- To give a better service to customers.
- To become more efficient.
- As a record of accounts and sales.

Whenever you collect information make sure that it is correct. Always say when and where you got the information.

Data Protection Act 1984

The Data Protection Act controls the way in which data stored on computer about indivi-duals is used. People can ask to see what information about themselves is on file. The Act tries to ensure that the data is:

▸ Accurate.
▸ Used only for specific purposes.
▸ Not given to other users.
▸ Limited to certain items.
▸ Only stored for a particular time
▸ Not freely available.
▸ Not misused.

An office will get its information from many sources. Examples include facscimile (fax) machines, telephones, letters, quotations, employees, etc. The office must collect the data regularly and keep it up to date. Sometimes office staff are asked to collect data or information over the phone.

ACTIVITY

1 Construct a bar chart showing the number of telephone calls received by your workplace during a typical day. Use axes like those below.

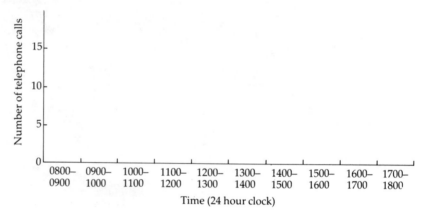

2 Do the same for the number of calls made from your workplace. Can you say anything about the pattern of the calls?

3 You arrive back from lunch and find this message on your desk:

Message
JM Thomson at Portsmouth Rd., Woking, phoned to say they wanted 2 doz stainless steel table knives, and 2 doz steel spoons and forks (the ones which sell at £7·50, £6·50 and £3·50 each). Their order JMT 1121. They want delivery 2 weeks today. I said yes. Can you complete the telephone order and send an acknowledgement?   Thanks PJ

TELEPHONE ORDER

DELIVERY ADDRESS

DATE DELIVERY REQUIRED	DELIVERY DATE GIVEN	TODAYS DATE	
CUSTOMER ORDER NUMBER	ORDER TAKEN BY	OUR REFERENCE NUMBER	
QUANTITY	DESCRIPTION		UNIT PRICE	AMOUNT

ACKNOWLEDGEMENT OF ORDER

| TODAYS DATE | YOUR ORDER DATE | YOUR ORDER NUMBER |
| GOODS TO BE SENT BY | EXPECTED DELIVERY DATE | |

COMMENTS

Storing information

Information storage and retrieval systems

We have seen that there are many reasons why organisations store information. A good filing or storage system should be:

- Simple to use with easy access.
- Safe and secure.
- Known and understood by everyone who will use it.
- Efficient and easy to see.
- Up to date.
- Well organised and arranged.
- Logical and easy to maintain.

There are several ways of storing information. Many offices file their information in a computer. Some of these have special passwords so that only certain people will be able to look at all the data. Manual filing (filing by hand) however, is still very important.

Manual methods of filing

Box files

- Useful for storing old documents.
- Difficult to find documents quickly.
- Get very dusty if not cleaned or used.

Ring binders

- Secure and easy to use.
- Documents can be torn and damaged if punched holes in the paper are not protected.

Vertical filing cabinet

- Safe, secure and simple to use.
- Large amounts of information can be stored.
- Can be unstable if the top drawers are overloaded.

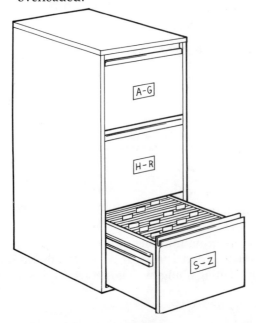

Card index

- Useful for telephone numbers, suppliers names and addresses.
- Cards are easy to find.
- No good for large amounts of information.

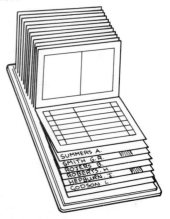

Strip index

- Information is stored on thin strips of paper.
- Easily seen.
- Little information can be recorded (they are often used in libraries for book titles and authors).

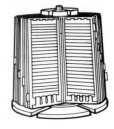

Lateral filing

- Safe and simple to use.
- Documents are placed horizontally.
- Large amounts of information can b stored.

Rotary card index

- Easy to use.
- Holds a large number of cards.
- Can stand on a desk.

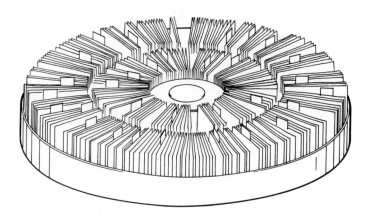

How to file

Numerical order   Filing by numerical order is useful for filing invoices or orders. The invoice or order number is usually at the top corner of the form. The documents are then filed so that the numbers are in order.

Subject order   Documents are filed alphabetically according to the contents of the document, e.g. **A**ccident reports, **B**uildings, **C**leaning.

Alphabetical order   Filing according to the position of letters in the alphabet. File of customers' names would usually be kept in alphabetical order.

Basic rules for filing

1 File by surname   Collins Joan
                     Davies Edward
                     Dodson Helen
2 When surnames are the same then file by the first letter or initial of the forename, e.g.
                     Collins Joan or Collins J
                     Collins Kenneth or Collins K.
                     Collins Martin or Collins M.
3 If surnames and forenames or initials are the same, then file by the first letter of the address
                     Collins J 15 Albany Rd.
                     Collins J 27 Bure St.
                     Collins J 87 Cross Way
4 If surnames and forenames or initials and the first letter of the address are the same, use the second letter of the address
                     Collins J 21 Abott Rd.
                     Collins J 40 Acorn Dr.
                     Collins J 15 Albany Rd.
5 St names come after Saint
                     Saint P J
                     St Josephs School
6 Scottish or Irish names, e.g. Mac or Mc or MC are all filed as if they were Mac.
7 Names which are abbreviated should be filed as if they are written in full, e.g. BTEC will be filed Business and Technology Education Council.
8 When there are geographical names, e.g. a town or country, file under the name of the place, Brazilian Embassy.

1   The filing system in your office has the following categories:

Accidents	Gas
Accounts	Health
Building	Personnel
Burglary reports	Sales
Chemicals	Security
Cleaning	Telephones
Electricity	

Under which heading would you file the following documents:

- A bill from BT.
- A theft from the finance department.
- An application for a job.
- A report on mice in the canteen.
- A government report on storing flammable liquid.
- A broken window pane needs mending.
- A letter of resignation.
- An invoice from Sprite Office Equipment.
- A complaint about a sales assistant.
- A rent demand from the landlord.
- A request to change holiday dates.
- A suspected break in.

2   File the following in the correct order:

K J Motors	RAC Motoring Services
Prudential Insurance	McKay K
Ng Brothers	Mackay A A
Barnes R G	Saint A
Zychski M Z	St John Ambulance
Barnes W F	Save the Children Fund
Edmundson P	Zysemil P J
Kamara Y	Barnes E M
Pater D F	Zychski M Y
Kean-Hammersley	

Electronic office

In the last five years a large part of traditional office work has been taken over by computer and other electronic machines. Information can now be received electronic by fax and electronic mail. It can be processed and filed on a computer. Compu software packages such as databases and spreadsheets can handle and examine la amounts of data quickly and easily. Forms and letters can be produced using dedica word processors or computers. You will probably have received personal letters wh have been produced on a computer which say 'Dear (your name), you could win a car .

It was thought that doing everything on screen and storing information and docum electronically would end the need for paper documents in an office. The introductic electronic equipment should have led to the 'paperless office'. However, if you spea anyone who works with computers they will say: 'We have more paper than ever before – everyone wants 'hardcopy' of what they see on the screen. Then they want several more copies to show and give to their colleagues. This paper costs more.'

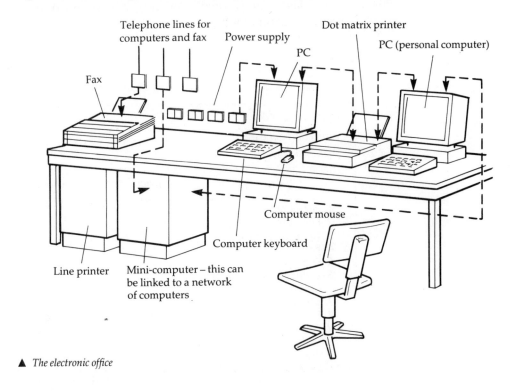

▲ *The electronic office*

Electronic mail

Messages are sent over computer links instead of by letter. Messages are keyed into the computer and stored in its memory. To 'read' or collect the message the person to whom it is sent must access or call the computer. They can then receive the messages on their computer screen.

Computer filing

When data is entered into a computer it is stored on a disk. Disks can be 'hard' or 'floppy' pieces of plastic. (You will probably have your own disk as part of this course.) Groups of data will be stored or filed under the same name. To look at, or retrieve this data, it has to be moved from the disk into the computer memory. The file can then be seen and read. This process is exactly the same as manually filing paper documents.

Paper filing

| Paper file put into a filing cabinet | → | File stored in cabinet | → | File taken out of filing cabinet |

Computer filing

| Data keyed into the computer | → | File stored on disk | → | File retrieved from the disk |

There are differences between computer and manual filing. The computer file stays where it is on the disk as well as being stored in a computers memory if it is being used. This means that the file cannot be taken away. It can be read by many people at the same time (if the PCs are linked or networked). The file can be accessed, or called up and read from anywhere there is a computer link.

Date of inspection: Inspection done by: Action checked by:			
Safety checklist	Action needed	By whom	Date
1 Fire doors 2 Fire exits 3 Fire extinguishers 4 Fire alarms 5 Fire notices 6 Bomb and flood warning notices 7 Safety notices 8 First aid notices 9 First aiders and kit 10 Storage flammable liquids (these burn very easily) 11 Heating and ventilation Structure 1 Floor covering 2 Stairs Offices 1 Photocopying and duplicating 2 Flammable liquids 3 Non-flammable chemicals 4 Electrical equipment			

▲ Safety checklist for the assignment

8 *Business documents*

Summary

This chapter examines the processes and documents used in buying supplies and selling goods. The assignments and related activities place you in a job role with a variety of tasks within a typical business transaction. The following topics are covered:

▸ Finding and choosing suppliers
▸ Making and dealing with enquiries
▸ Preparing quotations and tenders
▸ Ordering
▸ Invoices and paying for quotes
▸ Advice, credit and debit notes.

This chapter will help you to achieve the following outcomes:

Core Module 1   Business World
Outcome 1.4   Examine the relationships between an organisation and its customers
Core Module 2   Administrative Systems and Procedures
Outcome 2.2   Identify and use different communication systems and methods of a selected organisation
Outcome 2.3   Produce documents and material and process data

Core Module 3   Business Resources and Procedures
Outcome 3.3   Record financial transactions

Core Module 4   People in Business
Outcome 4.3   Examine and compare the main job roles in different organisations
Outcome 4.4   Contribute to achievement of organisational goals by fulfilling job role

The assignments can be used to cover the following performance criteria:

1.1e	the need for businesses to be dynamic in order to survive recognised
1.4a	importance of customers recognised
1.4b	types of customers identified
1.4c	changes in customer needs and business response identified
1.4d	need for employees to present positive image of the organisation fully understood.
2.2a	oral and written messages received and acted upon
2.2b	information obtained from appropriate sources
2.2c	routine business communications produced
2.2d	channels of communication identified and used
2.2e	incoming and outgoing mail processed
2.2f	electronic telecommunications used to receive and send information
2.3a	business documents produced using a word processing package
2.3b	information processing equipment used to run standard applications
2.3c	data examined and analysed using a spreadsheet package
2.4b	equipment used in accordance with operating instructions and procedures
2.4c	work area kept free from hazards
2.5b	polite and effective responses made to a range of customer/client situations
2.5c	liaison and communication with peers and senior colleagues conducted effectively
2.5d	rapport and mutual respect between colleagues and customers/clients established
3.1d	methods of acquiring the necessary resources for a business examined

3.3a	flow of money in the organisation charted and explained
3.3b	recording documents and systems identified and their purpose described
3.3c	correct systems and documents or files chosen or accessed
3.3d	information recorded neatly and accurately
3.3e	necessary calculations made accurately
3.3f	recording and calculations checked for accuracy
4.1b	the nature of work examined and different types compared
4.3a	functional areas within organisations identified
4.3b	job roles in different functional areas of organisations identified
4.3c	job roles compared
4.4a	relationship between organisational objectives and job role identified
4.4b	given tasks completed to agreed criteria
4.4c	contribution made both as an individual and as a member of a team to the achievement of agreed targets and goals

The assignment will help you with the development of all Common Skills, these are:

Managing and Developing Self
Outcome 1   Manage own roles and responsibilities
Outcome 2   Manage own time in achieving objectives
Outcome 3   Undertake personal and career development
Outcome 4   Transfer skills gained to new and changing situations and contexts

Working with and Relating to Others
Outcome 5   Treat others' values, beliefs and opinions with respect
Outcome 6   Relate to and interact effectively with individuals and groups
Outcome 7   Work effectively as a member of a team

Communicating
Outcome 8   Receive and respond to a variety of information
Outcome 9   Present information in a variety of visual forms
Outcome 10   Communicate in writing
Outcome 11   Participate in oral and non-verbal communication

Managing Tasks and Solving Problems
Outcome 12   Use information sources
Outcome 13   Deal with a combination of routine and non-routine tasks
Outcome 14   Identify and solve routine and non-routine problems

Applying Numeracy
Outcome 15   Apply numerical skills and techniques

Applying Technology
Outcome 16   Use a range of technological equipment and systems

Applying Design and Creativity
Outcome 17   Apply a range of skills and techniques to develop a variety of ideas the creation of new/modified products, services or situations
Outcome 18   Use a range of thought processes

Read the following assignment to help you to understand some of the things you sho be able to do by the end of the chapter. Normally it will be best to read the chapter carry out the set activities before you tackle the assignment.

Check whether you can do the assignment on your own or with one or more colleagu Some assignments will require organising by your tutor. Seek guidance, where need from your tutor.

The Trend Fashion Co. Ltd.

The Trend Fashion Co. Ltd. is based at Studio 2000, The Bull Ring, Birmingham. It specialises in selling to in-store boutiques in large department stores. It is well known for leading fashion in children's clothing. It has just obtained a large contract to supply clothing under its own label, The Trend, to a mail-order company.

The mail-order company distributes its catalogues nationwide. 'Trend' clothes will now be available to every child. The company will concentrate on two age groups, 5 to 10 year olds, and 10 into teens.

To meet its contract The Trend requires more fabrics. Most of its material will be bought plain and unbleached. These fabrics will then be dyed, using only natural colours. Their designers are currently working on two themes which are cultural diversity and seasons. The result is patterns with names such as Caribbean Autumn, Eastern Spring and Mediterranean Summer. The same patterns are used in both the boys' and the girls' clothing ranges.

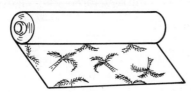 

You work in the purchasing department of the company as one of the assistants to the fabrics buyer. Your job description says that you have to work closely with other members of the team, have a good telephone manner and be able to work neatly and accurately under pressure.

There are three firms which provide the fabrics you want. They are:

▸ Hose and Rubble
Bermondsey St
London SE1

▸ Studio Collection
Design House
Bath
Avon

▸ Cali Co
Coin Market St
Liverpool 4

Task 1

Memorandum

To: Assistant
From: M Patel

Date: Today

Can you please type or word process a letter to each of the suppliers. Say what type of and how much material we need – the purchase requisition form attached tells you this information. You must ask for a quotation and stress the importance of an early and guaranteed delivery date. The material must not burn easily, it must be **flame retardant.**

Purchase Requisition Form

To: Purchasing	PR 0133
From: Production	LM

Qty	Description
700 yds	Plain Polycotton Width 1 yard
300 yds	Plain Polycotton Width 1 ½ yards

Task 2 Complete a quotation request form and enclose this with your letter.

QUOTATION REQUEST

To:	From:

Please quote for your best price and delivery on these goods

Quantity	Description
	Date:
	Authorised by:
	Position:

Task 3 As a result of your letter, The Trend Fashion Co. Ltd. get back three price lists.

Hose and Rubble Price List

Material	Width	PRICE PER LINEAR METRE Length			
		0–50 m	51–100 m	101–500 m	Over 500 m
Polycotton	0.5 m	£1.50	£1.40	£1.30	£1.20
Polycotton	1.0 m	£3.00	£2.90	£2.80	£2.70
Polycotton	1.5 m	£4.50	£4.40	£4.30	£4.20

Guaranteed delivery within 21 days

5% discount for payment within 28 days

Studio Collection Price List

Material	Width	PRICE PER LINEAR METRE Length			
		0–100 m	101–500 m	501–1500 m	Over 1500 m
Polycotton	0.5 m	£1.50	£1.40	£1.35	£1.20
Polycotton	1.0 m	£3.00	£2.80	£2.70	£2.60
Polycotton	1.5 m	£4.50	£4.40	£4.30	£4.10

Delivery within 14 days

5% discount for payment within 21 days

Cali Co. Price List

Material	Width	PRICE PER LINEAR METRE Length			
		0–200 m	201–500 m	501–1000 m	Over 1000 m
Polycotton	0.5 m	£1.40	£1.30	£1.25	£1.20
Polycotton	1.0 m	£2.90	£2.70	£2.60	£2.50
Polycotton	1.5 m	£4.40	£4.20	£4.15	£4.10

Cali Co. Out of Stock

We are temporarily out of stock on the goods listed below.

Your order number	Date of order	Date

Goods sent by

Ready in 7 weeks

Comments *Sorry the 1m and 1½ m polycotton are out of stock   R.L.*

Decide which company offers you the best price (remember to change yards into metres). Type or word process a reply and fill in an order form. You will need to create your own order number but use your own name and today's date. Make copies and mark these for the various departments that need the information. Do all the calculations, including VAT.

Task 4 During your lunchbreak, you are talking to a friend. Both of you reckon that you can design better patterns than those currently available.

Choose one of the items from each theme list and working with your friend, design and colour your pattern. Remember that the design must be suitable for children's and teenager's clothing.

Themes:

- **Cultural diversity**   African, Eastern, Caribbean, Nordic, Mediterranean, American.
- **Seasons**   Spring, Summer, Autumn, Winter.

Introduction

The rest of this chapter provides information and activities which will help you to complete the assignment. Firstly it looks at:

- **Purchasing or buying**   The ordering of goods and services, and looks at the forms and documents which are needed to do this.
- **Supplying or selling**   The preparation and despatch of quotations, invoices and statements.

Ordering goods and services

Whatever the type of organisation, it will at some time have to select, order and buy goods and services from other companies. For instance, if stock has been used or become out of date, new stock will be needed. For example, an organisation could buy:

- **Goods**   e.g. stationery and supplies, computer consumables, furniture, equipment, anti-static carpets (to stop people getting electric shocks), etc.
- **Services**   e.g. plumber, carpenter, electrician, carpet layer, etc.

In ordering goods or services, there are a number of steps which an organisation needs to follow:

1 **Find suppliers.**
2 **Make enquiries.**
3 **Obtain a quotation or tender.**
4 **Choose a supplier.**
5 **Place an order.**
6 **Take delivery of the goods or service.**
7 **Pay for the goods or service.**

Sometimes the positions of steps 6 and 7 are reversed. Customers may be required to pay for the goods or services before they receive them. We will now take each of these seven steps in turn and explore them in detail.

1   Find suppliers

Before a company places an order, it will want to ensure that it gets the best deal at the best price. It will want value for the money it spends. Ideally it would visit the suppliers or see the goods in advance to check to see whether they are suitable. But before the company can visit it has to find suitable suppliers. There are several sources of information available to help you to do this:

- The company may have its own records of existing suppliers.
- *Yellow Pages* list the names of businesses alphabetically under specific headings, e.g. plumbers.
- Exhibitions, trade fairs and conferences where firms can show their latest products and designs
- Trade directories which list firms in a particular trade or occupation.
- Registers of approved organisations which list firms whose work meets minimum standards as laid down by the industry in which they work.
- Trade associations and local Chamber of Commerce.
- Sales representatives from firms trying to sell their products.
- Catalogues, price lists and publicity sent out by suppliers to possible customers.

Take great care when looking at price lists from different companies. They are often presented differently so that it is difficult to tell which is the cheapest. The price will often depend on how many items are wanted and how quickly payment is made, e.g.

Bob's Office Supplies
Boxes of staples (100 per box)

Number of boxes purchased	Price per box £
0–50	1.70
51–100	1.60
101–500	1.50
over 500	1.40

Lin's Office Supplies

Boxes of staples (100 stapes per box)	Number of Boxes purchased price per box			
	0–100	101–250	251–500	Over 500
	£1.70	£1.60	£1.50	£1.40

When you first look at the information, the prices of both Bob's and Lin's Office Supplies look the same. If you buy 40 boxes the price is the same – £1.70 per box, but if you buy 60 boxes Bob's Office Supplies is cheaper at £1.60 compared to £1.70 and for 110 boxes Bob's Office Supplies is still the cheapest. For orders over 500 boxes the price is the same from both suppliers.

If prices appear to be similar, check to see if there are differences in delivery charges, discounts, etc.

---/ ACTIVITY /--

1 Find the names of four companies in your area which sell computer consumables.
2 Find the names of four builders in your area which belong to the NHBC.
3 Obtain three catalogues of office supplies.

2   Make enquiries

Telephone enquiries

A telephone enquiry is one made by telephone. Before you make an enquiry, write notes of what you want to ask. This rule applies whether you are buying small or large items, typewriter ribbons or typewriters, e.g.:

● Do they have the size, style, colour you want?
● Does the product meet your needs?
● Do they have the items in stock?
● What is the delivery date?
● Is there a guarantee or warranty?
● What is the price – is it fixed?
● Is there a service contract?
● Is there a discount?
● Is there a delivery charge?
● Is there an installation charge?
● What is the payment method?

▲ *Making telephone enquiries*

Always be clear and direct; give the name of your company, know what you want an how much you are prepared to pay. If you offer a company your business they will ofte reduce the price for you. You should always follow company rules when dealing wit suppliers. Junior staff are not normally allowed to talk with suppliers unless supervise by a buyer or purchasing officer.

One standard procedure is:

a) Take the name, position and telephone number of the person to whom you speak.
b) Make a note of the information obtained.
c) Note the day and time of the phone call.
d) Put this information on a card.
e) Copy the information to a supervisor.
f) File the card.

Written enquiries

A written enquiry is a business letter which is sent to possible suppliers. Again it m follow the normal rules of the organisation. It should cover all the points noted for telephone enquiry and be signed by a supervisor. If you have already telephone company, you can address the letter to the person you spoke with, including the day a time of the conversation.

/ **ACTIVITY** /

New typewriter ribbons (they can be cartridges or cassettes) are needed for your workpl
Make notes of all the details you need to ask a supplier, then write a letter which coul
sent to possible suppliers. Use the catalogues you obtained for the previous activity.

---

3 Obtain a quotation or tender

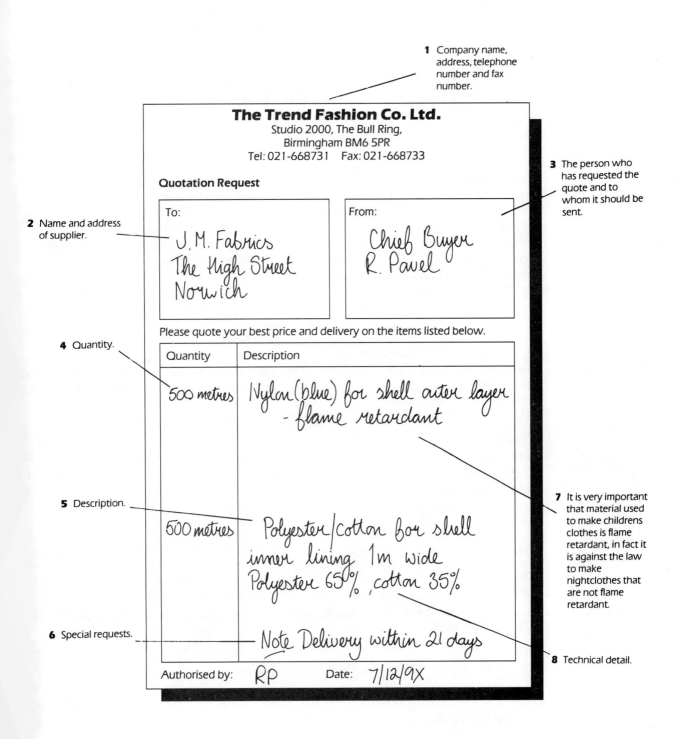

1 Company name, address, telephone number and fax number.

2 Name and address of supplier.

3 The person who has requested the quote and to whom it should be sent.

4 Quantity.

5 Description.

6 Special requests.

7 It is very important that material used to make childrens clothes is flame retardant, in fact it is against the law to make nightclothes that are not flame retardant.

8 Technical detail.

The Trend Fashion Co. Ltd.
Studio 2000, The Bull Ring,
Birmingham BM6 5PR
Tel: 021-668731   Fax: 021-668733

Quotation Request

To:

J. M. Fabrics
The High Street
Norwich

From:

Chief Buyer
R. Pavel

Please quote your best price and delivery on the items listed below.

Quantity	Description
500 metres	Nylon (blue) for shell outer layer - flame retardant
500 metres	Polyester/cotton for shell inner lining 1m wide Polyester 65%, cotton 35%
	Note Delivery within 21 days

Authorised by: RP   Date: 7/12/9X

▲ *Example of how a quotation request should be completed*

131

A quotation request is a formal invitation from one company to another to quote – give its best or lowest price – for supplying specific goods or services. The request for a quotation should be sent with a letter to a number of selected companies. The company buyer or purchasing officer is usually responsible for preparing the quotation request. The description can be very detailed and technical and is sometimes called a specification, i.e. the company specifies exactly what it wants.

The production department will complete a **purchase requisition form** showing the item, quantity, production details and delivery date required. This is sent to the purchasing department and is the basis for the **quotation request.** The purchasing department finds suppliers, obtains quotes, decides which supplier to use and places the order.

Tender request

A **tender** is a formal offer or bid to supply specific goods or services at a stated cost or price. The process of requesting a tender is similar to that for obtaining a quote. With large contracts it is often compulsory for the work to be put out to tender. In local authorities compulsory competitive tendering is now standard practice. The work to be done or the service to be provided must be advertised. Look in the Public Notices section of your local newspaper to see advertised tenders.

4 Choosing a supplier

Junior employees are not normally involved in choosing a supplier. Choosing suppliers is the responsibility of a manager, but you do have to know why and how the decision is made. The choice will depend on the type of product or service a company wants to buy. Remember, it is value for money which is wanted, not simply the lowest price. For example suppliers could be compared on the basis of any (or all) of the following:

- Price.
- Quality.
- Type of material used.
- Delivery date.
- Method of delivery.
- Delivery charges.
- Installation costs.
- Discounts available.

Each of the companies being considered as a possible supplier could be given marks out of 10 under each feature. The winner would be the company with the most marks. (You could use this method to compare or evaluate the possible suppliers of typewriter ribbons/cassettes/cartridges in the previous activity.)

The quotation or tender chosen by a company is usually the one that gives the best value for money. It is not necessarily the cheapest.

ACTIVITY

1   Your office needs to replace its stock of computer consumables. It is not unhappy with present supplier but is interested to find out if the items can be bought more cheap Quality and guaranteed delivery are also essential.

You are asked to prepare a quotation request for 100 floppy disks, 50 printer ribbons a continuous stationery. (Check the size, make, etc. used in your office. The paper m have perforations down both sprocket hole margins and at the folds.)

2 As trusted members of the junior office staff team you and your colleagues have been asked to recommend a supplier for the new desks that you require. You have received these quotations as summarised below. Which of these quotes would you choose? You must reply with a typed memo to your supervisor Ms M Lester giving reasons for your choice (remember that you would have to assemble the desks). Ms Lester will make the decision.

Top Desks
Price £114; delivery date 10 days; delivery charge £25; installation charge £30 (flat rate which does not depend on the number of desks).

Great Desks
Price £120; delivery date 10 days; flat packed ready for easy assembly.

Sky Desks
Rock bottom price £99; delivery 5 weeks; no hidden extras

On the carpet

The office you work in measures 18 feet by 32 feet. The floor area is $18 \times 32 = 576$ square feet, or 64 square yards (there are 9 square feet in 1 square yard). You contact the carpet company and are quoted a price of £25.00 for a square metre of carpet. How much would you have to pay to have the office carpeted?

To work out how much the carpet will cost we must change (convert) square yards into square metres. We need a number that will tell us how many square yards there are in a square metre to help us do this conversion. You can work this out on a calculator, but often you can find these numbers in diaries or the back of dictionaries. For this calculation we find:

1 square yard = 0.836 square metres

i.e. a square yard is smaller than a square metre.
Therefore:

64 square yards = 64 × 0.836 square metres
　　　　　　　 = 53.504 square metres

The cost of the carpet is calculated by multiplying the number of square metres by the cost of carpet per square metre. 1 square metre costs £25.00, therefore 53.504 square metres will cost:

53.504 × £25.00 = £1337.60

Other useful conversions are:

- 1 inch = 2.54 centimetres = 25.4 millimetres
- 1 yard = 3 feet = 0.9144 metres
- 1 mile = 1.609 kilometres
- 1 pint = 20 fluid ozs = 0.568 litres
- 1 gallon = 4.546 litres

Example
Change 200 yards into metres.

1 yard = 0.9144 metres

i.e. for every 1 yard there are 0.9144 metres (nearly 1 metre) Therefore for 200 yards there are

200 × 0.9144 = 182.88 metres

Example
Change 300 metres into yards.

This time we divide by 0.9144 because there will be more yards than metres. Therefore, for 300 metres there are

300 ÷ 0.9144 = 328.08 yards

R.B.JACKSON

┌─ **ACTIVITY** ─────────────────────────────────

Your boss bursts into the office one morning saying, 'We have to get into Europe. We can't ⸏
on producing our drinks in pints any more – we have to start using litres. We'll begin ⸏
changing our expected sales figures into litres. We have to start somewhere.'

You are given the job of changing the figures:

	Sales in pints	Sales in litres
May	21 300	
June	22 800	
July	26 520	
Aug	29 200	
Sept	24 000	
Oct	18 100	
Nov	17 900	
Dec	23 540	

5 Place an order

Once a decision has been made as to which quote to accept, an official company order can be made out. The design of the order form would depend on the needs of the company.

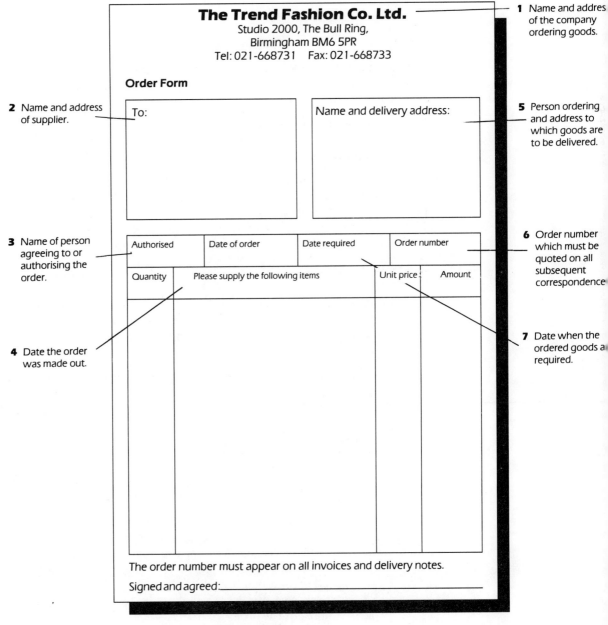

The Trend Fashion Co. Ltd.
Studio 2000, The Bull Ring,
Birmingham BM6 5PR
Tel: 021-668731   Fax: 021-668733

Order Form

To:

Name and delivery address:

Authorised	Date of order	Date required	Order number

Quantity	Please supply the following items	Unit price	Amount

The order number must appear on all invoices and delivery notes.

Signed and agreed:_____

1 Name and address of the company ordering goods.

2 Name and address of supplier.

3 Name of person agreeing to or authorising the order.

4 Date the order was made out.

5 Person ordering and address to which goods are to be delivered.

6 Order number which must be quoted on all subsequent correspondence.

7 Date when the ordered goods are required.

▲ *Example of how an order form should be completed*

The order number, for example, can show which department has placed the order and which expenditure heading it should be charged to (see Chapter 12, Keeping the Books).

Everything written on the order form must be correct as it is a legal document. The order form must only be signed by someone with the responsibility or authority to do so. The order can now be sent to the supplier. Copies should be filed either by alphabetical listing, under the company name, or by order number. Other departments in the organisation should be sent copies so that they:

a) Know what is happening.
b) Can chase up the supplier if something goes wrong.
c) Can prepare for the delivery.

How to make an order number

Department	Expenditure	Number
Sales	Stationery	
Clerical	Furniture	
Transport	Office equipment	
Production	Postage	
Computing	Consumables	

The basis for a very simple order number system can be made by taking the first letter of the department, then the first letter of the expenditure heading and assigning a number for the orders already placed, e.g.

SF 0012   Sales department, furniture order number 12
TO 0029   Transport department, office equipment order number 29
CS 0187   Clerical department, stationery order number 187

This type of system enables the finance section to debit or charge the order to the correct department and expenditure code, e.g. order number CS 0188 for £20.70 is an expenditure on stationery made by the clerical dept. It is this account which would be debited (have the money taken away) to pay the order.

ACTIVITY

1   Blaser Computing, Banbury Road, Oxford, OX0 3NY, have won the order from you company for 700 Floppy Disks at £0.85 each, 50 printer ribbons at £3.50 each and 30 reams of photocopy paper at £11 per ream.

You work in the computer department of The Steel Co. of Wales, Margam, S. Wales. Please complete the order, you must calculate VAT. Give todays date. The items are required in ten days time.

2

> ### *Gosport Electronics*
> Unit 6
> Bay Road
> Southampton
> #### Internal memo
>
> Can you please make out the following order
> 6 Reams A4 Bank Paper; 3 reams A4 Bond paper; 3 reams A5; 100 envelopes A4 size; 100 envelopes with windows for A5; 40 bottles of correcting fluid; 5 doz ballpoint pens (blue); 5 doz ballpoint pens (black).
> Please check with the local suppliers as to which is the cheapest. Then please make out the order to them.

ORDER FORM

TO		DELIVERY ADDRESS	

ORDER NUMBER	DATE OF ORDER	DATE REQUIRED	AGREED BY

QUANTITY	DESCRIPTION	UNIT PRICE	TOTAL	

	Total excluding VAT	
	VAT at 17½%	
	Total including VAT	

ORDER NUMBER MUST APPEAR ON ALL INVOICES AND DELIVERY NOTES

6 Take delivery of the goods

The stock or stores section will normally take delivery of goods. It is important that the goods delivered, as shown on the **delivery note** match the order form. The goods must be in perfect condition.

7 Paying for the goods

Once the goods have been received the finance department is informed. This will enable payment to be made to the seller.

What to do if something goes wrong

1 Never be afraid to ask someone if you do not know what to do.
2 Always ask for help if you do not understand an instruction. Remember that this happens to everyone.
3 Always find out the company rules on buying goods or services.
4 Always follow the company rules completely.
5 Always ask people to repeat their name and spell it if you are making a telephone enquiry.
6 Keep files and records up to date. Know where the information is kept.
7 Companies sometimes do not deliver when they say they will. Always be prepared to ring

them and find out why they have not delivered. Ask them to give you a new delivery date.

8 Check and double check whenever you fill in a form. You need quiet conditions to be able to concentrate on filling in forms, so do not be afraid to ask people around you, 'Please could you be quiet, I'm trying to work.'

Preparing and dispatching business documents

Having looked at documentation from the purchasing side we now turn to documentation used by the supplier of goods/services. We will now look at:

1 How quotations and invoices are prepared, completed, filed and distributed to other departments.
2 The use of advice notes and credit and debit notes.
3 How enquiries and complaints can be dealt with.

The diagram opposite shows how the departments in an organisation all work together. They are like the links in a chain – the organisation is only as strong as the weakest department. Forms and documents pass or flow from one department to another. A bottleneck in one part of an organisation will create problems everywhere else.

The sales section is no exception, it relies heavily on the work done elsewhere in the organisation, e.g. in purchasing, production, accounts, and stock control. To be successful it must have up-to-date information and a proper system for keeping records and dealing with documents and customers.

Whilst in large companies each department might have just one function, in small organisations a general office might perform all the tasks.

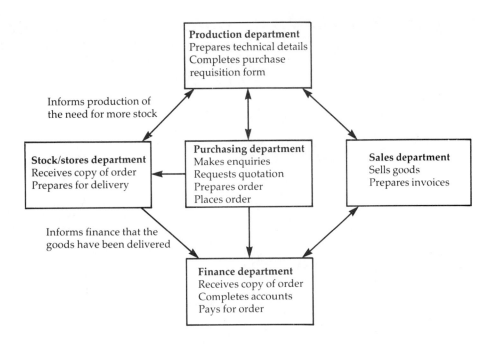

▲ *How departments of an organisation work together*

Where the sales department gets its information

Information for the sales department comes from:

- Existing and possible customers.
- Telephone and written enquiries.
- Requests for price lists and quotations.
- Its sales people.
- Replies to publicity or promotional brochures and leaflets which have been sent directly to the key people in companies they are trying to sell to.
- By asking people for their views and ideas.

1 Dealing with enquiries

If a telephone or written enquiry is received, it should be dealt with immediately. Organisations will have their own method of handling queries and requests and these must always be followed. For example, companies may type or word process individual replies, or they may adapt or customise standard letters by selecting particular paragraphs for inclusion in the final letter. Always check the final letter thoroughly, for the accuracy of the information and the spelling. Take great care if you use a word checking program on a word processor because it will not tell you if you have used the wrong word, e.g. a common error found in letters sent to colleges is to use the incorrect word 'principle' when addressing the 'principal'. However, word processors do have many advantages. By using a word processor you can:

- Change the typeface of a letter.
- Shift words, sentences and paragraphs up or down.
- Delete words, sentences or paragraphs.
- Put in graphs and diagrams.
- Use a mailmerge program to address a standard letter to many customers.
- Check everything before it is printed.

Publicity leaflets and brochures would normally be enclosed with any written reply to an enquiry.

> RIGHT – WHO'S NEXT?

ENQUIRIES

R.B.JACKSON

▲ *Dealing with enquiries*

2 The quotation

A quotation is a document showing a firm list of prices and costs at which goods or services will be supplied, or at which work will be done. This information is given by the seller to possible buyers. It can also show whether the seller is willing to give a discount or reduced price for payment by cash, prompt payment or large purchases. If a quotation is accepted by the buyer, the goods must be supplied at the quoted price.

A simple quotation may be completed by one or two people. However, to prepare a complex quotation, the sales department may have to work with other sections of the organisation to prepare a quote.

Preparing a quotation

Information comes from:

- ▸ Production department, e.g. delivery dates, types of material, technical data.
- ▸ Distribution/Dispatch department, e.g. method, cost, time of delivery
- ▸ Accounts department, e.g. prices, costs, method of payment.

A quotation will usually show:
- ▸ Quantity to be supplied.
- ▸ Unit or each price and the total.
- ▸ Method and date of delivery.

140

- Materials used and technical data.
- Method and terms of payment.

A letter is usually sent with the quotation. Sometimes the quotation itself can be in the form of a letter or it can be a large document if a big, complex order is involved. This quotation below is the sellers reply to the quotation request made by The Trend Fashion Co. Ltd. on page 131.

Copies of the quotation and the accompanying letter will be filed by the sales department. If the sales department does not get a reply within a few days it will contact the company to see if the quotation has been accepted.

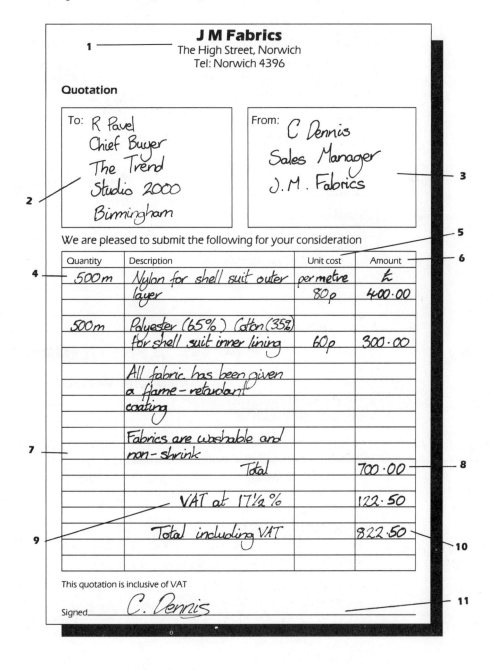

J M Fabrics
The High Street, Norwich
Tel: Norwich 4396

1

Quotation

To: R Pavel
Chief Buyer
The Trend
Studio 2000
Birmingham

2

From: C Dennis
Sales Manager
J.M. Fabrics

3

We are pleased to submit the following for your consideration

5

Quantity	Description	Unit cost	Amount
500m	Nylon for shell suit outer layer	per metre 80p	£ 400.00
500m	Polyester (65%) Cotton (35%) for shell suit inner lining	60p	300.00
	All fabric has been given a flame-retardant coating		
	Fabrics are washable and non-shrink		
	Total		700.00
	VAT at 17½%		122.50
	Total including VAT		822.50

4

6

7

8

9

10

This quotation is inclusive of VAT

Signed C. Dennis

11

▲ *Example of how a quotation should be completed*

1 Name and address of the supplier.

2 Name and address of company requesting the quote.

3 Name and position of the person sending the quote. This is the person who should be contacted if there is a query about the information. In this case there are two queries:

   Firstly, the suppliers have not specified whether the material for the shell suit outer layer is blue. Secondly, they have not said whether they can deliver in 21 days?

4 Quantity in metres.

5 The price per metre of cloth. This is a trade price from one company to another. It is not the price at which it could be bought in a shop – shop or retail prices are much higher.

6 The total figure for each item. In this case, for the nylon.

   Total for 500 metres at 80p (£0.80) per metre
   $= 500 \times 0.80 = £400.00$

7 Special details in reply to special requests.

8 The total amount of all items. Here it is £400 + £300 = £700 excluding VAT (i.e. no VAT has been added).

9 Value Added Tax (VAT) at 17½%. 17½% of the total price must be added to the total to give the **total including VAT**. In this case

   $$VAT = £700.00 \times \frac{17.5}{100} = £122.50$$

10 Total inclusive of VAT = £700.00 + £122.50 = £822.50

11 Name of person responsible for the quote.

/ **ACTIVITY** /

You work for Hose and Rubble. You arrive back from lunch one day to find two telephone messages. There is a Hose and Rubble price list on page 126, use it to action the messages.

HOSE AND RUBBLE

Telephone Message

To: You   Time: 12·00

From: Mountain Clothes   Date: Today
   Llanfair, N.Wales.
Contact G. Owen, Sales.
              Message
They want a quote for 800 metres of
Polycotton ·5 metres wide and 200 metres
of our 1·5 metres width.
Can you do the quote please? You can
give a 5% discount, they are good
customers of ours.   M.L. Supervisor

HOSE AND RUBBLE

Telephone Message

To: *You* Time: *12·20*
From: *Todders World, Lincoln* Date: *Today*

Contact *B. Rich*

Message

Can you please quote for 50 metres of each width?
URGENT — They are ringing back in an hour. M.L.

---

3 Receiving the order

Once a firm order has been received the sales department will:

1 Find out from the stock/stores department if the goods are in stock.
2 Inform production if they have to be made.
3 Inform distribution that they have to delivery goods.
4 Inform accounts so that an invoice can be made out. This will enable the company to be paid. Sometimes the supplier is not sure whether the buyer can afford to pay for goods which have been ordered. In this case it might ask the buyer for a banker's reference. This would be provided by the buyer's bank and would show if the customer could afford to pay. A banker's reference is normally only requested from customers the supplier has not dealt with before. Whilst this is happening the supplier may send an **acknowledgement of order** form to show that the order has been received and is progressing.

ACKNOWLEDGEMENT OF ORDER

DATE	YOUR ORDER NUMBER	YOUR ORDER DATE
EXPECTED DELIVERY DATE	GOODS TO BE SENT BY	

COMMENTS *Received with thanks your order 500m nylon, 500m polycotton*

▲ *Example of an acknowledgement of order form*

Other documents

Advice note

Once the buyer has been checked out and found to be satisfactory, the supplier may send out an advice note. The advice note advises the customer that goods are going to be delivered. The advice note should arrive ahead of the goods. It contains the same information as the invoice. The buyer can, therefore, check that the items that have been ordered are the same as those that are being delivered. Any errors can be put right at this stage.

J M Fabrics
The High Street, Norwich
Tel: Norwich 4396

Advice Note

TO:	DELIVERED TO:

YOUR ORDER NUMBER	DATE SENT	INVOICE DATE	INVOICE NUMBER

QUANTITY	DESCRIPTION	UNIT PRICE	AMOUNT

GOODS RECEIVED IN GOOD CONDITION BY:

▲ *Example of an advice note*

Invoice

This is a form or document sent by a supplier to a buyer. It lists the goods or services which have been supplied. It states the total sum of money now due for payment from the buyer to the seller.

This is how you would complete an invoice:

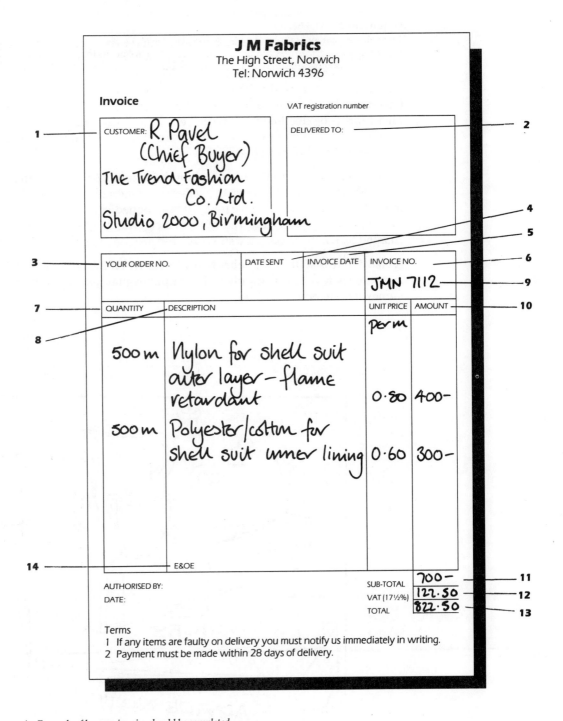

J M Fabrics
The High Street, Norwich
Tel: Norwich 4396

Invoice

VAT registration number

1 — CUSTOMER: R. Pavel (Chief Buyer) The Trend Fashion Co. Ltd. Studio 2000, Birmingham

2 — DELIVERED TO:

YOUR ORDER NO.		DATE SENT	INVOICE DATE	INVOICE NO.
				JMN 7112

3 —   4 —   5 —   6 —   9 —

QUANTITY	DESCRIPTION	UNIT PRICE	AMOUNT
		per m	
500 m	Nylon for shell suit outer layer – flame retardant	0.80	400 –
500 m	Polyester/cotton for shell suit inner lining	0.60	300 –

7 —   8 —   10 —

E&OE

AUTHORISED BY:
DATE:

SUB-TOTAL	700 –
VAT (17½%)	122.50
TOTAL	822.50

11 —   12 —   13 —   14 —

Terms
1 If any items are faulty on delivery you must notify us immediately in writing.
2 Payment must be made within 28 days of delivery.

▲ *Example of how an invoice should be completed*

1 Put in the customer's/buyer's name and address and perhaps a contact name.
2 The address where the items were delivered.
3 The customers order number as it appeared on the order form.
4 Date on which goods were sent.
5 Date on which the invoice was completed.
6 The number of the invoice, here it is JMN 7112. JM – the company name, N – the product code for nylon, 7122 – the number for this order, (for filing and as a reference). The order number and invoice number are important if any queries are made.
7 Quantity, e.g. 500 m.
8 Description – what the items are, e.g. flame retardant nylon for shell suit outer layer.
9 Unit price – price for one item, e.g. 80p for each metre.

145

10 Amount – total to be paid for a particular item, e.g. £400.00 without VAT for the nylon.

11 Sub total – the amount for all the items, without (exclusive of) VAT. Here it is £700.00.

12 Amount of VAT – here it is £122.50.

13 Total – the amount with (inclusive of) VAT. Here it is £822.50.

14 E&OE stands for 'Errors and Omissions Excepted'. This means that if a mistake has been made on the form, the seller cannot be bound by it, that is to say, cannot be held responsible.

Credit notes and debit notes

These forms or documents may be sent by a seller to a buyer after the invoice. Their purpose is to rectify or put right any difference between the amount actually paid and the amount that should have been paid.

A **debit note** is sent to the buyer when the amount paid is less than the value of goods received. The buyer still owes the seller some money. For example, Clare's Computers, the seller, have sent an invoice for £110.80 to Benedict's Medical Co., the buyer. However, the value of the goods received by Benedict's was £115.80. Benedict's have been undercharged by £5, therefore they still owe, and are sent a debit note for, this amount.

A **credit note** is sent by the seller to the buyer when the buyer has been overcharged. The buyer owes less to the supplier. The supplier may pay the buyer the difference if the money has already been paid.

R.B.JACKSON

1 You are working as trainee assistant to R Andrew, an invoice clerk at Southwark Commodities. You deal mainly with documents concerning sales to customers. You also handle the buying of supplies for general use in the office. Today you have received two invoices from Reap Office Supplies Ltd.

- Check all the items on the invoices against the copies of the delivery notes filed in the office.
- Check all prices and arithmetic against the price list; correct any errors.
- If you think that an invoice is correct and should be paid, sign it and complete a cheque ready for signature.
- If you think an invoice is incorrect, write a short letter, suitable for signature by R Andrew, pointing out any mistakes.

Reap Office Supplies Ltd.
Delivery Note

Date_____ Our Ref: _1362_
To____ Southwark Commodities ____
____ Your order No. SC 7865 ____

Qty.	Description
3 Reams	A4 Bond
5 Reams	A4 Bank
2 Reams	A4 Narrow margin feint ruled
4 Reams	A4 Wide margin feint ruled

Signed   _J Goddard_

Reap Office Supplies Ltd.
Invoice

VAT No. **65 1 93122**

Customer:	Delivered to:
Southwark Commodities	7–11 Riley Rd. LONDON SE1

Your Order Number	Date Sent	Invoice Date	Invoice Number
SC 7865			1362

Quantity	Description	Unit Price	Amount
3 Reams	A4 Bond paper	9.20	27.60
4 Reams	A4 Bank paper	9.40	47.00
2 Reams	A4 Narrow margin feint ruled	7.50	15.50
4 Reams	A4 Wide margin feint ruled	7.50	29.00

E&OE

Authorised by:	Sub-Total	119.10
Date:	VAT (17½%)	20.84
	Total	139.94

Terms
1 If any items are faulty on delivery you must notify us immediately in writing.
2 Payment must be made full within 28 days of delivery.

Reap Office Supplies Ltd.
Selected Price List
Papers

Qty.	Item	Price
Ream	A4 Wide ruled	7.50
"	A4 Bond	9.20
"	A4 Bank	9.40
"	A4 Narrow margin	7.50
"	A4 Wide margin	7.50
"	A5 Narrow margin	3.80
"	A5 Wide margin	3.80

Reap Office Supplies Ltd.
Delivery Note

Date_____ Our Ref: _No 1363_

To_ Southwark Commodities_

Your order no. SC 7866

Qty.	Description
5	A4 Wide ruled
9	A5 Narrow margin
7	A5 Wide margin

Signed   *F Goddard*

Reap Office Supplies Ltd.
Invoice

VAT No.

Customer:	Delivered to:
Southwark Commodities	7-11 Riley Road LONDON SE7

Your Order Number	Date Sent	Invoice Date	Invoice Number
SC 7866			1363

Quantity	Description	Unit Price	Amount
5	A4 Wide margin	9.50	47.50
9	A4 Narrow margin	3.80	27.60
9	A5 Narrow margin	3.80	34.20

E&OE

Authorised by:	Sub-Total 109.30
Date:	VAT (17½%) 19.08
	Total 128.38

Terms
1 If any items are faulty on delivery you must notify us immediately in writing.
2 Payment must be made full within 28 days of delivery.

148

2 Please check this invoice and correct any errors.

Bridge Business
BOLTON

Invoice

TO: Benedicts New Road Tonbridge Kent	DELIVERY ADDRESS: Benedicts Long Acre Birchington Kent

YOUR ORDER No.	DATE SENT	INVOICE DATE	INVOICE No.

QUANTITY	DESCRIPTION	UNIT PRICE	AMOUNT
50	Ring Binders	– 85	42·50
200	Document Wallets	– 10	20·00
800	Square Cut Folders	– 03	24·00
60	Jiffy Bags 4" x 8"	– 15	10·50
150	Jiffy Bags 14" x 12"	– 45	82·50
35	Soft Cover Display Books	2-25	18·75

E&OE

AUTHORISED BY:
DATE:

SUB-TOTAL	258·25
VAT (17½%)	45·46
TOTAL	304·21

Terms
1 If any items are faulty on delivery you must notify us immediately in writing.
2 Payment must be made within 28 days of delivery.
** Free video tape if you pay within 10 days.

ACTIVITY

1 Following the highly successful launch of the MENSA range of 'educational furniture for intelligent people', you receive the following requests for quotes. Use the press release and price list on page 59 to prepare the quotes.

a)

> Port Talbot College
> Station Rd.
> Port Talbot
> West Glam
> SW13 4JN
>
> The Worldwide Furniture Co.
>
> Dear Sir/Madam
>
> We are very interested in your new range of MENSA furniture which can be recycled. Could you please send a quote for 55 Alpine chairs in ice blue and for 18 chairs in sunset red.
>
> Yours faithfully
>
> *M. Paul*
>
> M. Paul

b)

> St Martins Junior School
> Bromley
> Kent
> BR1 5ZY
>
> Worldwide Furniture Co.
>
> Dear BTEC Trainee
>
> We were very impressed with your new chairs, which we saw advertised recently. Could you please give us a quote for 10 Mont Blanc in Forest Green, and 80 Continental in sunripe yellow.
>
> Yours sincerely
>
> *A. Burton*
>
> A. Burton

c)

> Abbey Local Education Authority
> County Hall
> Abbey
>
> Worldwide Furniture Co.
>
> Dear BTEC Trainee
>
> We are attempting to refurnish many of our secondary schools in an attempt to stop them from opting out. Could you please provide us with a quote for your new MENSA range of furniture.

We are looking for a special discount given the size of the order.
We would require:
800 21st Century chairs in Deep Space
700 21st Century chairs in Ice Blue
850 21st Century chairs in Sunset Red
400 Alpine chairs in Forest Green
475 Alpine Chairs in Sunripe Yellow

Yours sincerely

J. Thomas
Chief Executive

2   Each organisation which received a quotation places an order. Can you now make out an invoice for each organisation. Carry out all calculations including VAT. Make copies of the invoices and mark each of them with the name of the department which should receive it.

⎯/ ACTIVITY /⎯Buying and selling role play ⎯⎯⎯⎯

For this assignment you will need to work in groups of three. There are three roles, two suppliers of office and business furniture and one buyer.

- Person A works in a well known established company which supplies office and business furniture.
- Person B works for a new company which has just started business. It also is a supplier of office and business goods and furniture.
- Person C works in an organisation which wants to buy the products. You are the customer.

You can choose your own role, or put the letters A, B, C into a bag and take your chances with which role you get. Each person will need to complete the tasks needed to buy or sell the goods. All documents must be sent to the suppliers and buyer. Copies must be kept. Suppliers can offer discounts and special terms for prompt payment.

Person A   You work as a clerical assistant for Gordon Brown Furniture, Scotts Lane, Scotts Industrial Park, Salisbury. Your job is to complete any documents necessary to sell the goods. The company distributes nationwide. There is a packing and carriage charge of 10% of the gross value of the order.

Person B   You work at Dynamic Trading, New Road, Blackpool. Your company charges 10% of the gross value of the order for packing and carriage. It distributes free within a 50 mile radius. Your job is to prepare all the documents required to sell the goods. Your supervisor has the responsibility for signing or authorising any document.

Person C   You work as a clerical officer at Mutual Electronics, Lea Trading Estate, Preston. Mutual Electronics want to purchase 38 new chairs for its canteen. Your job is to do all the paperwork required to buy the chairs. Your supervisor will need to authorise any proposals you make and sign the final order.

A budget of about £24.00 per chair has been allocated to the purchase. The chairs should be strong and attractive.

1 You work for Mutual Electronics. Prepare a quotation request for the 38 chairs that are needed. Type or word process a letter to accompany the request. There are two suppliers. Make and keep copies for the files. You must send the request and letter to the suppliers.

2 You work for a supplier. Once you have received the quotation request prepare and complete a quotation and send a suitable letter in reply. Make copies for the files. Your replies must be sent to Mutual Electronics. Your price list is shown here

Gordon Brown Furniture Price List
(exclusive of VAT)

	Price per chair		
	0–10	10–50	Over 50
Cherokee Chair (Black stacking)	£12.40	£10.75	£9.50
Apache Chair (Primary colours, stacking with arms)	£20.65	£22.30	£20.60
Navajo (Green and black)	£21.45	£21.00	£19.00

Packing and carriage charge 10% of gross value of order.

Dynamic Trading Price List
(exclusive of VAT)

	Price per chair	
	0–50	Over 50
Dyno Chair (Coloured and padded)	£23.10	£19.15
Action Chair (Coloured and stacking)	£21.95	£18.20

Packing and carriage charge 10% of gross value of order.
Free delivery within 50 mile radius.

3 Mutual Electronics receive two quotes back. Study the quotes carefully and recomm… one to your supervisor. Once a decision has been made, complete an order form for supplier and write an appropriate letter. Send these to the supplier and make copies.

4 You work for the company which has won the order. Draft a reply. This should say:

● Thank you for the order.
● When and how you will despatch the goods.
● How the goods are to be paid for.

Additionally you should also send an acknowledgement of order form. Check every… with your supervisor and keep copies.

5   Complete and send an advice note. Make copies. Make out an invoice ready for your supervisor. Now send out the invoice to Mutual Electronics.

6   You work for the company that failed to get the order. Prepare some notes which you could use at a meeting with your supervisor.

7   Mutual Electronics have now received the chairs and the invoice. Check that the invoice is correct. Make sure that the chairs you receive are the ones you ordered.

    You discover that only 36 chairs have arrived and have to make a complaint.

    a)   Write a memo to your supervisor.
    b)   Write notes for a telephone message to the company – make the telephone call.
    c)   Write/type/WP a fax message.

8   You have to deal with the complaint. What action should you take.

9   The supplier has now dealt with the complaint to your satisfaction. Prepare a cheque ready for signature and enclose an appropriate letter.

10 You work for the company which did not get the order (you don't stop work when you fail to get an order – you have to work harder). You have heard about your competitors failure to deliver all 38 chairs. How could you get the order the next time your company is asked to quote?

11 If instead of being based at Preston, Mutual Electronics were next door to where you work or study, would your choice of supplier still be the same?

MODULE 3

Business Resources
and Procedures

Production

Summary

In this chapter you will learn about the work of a production department in a manufacturing company. The assignment involves you in investigating how a business organisation uses resources to produce its product. The following topics are covered:

▸ Business resources
▸ Interdepartment processes
▸ Large and small firms
▸ Production documents
▸ The workplace environment

This chapter will help you to achieve the following outcomes

Core Module 2   Administrative Systems and Procedures
Outcome 2.4   Understand and follow health and safety procedures

Core Module 3   Business Resources and Procedures
Outcome 3.1   Investigate the resources used in operating a business
Outcome 3.2   Contribute to the effective use of physical resources
Outcome 3.4   Investigate and apply simple measures of performance

The assignment can be used to cover the following performance criteria:

2.3b   information processing equipment used to run standard applications
2.3c   data examined and analysed using a spreadsheet package
2.4a   potential hazards to the well-being of self and others recognised and reported
2.4b   equipment used in accordance with operating instructions and procedures
2.4c   work area kept free from hazards
3.1a   scope, size, nature and aims of a business identified
3.1b   mix of financial, physical and human resources used in the business identified and explained
3.1c   reasons for the balance of resources used in the organisation elicited
3.2a   audit of physical resources carried out
3.2b   resources used cost effectively and safely
3.2c   own performance measured and recorded
3.2d   suggestions made or implemented to improve the use of physical resources
3.4a   meaning of performance investigated and explained
3.4b   methods of measurement of performance investigated and described
3.4c   suitable method chosen to gauge performance in identified jobs, tasks of operations
3.4d   methods applied to job/task/operation selected and conclusions drawn from results

The assignment will help with the development of Common Skills, especially the following:

Managing and Developing Self
Outcome 1   Manage own roles and responsibilities
Outcome 2   Manage own time in achieving objectives

Communicating
Outcome 9   Present information in a variety of visual forms

Managing Tasks and Solving Problems
Outcome 13   Deal with a combination of routine and non-routine tasks

Applying Numeracy
Outcome 15   Apply numerical skills and techniques

Applying Technology
Outcome 16   Use a range of technological equipment and systems

Applying Design and Creativity
Outcome 17   Apply a range of skills and techniques to develop a variety of ideas in the creation of new/modified products, services or situations

Read the following assignment to help you to understand some of the things you should be able to do by the end of the chapter. Normally it will be best to read the chapter and carry out the set activities before you tackle the assignment.

Check whether you can do the assignment on your own or with one or more colleagues. Some assignments will require organising by your tutor. Seek guidance, where needed, from your tutor.

Assignment   **Taking the biscuit!** ——————————————————

Task 1   Local schools often arrange visits for their pupils to your place of work. Pupils are normally age 11 to 15. Your manager asks you to compile a fact sheet, including diagrams and pictures explain how your section works. If your company produces goods, you can explain how th are made. However, if it provides a service, you will have to describe how this is done.

Whilst talking with your manager you suggest that pupils like to have activity sheets complete during a visit. She thinks this is a good idea and asks if you could design one.

▸ Design the activity sheet to fit on one side of A4 paper.

Task 2   You work in the Wellmade Biscuit factory which makes biscuits. (Try and get your tutor arrange a visit to a biscuit factory.) The firm's food scientists have been working on a n product, Home Bake Biscuits. These are biscuits which are already prepared, but have not b cooked. Customers will be able to bake them at home. The production manager thinks it wo be fun if the department had a competition to see which employee can cook the best biscui

You are required to make and bake sufficient biscuits for your work group to sample. In addi you must write out the recipe for your biscuits and say how much they cost to make. You need to work out the cost of all the inputs, including the raw materials, labour costs, ga electricity, etc.

Task 3

☎ MEMO

From: Stock Control

To: Purchasing

    The following items need to be re-ordered. Can you place our usual order with Better Flour Ltd?

Peanuts	200 kg
Plain Flour (A)	3,000 kg
" " (B)	6,000 kg
Brazils	360 kg

Many Thanks

ML

You receive this memo from stock control which you are required to action. You will need to take the following steps:

▸ Complete a purchase requisition form.

▸ Complete an order form from the purchasing department using the prices on page 164.

▸ Make three copies of the documents – one for stock control, one for production and one for your file.

REQUISITION

TO	FROM	DEPT	DATE	
REFERENCE NUMBER	DESCRIPTION		QUANTITY REQUESTED	QUANTITY RECEIVED

AUTHORISED BY   RECEIVED BY

Wellmade Biscuit Co.
Main Road,
Reading

Order

To:	Delivery address:

	Date required	Date of order	Order number
Quantity	Please supply the following		Unit price	Amount

The order number must appear on all invoices and delivery notes.

Signed:_____

Business resources

When you look around you, almost everything you see has been manufactured. company which makes goods is called a manufacturing company. Tables, chairs, per pencils and cookers are all manufactured. To make any product a company will ne resources. Here are some examples of resources:

- Raw materials
- Buildings and land
- Machines
- Workers
- Power to operate machines
- Management
- Finance

All resources must be bought or purchased by the company. Any resource which is needed to make a product is called an **input**. What inputs does your organisation use? A bank which provides a financial service would need staff, premises, computers, cheque cards, cheque books, telephones, cash, etc. as inputs.

A furniture making company would need workers, wood, machines, storage facilities, power, etc.

What inputs are needed to make biscuits? To make biscuits we need the factory, raw materials (e.g. flour, fat, sugar, nuts, chocolate, etc.), machinery for mixing, stirring, cutting, cooking, cooling, wrapping and packing, and people. Even if the biscuits were made at home you would still need the resources.

The production department

All the departments in an organisation have a part to play in the making of the product. But the production department has a special role, it must:

● Make the goods.
● Make sure that the quantity of goods produced is correct.
● Make sure that the quality of goods produced is correct.
● Use the resources efficiently.
● Produce the goods on time.

To make biscuits successfully the production department will have to work with:

● **The sales department**   This department has the job of getting the orders. Once these are known the production department can then fix its own targets, e.g. how many nutty, plain or chocolate biscuits to produce.
● **The purchasing department**   This section must buy the raw materials and make sure that there is enough of them. It must reorder materials used already, and place orders for any new materials which are required. So, if the company has introduced a new coconut biscuit, there must be enough coconut available.
● **The personnel department**   This department hires new people, looks after the welfare of existing staff, and arranges training. To make biscuits there must be enough staff. They must be properly trained and be able to work the machines. If there is a large increase in orders then production will have to increase. Either people will have to work longer hours or more people will need to be employed.
● **Finance section**   The people here work out the cost of producing biscuits, the cost of the raw materials, the wages of the people employed to make the biscuits, how much heating and electricity is used in the process and all the other costs.

Fixed costs or overheads

Fixed costs are costs which do not change with the level of output produced. Fixed costs have to be paid even if nothing is produced – they are inescapable. Good examples are rent, business rates, insurance and some key maintenance and management staff costs. In capital-intensive industry the fixed costs can be very high, and a large amount must be produced to 'cover your costs'.

The departments will all have to work together to make perfect biscuits. The ingredients must all be available. They must be mixed and cooked properly for the right amount of time and at the right temperature.

The process of mixing and baking (producing) the biscuits is the production process. A variety of (inputs) resources are used to produce the output (biscuits).

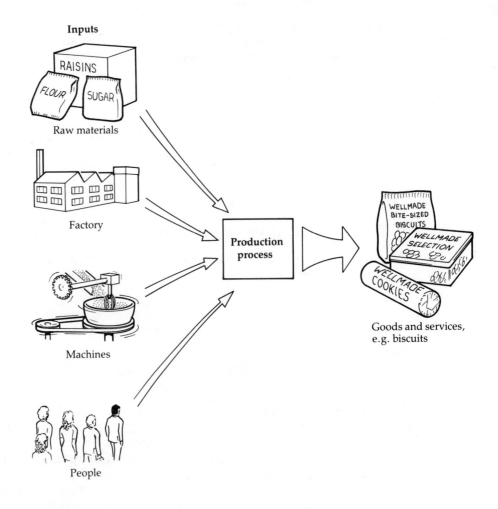

Inputs

RAISINS
FLOUR   SUGAR

Raw materials

Factory

Machines

People

Production process

Goods and services, e.g. biscuits

▲ *The production process*

You can imagine the production process for making biscuits as a series of stages:

Obtain raw materials (purchasing)
↓
Weigh and choose right quantity
↓
Mix the ingredients
↓
Make into biscuit shape
↓
Put onto baking tray
↓
Put into oven
↓
Cook and remove

We would have to go through these stages whether the biscuits were made at home or factory. The real difference is the size or scale of the production. In the factory million biscuits are made. Therefore the stages or flow of production have to be simple efficient. Many companies employ someone whose job it is to sort out difficulties in production process. They may be called 'trouble shooters', 'progress chasers' or protion controllers. Their job is to identify problems and find solutions.

For an organisation to operate smoothly the administration section must make sure the resources which are needed are in the right place at the right time.

Large and small firms

The bigger the better?

Small firms

Advantages	Disadvantages
Better communication with customers, employees and suppliers	Are unable to produce very large orders
Able to respond quickly to changing trends	Do not have access to large amounts of capital, therefore unable to expand
Can take account of personal needs	May not have a range of expertise among its employees
Can produce on a small scale	Cannot take advantage of bulk buying discounts
Close control over all aspects of the business	

Large firms

Advantages	Disadvantages
Able to obtain discounts through buying in bulk	May find it difficult to make decisions quickly
Can use specialist machines and employ specialist people	Can have difficulty with communication within the organisation
Can use their size to negotiate better prices	May be slow in responding to market changes
Can reduce their costs by producing large quantities	Can experience problems with control and coordination
Able to obtain extra cash through a wide range of sources	

Documents used in the production process

The production department will know how much material it uses. To order more it will make a request to the purchasing department on a **purchase requisition form.** This will state:

- The item required
- Quantity
- Date needed
- Delivery site
- Possible supplier
- Name of the person who needs it

Wellmade Biscuit Company

Purchase Requisition Form

Date   Reg. No.

To Purchasing	Section	From Prod.	Date Needed Aug '92
Agreed by A. King		Job Title Christmas '92 'Nutty'	

Reference Number	Description	Quantity Requested	Quantity Received
P92N130	Hazel Nuts	900 kg	
P92N131	Brazil Nuts	400 kg	
P92N131	Peanuts	2000 kg	
P92F200	Wholemeal Flour	4000 kg	
P92F210	Plain Flour (Grade A)	7000 kg	
P92F220	Plain Flour (Grade B)	9000 kg	

Received by

Possible suppliers

◀ *Example of a requisition form*

Wellmade Biscuit Company

Main Road, Reading

Order form

From P. J. Olofu   Order No. WBC 3441

Address As Above   To Better Flour Ltd
                              Tanner St.
                              London SE1

Tel No 0923 54636

Fax No

Item Required	Quantity kg	Unit Price	Total Price
Hazel Nuts	900	.30	270.00
Brazil Nuts	400	.40	160.00
Wholemeal Flour	4000	.25	1,000.00
Plain Flour (A)	7000	.20	1,400.00
Plain Flour (B)	9000	.15	1,3500.00
Peanuts	2000	.20	400.00
			4,580.00

Signature R.J Olofu

Date   9.11.199X

Authorised by

R.M.M.

▶ *Example of an order form*

VAT at 17½%   801.50

Total incl. VAT   5 301.50

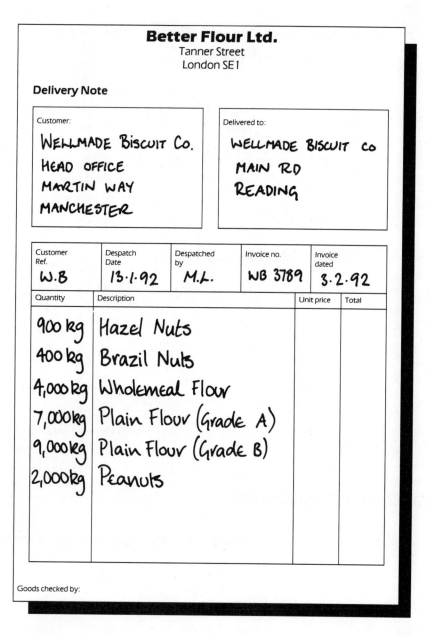

Better Flour Ltd.
Tanner Street
London SE1

Delivery Note

Customer:	Delivered to:
WELLMADE BISCUIT Co. HEAD OFFICE MARTIN WAY MANCHESTER	WELLMADE BISCUIT CO MAIN RD READING

Customer Ref.	Despatch Date	Despatched by	Invoice no.	Invoice dated
W.B	13·1·92	M.L.	WB 3789	3·2·92

Quantity	Description	Unit price	Total
900 kg	Hazel Nuts		
400 kg	Brazil Nuts		
4,000 kg	Wholemeal Flour		
7,000 kg	Plain Flour (Grade A)		
9,000 kg	Plain Flour (Grade B)		
2,000 kg	Peanuts		

Goods checked by:

▲ *Example of a delivery note*

On the basis of this information the purchasing department will make out an **order form** to the supplier

The supplier will be one specially chosen by the company. The basis of the choice will be:

- Price
- Quality
- Reliability
- Delivery on time
- Service

The order form is a legal document so all the details must be correct and accurate.

Better Flour Ltd.

Invoice

Tanner Street, London SE1

VAT No.

Customer:

Wellmade Biscuit Co
Head Office
Martin Way
Manchester

Customer Ref. No WB/ML
Despatch Date 3.1.92
Date 3.2.92
Invoice No. WB 3789

VAT Registration

Quantity	Description	Unit Price	Total	
900 kg	Hazel Nuts	30	270	00
400 kg	Brazil Nuts	40	160	00
4,000 kg	Wholemeal Flour	25	1,000	00
7,000 kg	Plain Flour (grade A)	20	1,400	00
9,000 kg	Plain Flour (grade B)	15	1,350	00
2,000 kg	Peanuts	20	400	00

E&OE

Sub-Total	4,580	00
VAT (17½%)	801	50
Total	5,381	50

▲ *Example of an invoice*

Some time later the company will receive the goods it has ordered. With the goods will b
a **delivery note**. In our example it will come from Better Flour Ltd. It is the responsibility
the company that orders the goods firstly to check that they have all arrived, secondly
check that they are in good condition. The delivery note is then signed to say that th
goods have been received.

The company which has ordered and obtained the goods – the Wellmade Biscuit Co – w
later receive an invoice. Once again this must be checked to make sure that everything
accurate. Ask yourself the questions:

- Are the goods correct?
- Is the quantity correct?
- Is the price right?
- Are the totals correct?

If the details are correct the customer should return the invoice with the payment. A co
of the invoice will be kept by the customer. This invoice will later be used as part of
company's accounts.

The working environment

Equipment and machinery

All companies want to produce efficiently. To do this the workplace must be well designed. If biscuits are produced at home or in the factory we want to achieve:

- Highest production.
- Best use of the space.
- Best use of machinery and equipment.
- Best use of the people.
- Lowest cost of the raw materials.
- Best use of the resources.

To achieve these objectives, we need the best working environment, the best workplace. Some of the items we must look at to achieve this are:

- How much noise is there likely to be? How can we reduce the noise?
- Is the workplace too hot, too cold, too humid or dry? Is there enough ventilation? Should there be air conditioning?
- Is there enough light in the whole area? Is there enough light where people are working? Is there too much light or glare, e.g. do the computer screens reflect the sunlight?
- Is there too much dust, e.g. in a biscuit factory this is likely to be a problem. There will need to be extractor fans to take the dust outside the building.
- Are the worksurfaces at the right height? (People are not all the same size.) Are the chairs the right size? Do they give enough support?
- Is there enough room for people to move around safely? Can fat and thin people move around?
- Are all the controls and switches within easy reach, e.g. is the electricity point hidden behind a filing cabinet (it usually is)?
- Can workers reach all the items they need easily?
- Do workers have to carry heavy objects? If so have they been trained to carry heavy items? There is European legislation about how much can be carried.
- Are the instructions on how to work the machines clear and simple? Is the writing large enough to be easily read?
- Are the emergency controls and signals clear? Can they be easily seen? Can they be heard? Can they be easily operated? Will the workers need any special training for emergencies? Will the workers need any special physical qualities to deal with emergencies?

Ergonomics

This is the study of workers in their working environment. It looks at the way that workers use the machinery, tools and furniture they have at work. The purpose of ergonomics is to increase productivity and efficiency. It does this by improving the design of the workplace, for example tables and chairs could be redesigned to suit the size and height of more people, tools could be made simpler to use, controls could be better placed and dials easier to read. The working environment could be improved to make it more pleasant and so increase motivation and make it more user friendly.

Ergonomics is commonly used to look at:

▸ Types of controls, dials, levers or keys on machinery.
▸ Types of information display, e.g. should they be colour, digital, liquid crystal (LCD)?
▸ Style of the environment, e.g. colour schemes and furniture.
▸ Car dashboard, e.g. can everything be reached; are the most important items most visible?
▸ Seating in trains, e.g. which way round; how much leg room?

ACTIVITY

1   Use the questions on this page to make a checklist which you could use to examine your own working environment. This may be the centre where you study or your workplace. If you discover something wrong, badly designed or which could be improved, type a memo to the person who is responsible for the working environment. Say what is wrong and how it could be improved, but remember to be polite, diplomatic and sensible.

2   You could assess the ergonomics of your home. Look at your kitchen and draw a simple plan of it on graph paper. Then answer the following questions:

1 Is everything in the best place?
2 Are the work tops the right height for all members of your family?
3 Is there enough general light?
4 Is there enough light where you work?
5 Is the temperature right?
6 Is there enough space?
7 Can all the members of your family that need to reach the cupboards?
8 Are items stored properly?
9 Do you move around much? How often? From where to where?
10 What equipment is there?

Draw a new plan showing what improvements you would make to your kitchen.

Stock control

Summary

In this chapter you will learn about the use of business resources and administration systems by looking at the process of stock control in an organisation. The assignment and related activities will involve you in carrying out various stock control procedures. The following topics are covered:

▸ The function and role of stock control
▸ Productivity
▸ Efficiency measures
▸ Computerised control
▸ Stock taking and inventories
▸ Stock movement and control

This chapter will help you to achieve the following outcome:

Core Module 2   Administrative Systems and Procedures
Outcome 2.1   Understand and be able to use established information storage and retrieval systems
Outcome 2.2   Identify and use different communication systems and methods of a selected organisation
Outcome 2.3   Produce documents and material and process data

Core Module 3   Business Resources and Procedures
Outcome 3.2   Contribute to the effective use of physical resources
Outcome 3.4   Investigate and apply simple measures of performance

The assignment can be used to cover the following performance criteria:

2.1c   explanation of importance of effective storage, control and retrieval of information given
2.1d   business records managed using a simple database
2.2a   oral and written messages received and acted upon
2.2c   routine business communications produced
2.3a   business documents produced using a word processing package
2.3d   copies of original documents produced using reprographic equipment
3.2a   audit of physical resources carried out
3.2d   suggestions made or implemented to improve the use of physical resources
3.4a   meaning of performance investigated and explained
3.4b   methods of measurement of performance investigated and described
3.4c   suitable method chosen to gauge performance in identified jobs, tasks of operations
3.4d   methods applied to job/task/operation selected and conclusions drawn from results

This assignment will help with the development of Common Skills, especially the following:

Managing and Developing Self
Outcome 1   Manage own roles and responsibilities
Outcome 2   Manage own time in achieving objectives
Outcome 3   Undertakes personal and career development
Outcome 4   Transfer skills gained to new and changing situations and contexts

Communicating
Outcome 8   Receive and respond to a variety of information
Outcome 9   Present information in a variety of visual forms

Managing Tasks and Solving Problems
Outcome 12   Use information sources
Outcome 13   Deal with a combination of routine and non-routine tasks
Outcome 14   Identify and solve routine and non-routine problems

Applying Numeracy
Outcome 15   Apply numerical skills and techniques

Applying Technology
Outcome 16   Use a range of technological equipment and systems

Read the following assignment to help you to understand some of the things you should be able to do by the end of the chapter. Normally it will be best to read the chapter and carry out the set activities before you tackle the assignment.

Check whether you can do the assignment on your own or with one or more colleagues. Some assignments will require organising by your tutor. Seek guidance, where needed, from your tutor.

Assignment

Taking stock

For this assignment you will have to:

▶ Count the stock you have.
▶ Make stock control cards.
▶ Receive and check stock.
▶ Issue, give out or release stock.
▶ Keep records.
▶ Keep an inventory of stock.
▶ Update the inventory regularly.

You are responsible for the stock used in your office or workplace. This could be kept in a store cupboard or cabinet. You have been asked to keep a record of the stock your office uses.

Task 1   Obtain an office supplies catalogue, this should include the range of paper and minor or sundry items used in any office. Examples of sundry items would include correction fluid, paper clips, erasers, etc.

Task 2   Put small items in 'bins' or boxes. Label each bin, and make a stock control card for it. You will have to count the stock you have.

Task 3   Carry out an inventory. This could be a big job, so allow plenty of time to carry it out. Use catalogues to find out the prices of the items.

Task 4   Issue stock as necessary, but only to those people who are allowed to take it out.

Task 5   Change your stock control cards whenever you issue stock. Enter the initials of the person whom you give the stock on the stock control cards.

Make sure that the stock cupboard is kept locked and secure. Check it regularly, keep the key in a safe place. Ensure that only authorised people take out stock. Make sure that your stock room or stock cupboard is safe – where there is paper, there is always a risk of fire.

Task 6   Keep a record of stock on a computer stock control program.

Productivity and efficiency

All organisations try to make the best use of their resources. They want to provide the best possible service, or make the most goods. All the inputs must be used for as much time as possible – workers should not be sitting about doing nothing, machines should always be working.

You are possibly on a bonus or incentive scheme. This is a system where you are paid extra if, for example, you complete a job early, or sell more than a particular amount. Both of these schemes are intended to increase productivity.

There are many ways of measuring productivity or efficiency within an organisation. Companies can calculate the value of their total output or production, then divide this figure by the number of workers. This will give the output made by each worker:

$$\frac{\text{Value of output}}{\text{Number of workers}} = \text{Output for each worker (or output per head)}$$

Another way is to take the total amount of sales and divide this by the number of workers, to give the sales per head:

$$\frac{\text{Value of sales}}{\text{Number of workers}} = \text{Sales per head (per means for each)}$$

Whatever method is chosen, the same idea is used each time. Organisations look at the output or the amount produced, look at the inputs (or resources), then see what resources are needed to produce that output.

Productivity increases if:

- More output is produced from the same number of resources.
- Fewer resources are needed to produce the same output.

Productivity falls if:

- More resources are used to get the same level of output.
- Less output is achieved from the same amount of resources.

Example
Five workers using five machines make 100 tables each day

$$\text{Output per worker} = \frac{\text{Output}}{\text{Number of workers}} = \frac{100}{5} = 20 \text{ tables}$$

If the five workers using five machines make 110 tables each day

$$\text{Output per worker} = \frac{110}{5} = 22 \text{ tables}$$

then productivity has increased.

If the five workers produce 90 tables a day

$$\text{Output per worker} = \frac{90}{5} = 18 \text{ tables}$$

productivity per head has gone down.

One way of increasing productivity is to control the amount of stock used in a firm more efficiently.

Stock control

The purpose of stock control is to make sure that the items needed to run a business are:

- In the right place . . .
- at the right time . . .
- in perfect condition.

Controlling stock properly can be very difficult. Some goods, such as foods, cannot be stored very easily for long periods. Fresh foods can 'go off'. Chemicals can become very dangerous. Clothes can go out of fashion. You can often see food being sold very cheaply at 5.30 p.m. on a Saturday evening because it will not last until Monday morning. It is also difficult to keep the right amount of stock available. Too little stock could mean that there is not enough for production to continue. Too much stock also causes problems – there may not be enough space to store it or it may not be used quickly enough.

It costs money to buy and store stock. For example, if a company buys 300 reams of photocopying paper costing £2000 and uses 50 reams a month, the paper would last six months. However, the company has lost the use of its money over that six month period. It could have been put into a bank to earn interest rather than left as paper to sit in a cupboard somewhere. The company should only buy the 50 reams of paper a month it needs if it wants to keep the use of its money.

To be successful the stock control department must work closely with other departments in the organisation.

How the stock control section links with other departments

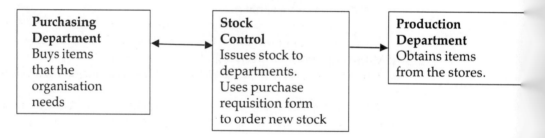

If any of the links in this chain break there could be major problems for the organisation. If extra stock is ordered there must be space to store it. If the purchasing department does not order stock, then the production department will not be able to make the goods.

ACTIVITY

Find out what type of stock is kept at your place of work or study. Make a list of the stock.

Stock control by computer

You have seen a chest of drawers in one of the large furniture stores that you would like. is in black and you would like it in pine. You ask the sales assistant, 'Do you have this f drawer chest in pine, please?'.

The assistant will look at the stock reference number attached to the item on display, th key this number into the computer. The VDU screen will display the computer version the stock record card. This usually only takes a few seconds to appear. The answer you may be, 'No, sorry. There is six weeks delivery time on that item.' It probably won't be answer you wanted but at least you know immediately how long you must wait to get item from that shop and that it is probably worth your while to look elsewhere.

Each member of your group should carry out a survey of the shops in your local area to find out which do and which don't use computers for stock control.

▸ Display the group results as a chart.
▸ Suggest some reasons for your results, e.g. type of shop, type of product, etc.

Advantages of using a computer

● Questions about stock levels can be answered quickly.
● The computer can be used to look at or analyse trends and patterns of demand for an item very quickly.
● Accurate records of stock levels and stock movement can be kept.
● Bar code readers at the check-out can be linked straight to a central computer. This will show how many items have been sold and makes reordering quick, simple and efficient.

ACTIVITY

Look at your own area of work in your organisation and choose a particular activity you undertake. In an office this may be a clerical routine.

1 Identify the amount of each resource which goes into that activity and the output which results. For example you may find a particular routine requires 30 minutes of an office worker's time and involves 20 different documents.
2 Examine the activity to see if less resources could be used to produce the same output or result.
3 If you genuinely have identified an improvement in efficiency then write a memo to your manager explaining how resources can be saved.

Stock taking – counting the stock

A manufacturing organisation will need to keep supplies of goods and raw materials on the premises. This is because they need to meet customer demand. A detailed list of articles, goods and property is called an inventory. There are three parts to the inventory. Taking examples from a company which makes blouses and shirts, these are:

● Raw materials – buttons, thread, cloth, etc.
● Work in progress (or goods which are being made) – collars, cuffs, sleeves, etc.
● Finished goods – the shirts and blouses of all types.

Stock =   Raw materials   +   Work in progress   +   Finished goods

▲ *Stock*

To make an inventory every item of stock has to be counted. The process of doing this is called stock taking.

How to do stock control

- Count every item of stock you have and make a list, the inventory.
- Store the stock securely.
- Put small items in boxes or bins.
- Put a label on each bin, this must say how many items there are.
- Make a stock control card.

Stock control cards

Stock level minimum 25 maximum 150	Stock item computer paper			Supplier office supplies Delivery time 48 hrs
Date	Quantity received	Quantity given out	Name Department	Balance Opening Balance 28
2.3.92	80	20	Finance.	88
4.3.92		30	Wages.	58
5.3.92		20	Wages.	38
6.3.92	100	25	Admin.	113

How the card works.

- The supplier is the company from which you order new stock.
- The delivery time is the time taken between ordering and receiving the item. Th supplier must be reliable and must deliver within the agreed time.
- The minimum stock is the lowest level to which stock is allowed to fall before new stoc must be ordered. The minimum amount must be sufficient to allow the company continue making goods before the new stock arrives.
- The maximum stock is the highest level you decide you need to keep, based on the da use of the particular stock item. Larger amounts must be held if delivery times a longer, e.g. if deliveries are every ten days and twenty items are used each day you w need to start with at least 200.
- Quantity received is the amount of stock received after each delivery.
- Quantity issued is the number given out (this column can include the name of t person or the department to which the orders are issued or given). You will need practise giving out stock and keeping a record of what you issue.
- Opening balance is the amount in the bin when a new stock control card is started.

Stock movement

Each time an item of stock comes into or is sent out of the stock room, it must be record This change in the level or amount of stock is called stock movement. Both the amount movement of stock must be tightly controlled. The better this is done, the more effic and profitable an organisation will become.

▲ *How much stock do you normally have?*

Look at the stock control card on p. 174. The balance is the number of items in the bin at one particular time. When the stock card was started the opening balance was 28.

80 are received on 2 March 1992
therefore balance = 28 + 80 = 108
but 20 are given out on the same day
therefore 108 − 20 = 88 are in the bin at the end of 2 March 1992

On 4 March 1992, 30 are given out
therefore balance = 88 − 30 = 58

On 5 March 1992, 20 are given out
therefore balance = 58 − 20 = 38

On 6 March 1992, 100 are received and 25 are given out
therefore balance = 38 + 100 − 25 =. 113

The stock control card is always kept with the item.

ACTIVITY

Check these stock control cards. Do the figures add up? Correct any mistakes and make out new stock control cards. What procedure would you follow if there was a mistake?

Stock Control Card

Stock Level Min. 80 Max. 200		Stock Item Shirts Medium Pink		Supplier Koszule Balham Delivery 10 days
Date	Qty. Rec'd.	Qty. Issued	Name/ Dept.	Balance 80
12.11.92	60	30	PZ	110
13.11.92	—	10	LE	100
16.11.92	80	40	KL	140
17.11.92	—	10		120

Stock Control Card

Stock Level Min. 40 Max. 100		Stock Item Correction Fluid		Supplier Universal Office Delivery 5 days
Date	Qty. Rec'd.	Qty. Issued	Name/ Dept.	Balance 40
1.3.93				40
4.3.93	50	10	Admin.	80
6.3.93		4	Finance	84
9.3.93		6	Wages	75
10.3.93		15	Personnel	50

Memorandum

We appear to have mislaid our stock record card for boxes of staples (large). However, I have managed to trace the quantities received and issued using other records. The invoices were useful. Can you make a new card by 11 a.m. today? Min. 20 boxes, max. 80 boxes. Supplied by Steel Staple of Swindon. Opening balance 20.

we received	20	boxes on the	1. 8.	199X
	25	" " "	1. 9.	"
	20	" " "	1.10.	"
	40	" " "	1.11.	"
we issued	5	" " "	3. 8.	"
	5	" " "	7. 8.	"
	3	" " "	17. 8.	"
	3	" " "	29. 8.	"
	1	" " "	10.10.	"
	9	" " "	15.10.	"
	10	" " "	23.10.	"
	20	" " "	27.10.	"
	30	" " "	2.11.	"

For your assignment use an inventory sheet drawn up like the one shown below. There is also a stock record card for you to copy. On the inventory:

- In the box marked 'Department' write the name of your department.
- In the box marked 'Location' write where the items are, e.g. warehouse, stock room, etc.

INVENTORY		Sheet No.		Date Count Check	
Department	Location	Priced by		Checked by	
Counted by					
Checked by		Date		Date	
Item No.	Description	Quantity	Unit	Unit price	Total price
	Amount carried forward				

- 'Counted by/Checked by' – write in the names of the persons who did this.
- Sheet No. – 1, 2, 3, etc. Some inventories can be very long.
- Priced by – write the name of who did this.

Stock Record Card

Stock Item			Size Unit				Bin Shelf			Minimum Maximum			Stock No.
Received			Issued			Balance	Received			Issued			Balance
Date	Name	Qty.	Date	Name	Qty.		Date	Name	Qty.	Date	Name	Qty.	
											Balance carried forward		

Summary

This chapter will involve you in the work of the finance and accounts department of a business organisation. You will learn through the assignment and related activities how to make and record financial payments. The following topics are covered:

▸ The accounts department
▸ Petty cash
▸ Cash receipts
▸ Cheques and statements
▸ Banking transactions
▸ Plastic cards
▸ Foreign exchange

This chapter will help you to achieve the following outcomes:

Core Module 2   **Administrative Systems and Procedures**
   Outcome 2.5   Understand the importance of maintaining and developing good business relationships with callers, customers/clients and colleagues

Core Module 3   **Business Resources and Procedures**
   Outcome 3.3   Record financial transactions

Core Module 4   **People in Business**
   Outcome 4.3   Examine and compare the main job roles in different organisations
   Outcome 4.4   Contribute to achievement of organisational goals by fulfilling job role

The assignment can be used to cover the following performance criteria:

2.2a	oral and written messages received and acted upon
2.2b	information obtained from appropriate sources
2.2c	routine business communications produced
2.2d	channels of communication identified and used
2.2e	incoming and outgoing mail processed
2.5a	callers greeted promptly and courteously and dealt with appropriately
2.5b	polite and effective responses made to a range of customer/client situations
2.5c	liaison and communication with peers and senior colleagues conducted effectively
2.5d	rapport and mutual respect between colleagues and customers/clients established
3.3a	flow of money in the organisation charted and explained

3.3b	recording documents and systems identified and their purpose described
3.3c	correct systems and documents or files chosen or accessed
3.3d	information recorded neatly and accurately
3.3e	necessary calculations made accurately
3.3f	recording and calculations checked for accuracy
4.3a	functional areas within organisations identified
4.3b	job roles in different functional areas of organisations identified
4.3c	job roles compared
4.4a	relationship between organisational objectives and job role identified
4.4b	given tasks completed to agreed criteria
4.4c	contribution made both as an individual and as a member of a team to the achievement of agreed targets and goals

The assignment will help with the development of Common Skills, especially the following:

Managing and Developing Self
Outcome 1 Manage own roles and responsibilities
Outcome 2 Manage own time in achieving objectives
Outcome 3 Undertakes personal and career development
Outcome 4 Transfer skills gained to new and changing situations and contexts

Working with and Relating to Others
Outcome 5 Treat others' values, beliefs and opinions with respect
Outcome 6 Relate to and interact effectively with individuals and groups

Communicating
Outcome 8 Receive and respond to a variety of information
Outcome 9 Present information in a variety of visual forms
Outcome 10 Communicate in writing
Outcome 11 Participate in oral and non-verbal communication

Managing Tasks and Solving Problems
Outcome 12 Use information sources
Outcome 13 Deal with a combination of routine and non-routine tasks
Outcome 14 Identify and solve routine and non-routine problems

Applying Numeracy
Outcome 15 Apply numerical skills and techniques

Read the following assignment to help you to understand some of the things you should be able to do by the end of the chapter. Normally it will be best to read the chapter and carry out the set activities before you tackle the assignment.

Check whether you can do the assignment on your own or with one or more colleagues. Some assignments will require organising by your tutor. Seek guidance, where needed, from your tutor.

A day's financial work

You work in the reception area of the Hastings Palace, a small hotel in the CJ Enterprises Group. You have just come back from a week's holiday, part of your annual leave. You are keen to tell everyone about the wonderful time you have had. However, you look on your desk and there is a week's work waiting for you.

The in-tray is full. What do you do?

▸ Take all the mail out of your in-tray.
▸ Go through each item and sort these into two piles, 'urgent' and 'non urgent'.
▸ Urgent items are those which must be dealt with immediately. Go through the urgent pile and decide whether:
   a) you can deal with the matter yourself,
   b) you can give it to someone else (you can delegate),
   c) you have to refer the matter to your supervisor. Contact anyone you need to immediately.
▸ Put the items you can deal with yourself into order of importance. This means you will have to give them a priority – prioritise them. The items with the highest priority will need your immediate attention. Keep calm and deal with all items carefully . . .

Task 1

☎ **MEMO**

From: Manager
To: You

Please make out these
cheques for me to sign

(1) Shiny Window Cleaners £150

(2) Sparks Electrics Ltd   £75

Task 2

MEMORANDUM

Today 8 a.m.

Welcome back! Can you find the telephone numbers of some gardeners or odd job people who could tidy the front garden by tomorrow lunchtime?
Many thanks
J B

Task 3 Make out the following cash receipts using today's date. Don't forget to fill in the stub counterfoil, this is the hotel's record:

a) Ms J Hernandez who paid for 3 cream teas at £2.50 each.
b) Mr N G Ching who paid for 4 lunches at £11.50 each, 1 bottle of red wine at £9.60 and coffees at 80p each.
c) Ms S Ratanya who had coffee and biscuits at 90p a head for a party of 14.

Number_____ Date_____ From_____ _____ _____ _____ £ p	**CASH RECEIPT** Date_____ Received from_____ _____ _____ The sum of_____ _____ £
Number_____ Date_____ From_____ _____ _____ _____ £ p	**CASH RECEIPT** Date_____ Received from_____ _____ _____ The sum of_____ _____ £

Task 4   A cleaner comes to you with a receipt for £7.82 from Quick Kleen showing 'cleaning supplies'. Make out the petty cash slip to A. Smith. Make an entry in the petty cash book.

Task 5   A guest tells you that the tap in room T32 is not working. What are you going to do? (Don't forget that you have to prioritise.)

Task 6   The person who delivers the post is waiting outside and says that there is an 80p overdue payment on postage, i.e. the hotel owes the Post Office 80p. You pay this and get a receipt. Make the entry in the petty cash book.

Task 7   Your colleague turns to you and says 'I have to go out for five minutes. Can you please make up an invoice for the couple in room 26?' The invoice is for:

2 nights B&B (bed and breakfast)	£80.00
Newspapers	50p
Telephone calls	£1.75
Evening meal	£27
Bar	£4.50

Task 8   At the end of your shift (your day at work) you have to cash up or prepare the cash, etc. ready for banking. This is what you have in the till:

6 × £20 notes		75 × 10p coins
8 × £10 notes		40 × 20p coins
17 × £5 notes		65 × 5p coins
50 × 50p coins		10 × 2p coins
		29 × 1p coins

▸ 16 cheques to the value of:

£85.20	£400.10
£90.30	£75.90
£140.27	£200.20
£65.40	£15.00
£12.25	£80.25
£18.30	£110.09
£9.20	£35.00
£180.50	£42.11

You bank with the National Westminster, Lower Road, Hastings. Code No 01 15 26. The account number is 876589. Fill in a bank Giro credit slip and counterfoil.

Task 9   You should be going home in 15 minutes, but a German guest asks you to change German currency into pounds. Even though you are tired, you say 'yes'. You are given 300 DM. How much in pounds sterling would you have to give in exchange?

Your in-tray is now empty.

Accounts department

The accounts department of an organisation manages the finance. It will:

- Make payments to other companies for goods or supplies.
- Collect payments from customers to whom it sells goods or services.
- Keep a record of all payments made and received.
- Analyse or examine these records to see how well the business is doing.
- Make forecasts or work out future patterns of income (money coming in) and expenditure (money going out).
- Make financial reports to the management of the organisation.

In any accounts department, you will have to handle money. This can be cash or cheques or some other type of payment. All organisations will have to keep some cash on the premises. You will have to know how to keep the cash safe and secure. You will also need to keep a record of any cash which is received, or which is paid out. You will have to account for the cash you are responsible for. An organisation will have rules about:

- How much can be kept on the premises as petty cash.
- How much cash can be given out to people.
- The reasons why people could get cash.

Dealing with petty cash

Petty cash is a small amount of money kept to make payments to people for minor items of expenditure, e.g. company employees may use petty cash for bus fares or postage, but only if on company business. At the beginning of the day the money in the petty cash box is called the float. The same word is used for money in a cashier's till or cash register. Petty cash is usually kept in a metal cash box which is always locked. The office manager is normally responsible for keeping it secure. The box is often stored in a safe at night.

In your office you will probably only be allowed to claim petty cash for a few items of expenditure, e.g. taxi or bus fares, or office supplies. Whenever you make a payment for these when you are on company business, you must get a receipt. This will prove that you have spent company money. You will then be able to claim or obtain this money back from your organisation. You will probably need to fill in a petty cash voucher, form or slip. This must have a space for:

- A title.
- The date.
- A description of the expenditure.
- The amount spent.
- The signature of the person receiving the money.
- The signature of the person authorising the money.

ACTIVITY

1 You have bought some office sundries in your local shop. You spent £4.80 and obtained receipt. Fill in a Petty Cash Voucher to claim the money back.
2 Fill in a Petty Cash Voucher for £3.75 spent on postage and £1.10 on correction fluid.

PETTY CASH

RECEIVED BY		AUTHORISED BY	DEPARTMENT		
DATE	DESCRIPTION			JOB NO	AMOUNT
				TOTAL	

Keeping petty cash records

Using the petty cash book

At the start of each day you should count the money in your cash box – the float. The amount you have is called the opening balance.

During the day you must record all the money you pay out. Give the name of the person who received it. Show the amount and the purpose it was used for. Keep the receipts, these show that the money was used legally. The 'payments' columns can show whatever items are needed, e.g. K Athy used a taxi to deliver some documents. This cost £2.00, she obtained a receipt. She filled in a petty cash slip and received the money. The £2.00 was recorded in the petty cash book under the payment heading 'travel'.

£ Receipts	Date	Name	£ Total	Off. Supp.	Payments Travel	Post
30.00	13.4.91					
	13.4.91	P. Martin	7.00		7.00	
	13.4.91	C. Paul	4.00			4.00
	13.4.91	C. James	3.50	3.50		
	13.4.91	K. Athy	2.00		2.00	
	13.4.91	V. Patel	1.25			1.25
			17.75 =	3.50 +	9.00 +	5.25
	13.4.91	Balance	12.25			
			30.00			
12.25	14.4.91					

▲ *Petty cash book*

At the end of the day you should:

- Total (add up) the payments columns, e.g. 'post' total = £4.00 + £1.25 = £5.25.
- Total the total column.
- The total of the payments columns totals must be equal to the total of the total column. The easiest way to check this is to add the totals of the payments columns horizontally across the page. If the figures are not the same, do your calculations again.
- Next, you will have to find out how much money you have left – the balance. This is done by subtracting the total payments from the receipts.

  Balance = £30.00 – £17.75 = £12.25

  This figure is entered into the petty cash book.

- Check the money in the cash box, there should be £12.25. If there isn't, check your figures again.
- The balance from 13.4.91 becomes the receipts for 14.4.91. It is brought down to the receipts column.

ACTIVITY

When you count the money in the Petty Cash Box you find 8 × £1 coins, 3 × 50p coins, 10 × 20p coins, 11 × 10p coins and 3 × 2p coins. Enter this in the receipts column of your petty cash book as the opening balance.

On the 14.4.91, J Alabi claims £1.97 for postage with a valid receipt, M Lifu claims £4.23 for office supplies again with a receipt and J Jones claims £1.20 for bus fares but has no proof except the bus ticket.

- Record these payments.
- Find the balance for the 14.4.91 and bring the balance down for the 15.4.91.
- What would you do about J. Jones bus fares?

Handling cash

Do:

- Keep cash safe and secure.
- Check all the details on a petty cash voucher are correct.
- Make sure the receipt matches the claim for petty cash.
- Lock the cash box.
- Keep it hidden from the public.
- Lock it in a safe at night.
- Record payments promptly.
- Report any problems to your supervisor.
- Follow any rules laid down by your company.

Do not:

- Steal or attempt to steal from your company or colleagues.
- Give cash without a receipt.
- Give cash without checking the claim.

You will probably get training in handling cash. There will be special rules depending o where you work. For example, if you work for a department store you will not be allowe to carry cash on you when working on the shop floor.

Stealing is one reason why you could be instantly dismissed by the company. You cou be taken to court.

Giving or issuing receipts

A receipt is a written acknowledgement or proof that one person or organisation h received money or goods from another person or organisation, e.g. 'Castle Cabs ha received £4.20 from a customer who has paid for a cab ride', 'Brighton Supplies ha received £6.14 from L Tamara for the purchase of office supplies'. A receipt can be a sa slip, stub, voucher or counterfoil.

In many jobs you may be asked to issue receipts as a proof that someone has purchase paid for something. If you work on a till or check out point, receipts are printed au matically by the machine. If they are not, you will need to write out a receipt by ha Look at how this has been done in the previous examples.

BRIGHTON SUPPLIES
Cash Receipt

Number _313_   Date _27.5.1991_

Received from _L. TAMARA_

_____

_____

The sum of _£6.14_

FOR OFFICE SUPPLIES

W.H.SMITH   1870

BOOKS   7.65 A
TOTAL   7.65

98938 C014 R07 29/05/91

London Regional Transport **Londo**
NOT TRANSFERABLE

50 ADULT

Class	Ticket type	Adult	Child	
STD	RETURN	ONE	NIL	OUT

Date   Number
30·MAY·91   05647   2897e5148S06

From   Valid   Price
LONDON BRIT RAIL ON DATE SHOWN   £8·00M

To   Route
REDHILL *   0833

British Rail

**Only one ai
from London, l**

_Received
73·75 Taxi
Robs   unh_

CASTLE CABS

Received _27/5/1991_

the sum of
Four painds 20p

£ _4·20_   _B Driver_
Signed

1   These receipts are all given to you by L Tamara. If they are acceptable write out petty cash
     slips and record the details in the petty cash book.

2 You work at Bristol Electrics, St Andrews, Bristol. A customer has just bought and paid for three 13 amp plugs at 99p each, three metres of flex at £3.99 a metre and five 13 amp fuses at 24p each. Fill out a receipt for the customer. You will need to write in the words, 'Received from' (put the person's name here) the sum of £ (put the total amount here).

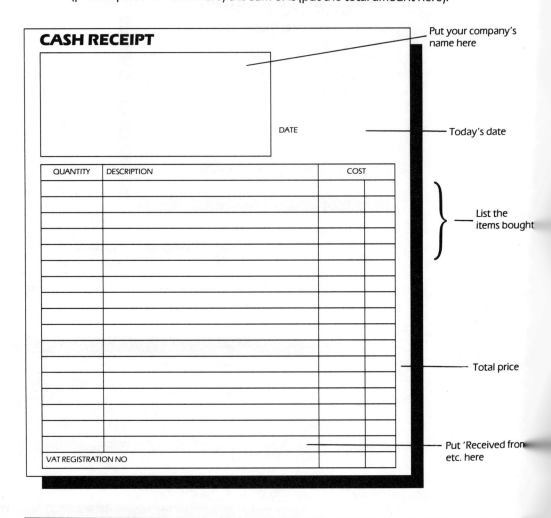

Going to the bank

Whenever organisations have a large amount of money on the premises, it must always kept in a safe. However, at some time it must be sent or taken to a bank. Before it leaves premises, it must be counted and checked against any receipts or paid invoices. paying-in slip should be completed which shows the amount of coins, notes, cheques, Double-check everything you do when handling money with your supervisor. Make s that no one sees the money who is not allowed to do so (security is very important).

If you use a security firm to collect the cash, always confirm the collection and agree details of the collection in advance, e.g. time and place.

If money is taken to a bank by employees, security precautions must be taken.

● Do not carry a bag labelled 'money', i.e. money bags from banks which often have 'f in £1 coins' or similar information written on them.
● Change the route you take to the bank frequently.
● Change the time of your departure frequently.
● Always go with a colleague.
● Check that everything is correct before you leave work.

- Try to behave as if you are not carrying money.
- Check that everything is correct at the bank.

Routine banking transactions

Writing out a cheque

Cheques are a type of payment. They can be used instead of cash. To have a cheque book you must have an account at a bank or building society. To open or start an account you must first put money into the bank or building society. If you have an account, you will have a personal cheque book. If a company has an account it will have a company cheque book. Company cheques often have to be signed by two people. This is to prevent theft or fraud. Most goods can now be bought with cheques, however retailers will usually only accept them as a means of payment if you have a cheque guarantee card or bankers card. This plastic card shows your own personal bank details. It guarantees that a retailer will be paid for the goods you buy up to a specified limit which is often £50 or £100.

The figure below shows a cheque correctly written out to City Office Supplies for £30.00. The numbers 1–11 refer to the different parts of a cheque.

1 Write the date here. It must be today's date, nobody will normally accept a cheque with the wrong date on it, particularly if it is a date in the future.
2 This is the bank sorting code. These numbers are unique to a particular branch and bank, e.g. 30–11–12 is unique to Boyds Bank, Big Branch, Victoria St, Bath.
3 Write the name of the person or organisation to whom the cheque will be paid here. This is the person (or payee) whose account will be credited. In this case the payee is City Office Supplies.
4 Write the amount to be paid out in words here.
5 Write the amount to be paid in figures here.
6 This is the name of the bank or building society and the name of the branch the account is at.
7 Write your signature here. If it is your personal account which will be debited you are the drawer. If you are signing a cheque on behalf of the company, the company is the drawer.
8 This is the cheque number and is the same as that on the stub or end slip. It will help you to keep a record of the payments made. On this cheque the cheque number is 512332.
9 This is the sorting code, in this example it is 30–1112. This is used for passing the cheque between banks.
10 This is the account number, in this case it is 875430. It tells Boyds Bank, Big Branch, Victoria St, Bath, which account to debit.
11 The crossing. This stops a cheque from being exchanged for cash. The cheque can only be paid into the account of the person named as the payee.

▲ Example of how a cheque should be completed

When you write a cheque do not leave any spaces. If it falls into the wrong hands someone else may add something (a cheque for £30 could be changed into one for £30,000!). This is why the lines have been put in and the word 'only' written in.

If you make a mistake when writing out a cheque, cross it out neatly and write in your initials. This will prove that you changed the information.

ACTIVITY

Draw up your own copies of the cheque on p. 189 and fill them in for the following (don't forget today's date):

a) Pay A Mendoza £1,233.20
b) Pay I Grabbit Ltd £5,200.90
c) Pay Baroness Buttons £9.27

The bank statement

A bank statement shows:

● The date when the account was debited or credited.
● The receipts or deposits – the money paid into or credited to the account.
● The withdrawals – the money paid out, or debited to the account.
● The balance, the actual amount in the account.
● The type of receipt or withdrawal (shown in the details column).

Types of withdrawal include:

● Cheques made out to a company or individual (e.g. cheques numbers 0196, 0197, 019⁙ on the statement below).

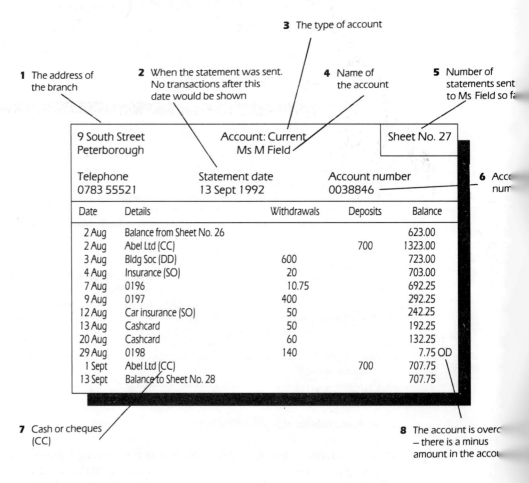

3 The type of account

1 The address of the branch

2 When the statement was sent. No transactions after this date would be shown

4 Name of the account

5 Number of statements sent to Ms Field so f⁙

9 South Street
Peterborough

Account: Current
Ms M Field

Sheet No. 27

Telephone
0783 55521

Statement date
13 Sept 1992

Account number
0038846

6 Acc⁙ num⁙

Date	Details	Withdrawals	Deposits	Balance
2 Aug	Balance from Sheet No. 26			623.00
2 Aug	Abel Ltd (CC)		700	1323.00
3 Aug	Bldg Soc (DD)	600		723.00
4 Aug	Insurance (SO)	20		703.00
7 Aug	0196	10.75		692.25
9 Aug	0197	400		292.25
12 Aug	Car insurance (SO)	50		242.25
13 Aug	Cashcard	50		192.25
20 Aug	Cashcard	60		132.25
29 Aug	0198	140		7.75 OD
1 Sept	Abel Ltd (CC)		700	707.75
13 Sept	Balance to Sheet No. 28			707.75

7 Cash or cheques (CC)

8 The account is over⁙ – there is a minus amount in the accou⁙

▲ Example of a bank statement

- Cash withdrawals made by a company or individual using a plastic cash card (e.g. cash card entries on statement).
- Personal cheques made out to pay cash.
- Standing order, where the financial institution makes a fixed payment on your behalf, at regular intervals (e.g. the transactions marked SO on the statement).
- Direct debit, when the payments made for you may be either fixed or variable (e.g. the transactions marked DD on the statement).

Types of receipt
- A cash payment made into the account.
- A cheque paid into the account.
- A transfer into your account from someone else's account. Wages are often paid like this.

The paying-in slip or bank giro credit

The paying-in slip which is shown here can be used to pay cash, cheques or postal orders into any account. The full amount will be credited to the account number filled in on the paying-in-slip. A company will usually have a printed paying-in-slip which shows the bank, branch and account to be credited. You should fill this in at your office, before you leave for the bank.

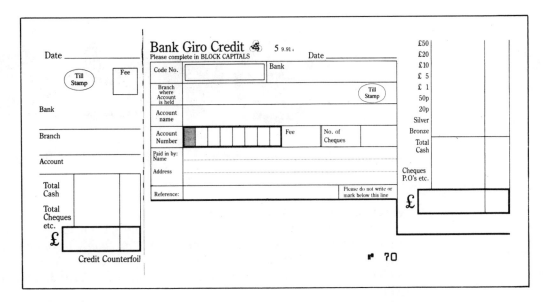

▲ Paying-in slip

ACTIVITY

Fill in a paying-in slip using this information:

- ▸ Bank: Floyds.
- ▸ Code: 30–20–26.
- ▸ Your name.
- ▸ Your address.
- ▸ Account name – your own name.
- ▸ Account number 28368090.
- ▸ Today's date.
- ▸ Number of cheques.

You have five cheques to pay in. These are the values £1,035.00, £675.00, £82.00, £39.83, £6.68. You have the following cash: 8 × £50 notes, 20 × £20 notes, 8 × £10 notes, 3 × £5 notes, 27 × £1 coins.

Keep a record of this information on the credit counterfoil.

Bank services

▸ Banks make payments for customers, e.g. when you write a cheque to pay someone, the bank will process it.
▸ Receive payments for customers, e.g. when you receive a cheque.
▸ Make loans to customers.
▸ Accept deposits/money from customers.

Other services a bank can provide include:

▸ Advice on how to invest your money.
▸ Travellers cheques and foreign currency.
▸ Night safe facilities (you see them on the outside wall of a bank).
▸ Facilities to buy and sell stocks and shares.
▸ Deposit box facilities for keeping valuables.

▲ The logos of the four major banks

Receiving and recording payments

You may already have a part-time or full-time job in, for example, a cafe, fast foo restaurant, garage or shop. Therefore you will probably have handled money or give receipts. This means that you will already have gained this competence. You should che with your tutor to see if you can be credited under the Accreditation of Prior Learning APL system.

Working as a cashier on a till

Cash transactions

If the purchase is for cash you will take the customer's money and check that it is correc it is, the money is put into the till in the right section. If there is not enough you will nee politely ask the customer for the extra money. If you are given more than the purch price, you will have to give change. For example, if the item costs £17.50 and you are gi £20.00, you will need to give £20.00 − 17.50 = £2.50 as change. This should be counted forwards to the amount the customer offered, e.g. you have 50p and two £1 coins rea Count, '£17.50,' give the customer 50p, '£18', give £1, '£19', give £1 and say '£20, thank very much.' Always be polite.

Cheque transactions

The customer must have a valid cheque guarantee or banker's card. You must ask for this before a cheque is made out. Then check that these items are correct:

- The date on the cheque.
- The amount in words.
- The amount in figures.
- Your company name.
- The signature on the cheque which must match the signature on the banker's card.
- That the bank details on the cheque and card match.
- That the date on the bankers card is valid.

If all the items are correct, then enter the details from the bankers card on to the back of the cheque.

Credit card payments

First check that the credit card is valid. You can also phone the credit card company to see if there is enough money in the account. A credit card inprinter is then used to transfer the credit card details on to the company receipts. Make sure that these receipts are filled out accurately – they are a legal document. The customer is given one copy for their own records and as proof of payment. You put your copy in the till.

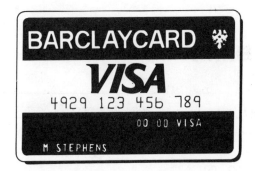 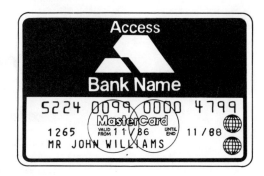

▲ *Credit cards*

▲ *Credit card imprinter*

Payments by electronic funds transfer

EFT systems

Many large organisations now use computerised till systems which print out cheques for the customer to sign. This is how you would use such a system:

- Ask the customer for the switch card, e.g. a plastic VISA card.
- Press EFT on the machine.
- Run the plastic card through the machine.
- Insert an EFT slip into the machine.
- Press 'print' so that the machine prints the details on to the slip, e.g. bank account number, date, amount to be paid, company name.
- Take the slip from the machine and give it to the customer to sign.
- Check the signature on the slip against the one on the card.
- If the signatures match, tear off the customer portion of slip and return it with the card and the receipt.
- Put the company copy in the till.

ACTIVITY

Would you accept this cheque with this bankers card? If you wouldn't say why.

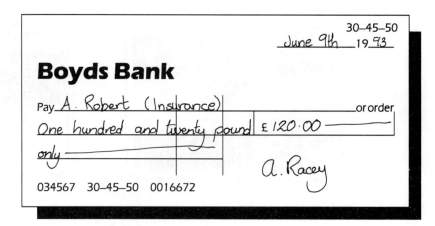

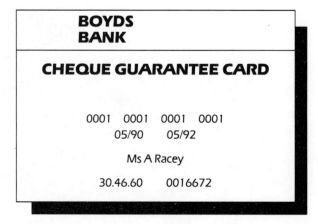

Foreign currency

To buy goods from another country you would normally use the currency of that country. For example, if you wanted to buy goods from an Italian company you would have to use the Italian currency which is the lira.

Sometimes the currency of the country from which you want to buy goods is very 'weak', e.g. the Polish zloty, and no-one outside that country wants the currency. When this happens trade will have to take place using a 'hard' currency that everyone wants, e.g. the US dollar. Poland can earn dollars by exporting their goods. These dollars can then be used to buy imports.

When a foreign company buys goods from a UK firm they have to pay in the UK currency which is pounds sterling.

Changing sterling into a foreign currency

Table 12.1   Exchange rates (correct as at 28 May 1992)

Country	Currency	Exchange rate, £1.00 =
Spain	Peseta (Pes)	183.45 Pes
France	Franc (Fr)	10.04 Fr
Germany	Mark (Dm)	2.95 Dm
Belgium	Belgian franc (Bfr)	60.90 Bfr
Netherland	Guilder (Gldr)	3.33 Gldr
Portugal	Escudo (Esc)	257.95 Esc
Poland	Zloty (Zl)	19,202.00 Zl
USA	Dollar ($)	1.73 $

Changing sterling into a foreign currency

If you look in any bank you will see a notice board headed 'Exchange Rates'. In the *Financial Times* newspaper you will find the FT Guide to World Currencies which gives the exchange rates of most of the currencies used around the world. The exchange rate or rate of exchange is the amount of foreign currency you would get after changing £1 sterling. To find out how many French francs you would get, look in the table above:

£1.00 = 10.04 francs, i.e. 10 francs and 4 centimes

To find the number of French francs you would get if you changed £5.00, you must multiply the number of pounds sterling by the exchange rate for French francs:

£5.00 = 5 × 10.04 = 50.2 French francs

Rule
To change pounds sterling into a foreign currency, multiply the number of pounds you want to change by the exchange rate of that currency. *Example* £1.00 = 60.90 Bfr (Belgian francs). Therefore to change £80.00 into Belgian francs

£80.00 = 80 × 60.90 = 4872 Bfr

Example £1.00 = 2.95 Dm (German marks). Therefore to change £17.20 into German marks

£17.20 = 17.20 × 2.95 = 50.74 Dm

Changing foreign currency into sterling

You have returned from France with 870 francs and want to change these back into pounds sterling. How many pounds sterling would you get?

Rule

To change a foreign currency into sterling pounds, divide the amount of foreign currency by the exchange rate for that currency.

$$\frac{\text{Amount of foreign currency}}{\text{Exchange rate}} = \text{Pounds sterling}$$

Example

How many pounds sterling would you get for 870 French francs?

$$870 \text{ French Francs} = \frac{870}{10.04} = \text{£86.65}$$

Example

You change 2,346,000 Italian lira into pounds sterling. How many pounds would you get?

$$2,346,000 \text{ lira} = \frac{2,346,000}{2199.50} = \text{£1,066.60}$$

Using exchange rates

Exchange rates are often used to convert currency in organisations.

QUOTATION

a. Dubois
Marte Subite
Brussels
Belgium

DATE May 28th 199–

QUANTITY	DESCRIPTION	AMOUNT
70	Alpine Chairs	74,602·5
180	Continental Chairs	165,526·2
	Prices based on an exchange rate of £1 = 60·90 Bfr.	

AUTHORISED BY: *aBM.*

Total 240,128·7 Bfr.

▲ Quotation

Example

A Dubois of the Morte Subite in Brussels (the capital of Belgium) wants to buy 70 Alpine chairs and 180 Continental chairs from the Worldwide Furniture Company. He would like a quotation for the chairs.

Assume that Alpine chairs cost £17.50 and Continental chairs cost £15.10.

For the Alpine chairs, each chair costs £17.50. (Remember that because he is buying 'in bulk' he gets a bulk discount.) The price of 70 Alpine chairs in pounds sterling is therefore

$$70 \times £17.50 = £1225.00$$

This needs to be converted into Belgian francs (Bfr)

$$£1225.00 = 1225.00 \times 60.90 = 74,602.5 \text{ Bfr}$$

The price of 180 Continental chairs in pounds sterling is

$$180 \times £15.10 = £2718.00$$

The price of 180 Continental chairs in Belgian francs is

$$2718 \times 60.90 = 165,526.2 \text{ Bfr}$$

The total price is found by adding the prices of the Alpine and Continental chairs

70 Alpine	74,602.5 Bfr
180 Continental	165,526.2 Bfr
Total price	240,128.7 Bfr

ACTIVITY

You receive the following requests for quotes for the Worldwide Furniture Company MENSA range of chairs. Find out the current rate of exchange for the currencies used in each country, then reply to the queries quoting the price in the correct foreign currency at today's exchange rate. You will have to find out in which country Lisbon, Madrid and Rome are situated. Use the price list on page 59.

1 A Zabrowski
  Av Estoril
  Lisbon

  requests a quote for 40 21st Century chairs and 110 Alpine chairs in sunset red.

2 P Lopez
  Av Fernandez
  Madrid

  requests a quote for 300 Mont Blanc chairs in ice blue.

3 C Ginelli
  Botticelli
  Rome

  requests 100 Mont Blanc chairs in Forest Green and 50 Continental chairs in sunripe yellow.

Statement of account

Statements are sent by a company to its regular customers. They can be sent weekly, monthly or quarterly (every three months). The time between the issue of statements depends on the amount of business and the number of transactions carried out in that time.

The statement will show:

- Customer's name, address and reference number.
- Company name, address and reference number.
- Description of items sold or business done.
- Dates of the transactions.
- Any money received by the company. This is shown as a credit.
- Any money owing to the company. This is shown as a debit or charges.

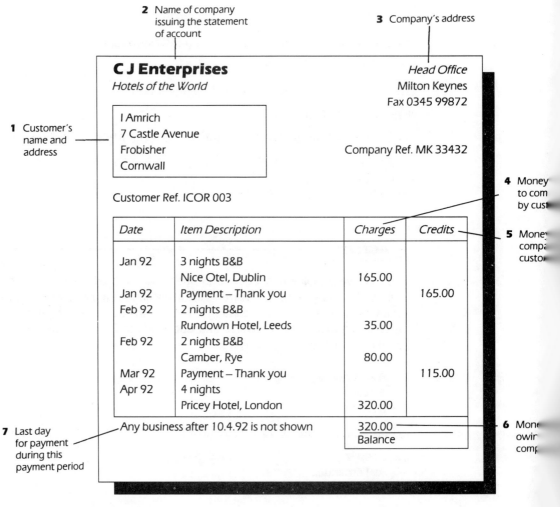

▲ Statement of account

C J Enterprises
Hotels of the World

Head Office
Milton Keynes
Fax 0345 99872

I Amrich
7 Castle Avenue
Frobisher
Cornwall

Company Ref. MK 33432

Customer Ref. ICOR 003

Date	Item Description	Charges	Credits
Jan 92	3 nights B&B Nice Otel, Dublin	165.00	
Jan 92	Payment – Thank you		165.00
Feb 92	2 nights B&B Rundown Hotel, Leeds	35.00	
Feb 92	2 nights B&B Camber, Rye	80.00	
Mar 92	Payment – Thank you		115.00
Apr 92	4 nights Pricey Hotel, London	320.00	

Any business after 10.4.92 is not shown

320.00
Balance

ACTIVITY

1 Copy and complete the Interflora McDonald statement for the orders below. You w have to work out the cost of each order – one dozen daffodils costs £6.00, 1 dozen ros cost £15.00.

1 March	CJE order 10 dozen daffodils
3 March	CJE order 5 dozen roses
4 March	CJE order 8 dozen roses
7 March	CJE pay £255.00 to InterFlora McDonald

9 March	CJE order 15 dozen daffodils		
9 March	CJE order 5 dozen daffodils		
14 March	CJE pay £50.00 to InterFlora McDonald		
16 March	CJE pay £70.00 to InterFlora McDonald		

INTERFLORA McDONALD

THE FLORISTS   The High, Harlow

STATEMENT

C J Enterprises
Hotels Inc.
Milton Keynes
Ref. MK33432

Date: 14.3.19

Date	Item Description	Debits	Credits
Payments received after the 15th are not included		Balance	

▲ Statement from InterFlora MacDonald to C J Enterprises

2   InterFlora McDonald receive a cheque for £70.00 from CJ Enterprises but it has not been signed. Write the letter explaining why you cannot accept the cheque.

Summary

In this chapter you will learn about keeping financial records or the accounts of an organisation. The assignment will involve you in running a mini business. The following topics are covered:

- Goals and objectives in business
- Health and safety
- Estimating
- Recording income and receipts
- Recording expenditure
- Day books
- Computerised account packages
- VAT calculations

This chapter will help you to achieve the following outcomes:

Core Module 2   Administrative Systems and Procedures
Outcome 2.3   Produce documents and material and process data
Outcome 2.4   Understand and follow health and safety procedures

Core Module 3   Business Resources and Procedures
Outcome 3.1   Investigate the resources used in operating a business
Outcome 3.3   Record financial transactions

Core Module 4   People in Business
Outcome 4.4   Contribute to achievement of organisational goals by fulfilling job role

The assignment and related activities can be used to cover the following performance criteria:

1.1d	goals of different types of business identified and compared
1.3a	reasons for community influence over business explained
1.3b	main forms of influence noted and outlined
2.2a	oral and written messages received and acted upon
2.2b	information obtained from appropriate sources
2.3a	business documents produced using a word processing package
2.3b	information processing equipment used to run standard applications
2.3c	data examined and analysed using a spreadsheet package
2.3d	copies of original documents produced using reprographic equipment
2.4a	potential hazards to the well-being of self and others recognised and reported
2.4b	equipment used in accordance with operating instructions and procedures
2.4c	work area kept free from hazards
3.1a	scope, size, nature and aims of a business identified
3.1b	mix of financial, physical and human resources used in the business identified and explained
3.1c	reasons for the balance of resources used in the organisation elicited
3.1d	methods of acquiring the necessary resources for a business examined
3.3a	flow of money in the organisation charted and explained
3.3b	recording documents and systems identified and their purpose described
3.3c	correct systems and documents or files chosen or accessed
3.3d	information recorded neatly and accurately
3.3e	necessary calculations made accurately

3.3f	recording and calculations checked for accuracy
3.4a	meaning of performance investigated and explained
3.4b	methods of measurement of performance investigated and described
4.4a	relationship between organisational objectives and job role identified
4.4b	given tasks completed to agreed criteria
4.4c	contribution made both as an individual and as a member of a team to the achievement of agreed targets and goals

The assignment will help with the development of Common Skills, especially the following:

Managing and Developing Self
Outcome 1   Manage own roles and responsibilities
Outcome 2   Manage own time in achieving objectives
Outcome 4   Transfer skills gained to new and changing situations and contexts

Working with and Relating to Others
Outcome 5   Treat others' values, beliefs and opinions with respect
Outcome 6   Relate to and interact effectively with individuals and groups
Outcome 7   Work effectively as a member of a team

Communicating
Outcome 8   Receive and respond to a variety of information
Outcome 9   Present information in a variety of visual forms
Outcome 10   Communicate in writing
Outcome 11   Participate in oral and non-verbal communication

Managing Tasks and Solving Problems
Outcome 12   Use information sources
Outcome 13   Deal with a combination of routine and non-routine tasks
Outcome 14   Identify and solve routine and non-routine problems

Applying Numeracy
Outcome 15   Apply numerical skills and techniques

Applying Technology
Outcome 16   Use a range of technological equipment and systems

Applying Design and Creativity
Outcome 17   Apply a range of skills and techniques to develop a variety of ideas in the creation of new/modified products, services or situations
Outcome 18   Use a range of thought processes

Read the following assignment to help you to understand some of the things you should be able to do by the end of the chapter. Normally it will be best to read the chapter and carry out the set activities before you tackle the assignment.

Check whether you can do the assignment on your own or with one or more colleagues. Some assignments will require organising by your tutor. Seek guidance, where needed, from your tutor.

:signment

The disco ──────────────────────────

For this assignment you must plan, organise and run a disco. You need to work in groups and need to plan well in advance, at least two months. You will have to hold meetings which must have an agenda to do with the disco. One item on the agenda must be objectives and targets of the disco. Proper minutes must be taken and you should follow the normal rules of meetings. The minutes must be typed and circulated – given – to all members.

R.B.JACKSON

Task 1   Decide and fix the price of the tickets. There could be special prices for men, women, groups.

Task 2   Design proper tickets and have them printed.

Task 3   Find and book a hall or other suitable venue.

Task 4   Estimate the number of people who could come.

Task 5   Estimate your income from ticket sales.

Task 6   Check the Health and Safety Regulations for your venue. Most importantly, check the numb
            people allowed in. You must meet the health and safety standards laid down.

Task 7   Organise a raffle with proper tickets and prizes.

Task 8   Find and book the entertainment. This could be a DJ, sound system, kareoke, etc.

Task 9   Provide food and drink for the disco.

Task 10   Sell the disco tickets.

Task 11   Sell the raffle tickets.

Task 12   Keep a cash book for transactions.

Task 13   Keep a sales day book for transactions.

Task 14   Keep a purchase day book for transactions.

Task 15   Keep a petty cash account and petty cash box.

Task 16   Books must be kept both manually (by hand) and by using a suitable computer program.

Task 17   Open a disco bank account if you can.

Task 18   Keep all receipts and records of everything.

Your accounts will be audited (checked) at various times during the planning stage and on completion of the disco. All your records and documents must be available for auditing at all times. All legal rules and regulations must be followed. Remember that you cannot sell alcoholic drinks unless you have a licence and then only to people over 18.

Remember, discos can make either a loss or a profit. How are you going to cope if your disco makes a loss? What if it makes a profit? Do you need to insure yourselves against the risks of running a disco in the venue?

Goals and objectives

Whatever the organisation it must ask itself the question, 'What do we want to achieve?' The answers to the question will help it to fix its objectives. Once these have been set, it will need to work out ways to achieve them. It will need targets to aim for and an action plan with policies to reach these targets.

Survival

The main objective of anyone who sets up a business is **survival**. Most people want their business to continue and succeed so that they can then earn a good living and possibly pass the business on to their children.

Profitability

Making profits is another objective. Some companies may only wish to earn enough or sufficient profits to allow them to survive, others attempt to make the most profit they can over a period of years. This does not mean that they try to earn the highest rate of profit in any one year, e.g. by charging very high prices, because this may turn customers away. Instead they charge a price which will continue to attract customers. These companies have the objective of trying to maximise (or make the most) profits.

FILE FACT

Profit can be defined as the difference between the total revenue (or money earned by a company) and Total Cost (or money paid out by a company).

Sales

Another objective which many companies have is to increase the value of their sales. They could do this by charging higher prices for their products. Companies may also want to increase the amount of their sales – the sales volume. However, to do this they might have to lower their prices. (What would this do to their profits?)

Market share

Companies often want to control the market in which they sell. They will then gain more power and influence to push the market in the direction they want it to go. To do this they will need to increase their share of the market. The market share is the fraction, or part, of the whole market for the product which the company has.

Growth

Another objective companies may have is to increase their overall size. They can achieve this by merging or joining with other firms, or by buying them out through a take-over: this way if one company takes over a competing company they can gain control of a larger share of the whole market and increase their power.

Other objectives

The type of market in which the company is working will also affect its objectives. The following is a list of other possible objectives:

- A good safety record.
- The best service.
- Reliable products.
- The best quality possible.
- Good after-sales service.
- Pleasant staff.
- Quick service.
- Low prices.

Whatever objectives an organisation chooses they must be able to be measured. To do this the organisation must have targets. These must be quite specific, for example:

- Increase profits by 10% next year.
- Sell 5% more in the Midlands.
- Reduce costs by 5%.

The organisation can then be managed so as to achieve these targets.

ACTIVITY

At your meeting discuss possible objectives and targets. Minute these carefully. Remember that you do not want to fix targets which are out of your reach, or which are too low.

Prices, people, income

Estimating

Fixing the right price is important for every business. Too high a price and people will not buy the product, too low a price and the organisation may not make sufficient money.

To estimate or forecast future income an organisation needs to carry out some market research. It will need to ask possible customers how much they would be willing to buy at a particular price. (In the case of the disco, you need to ask whether they would be willing to attend at the price you are asking for the tickets.)

Table 12.1   Estimating future income

Price (Column 1)	Estimated number sold (Column 2)	Estimated income (Column 3)
£1.80	90	£162
£2.20	85	£187
£2.50	80	£200
£3.00	65	£195

In Table 12.1:

- Column 1 shows various prices that could be charged.
- Column 2 shows how many items might be sold at a particular price.
- Column 3 shows the expected income from selling goods at a particular price, e.g. at a price of £2.20 the number expected to be sold is 85. Therefore
Estimated income = Price × Number sold
$$= £2.20 \times 85 = £187.00$$

For the case illustrated by Table 12.1 the best price would be:

a)   £2.50 if the organisation was trying to maximise (make the most) income.
b)   £1.80 if it was trying to sell as many items as possible.

The price chosen will depend on the objectives set by the organisation.

To run a disco successfully the potential customers would have to be asked if they would be willing to attend if the price were £2, £2.50, £3, £4 . . . £10 (well, you could offer free food and drinks).

/ **ACTIVITY** /

Carry out a market research survey of potential customers for the disco. You should ask a sample of people questions such as:

- How much are you willing to pay?
- Do you want food and/or drinks?
- What type of entertainment do you want?

Try and find out how many people are likely to go to the disco over a range of prices.

Keeping account of the business

Any business will want to know:

- How it gets its money.
- How it spends its money.
- How much money it is owed.
- How much money it owes.
- Whether it makes a profit.

To do this the company will have to keep records of each of these. These records are kept in books – the account books. In your job you might have to put information into these books. This job is called book-keeping. If you do the book-keeping you will have to be neat and tidy, honest, accurate and you cannot afford to make mistakes.

Companies have to keep books to:

- Report on the amount of value added tax which is to be paid or claimed.
- Meet any legal needs.
- Satisfy their accountant.
- Know how well or badly they are doing financially.
- Have a permanent record of the business. For this the company will need proper account books or ledgers.

Golden rules

Collect the information
A business must collect and keep all bills, receipts, invoices and cheques including:

- Customer and supplier invoices.
- Receipts for petty cash expenses.
- Cheques and cheque book receipts.

Record the information
All the paper you collect must be sorted out – it cannot just be put into a large cardboard box. Companies will keep a separate record of all:

- Customer invoices.
- Bills paid.
- Supplier invoices.
- Receipts.
- Cheques paid out, etc.

These records are its account books or ledgers. Small organisations can buy these already printed in any stationery shop. Large organisations are more likely to have their own specially printed books. There will be organisation rules about how these should be filled in. For example, all entries should be in ink. If any changes are made, these should have the initials of the person who made the change next to them. There should be no blank pages or pages torn out of the account books, if there are the accountant will probably (and perhaps rightly) suspect the organisation of dishonest practice. Always be totally honest and accurate.

/ **ACTIVITY** /

Find out the names of the account books kept by your organisation. This could be your permanent or work experience employer, or centre where you are studying.

Arrange for the finance department of your organisation to come and talk to your group.

Cash book

The cash book is used to keep a record of the organisation's income and expenditure. Income is the money your business receives. Expenditure is the money paid out by your business. Expenditure is always recorded on the right-hand page, whilst income is shown on the left-hand page.

Recording income or receipts

Income, or receipts, is the money received by a company after selling something.

We can use the example of a newsagents to show how income is recorded. Dorset Publications (DP), have four shops along the south coast of England. Each shop sells papers, household products such as cooking oil, batteries, cleaning materials, etc. The shops also sell sweets, chocolates and tobacco products.

All income is taken through the till, i.e. over the counter. Payments can be made by cash, cheque (if supported by a banker's card) and credit cards. Receipts are given to customers for every sale.

The shop owner divides the sales into groups, e.g. 1 stationery, 2 cards, 3 sweet products, 4 household products, etc. Whenever there is a sale, the code number 1, 2, 3, etc. is keyed into the till. At the end of the day the total sales are printed out by code number. These are then recorded in the cash book.

At the end of each week the sales are totalled. The amount of VAT paid by customers is also totalled. Money is paid into the bank each day.

The column headings for receipts in the cash book are:

- **Date**   When the income was received.
- **Item**   Where did the income come from (what was the source), e.g. £800.00 from the sale of stationery, £220.00 from the sales of sweets, etc.
- **Bank**   How much was paid into the bank. This figure includes the VAT and will appear as a credit on the organisation's bank statement. The VAT taken by the company selling the goods must be paid to Customs and Excise – the department responsible for collecting VAT.
- **Reference number (Ref)**   A simple number which can be used to store the information on manual or computer files, e.g. stationery is 1, cards are 2, etc. as defined above.
- **Value Added Tax (VAT)**   This figure must be shown separately for tax purposes.
- **Sales**   The headings here show the value of sales in each category (1, 2, 3, etc.). The price does not include VAT. Any headings could be used here, it depends on what is sold. It could be goods or services, including disco tickets, raffle tickets, etc.

Recording expenditure

Expenditure items are shown on the right hand page. This money is spent to purchase items, both stock and services. The column headings are:

- **Date**   When the expenditure took place.
- **Cheque number**   Number of the cheque used to make the expenditure (pay for the item).
- **Reference Number (Ref)**   A number useful for filing the document.
- **Bank**   The amount paid out. It will appear on the statement the company gets from its bank as a debit (withdrawal).
- **Value Added Tax (VAT)**   When the company buys an item it has to pay VAT to the seller. (It may claim this back at a later date.)
- **Stocks**   The price shown excludes VAT. The stock will be sold later. The headings for these columns can vary (in this case 'Sundries' includes sweets, cards and household products), it depends on the type of organisation. Other headings could include wages, rent, rates, gas, electricity, printing, hire of DJ, food, drink, tickets, etc. In fact whatever best suits the organisation.

Receipts

Income / Sales (£)

199X Date	Item	£ Bank	Ref.	£ VAT	Stat.	Cards	Sweets	House.
3/3	Till	940	1	140	800			
	Till	205.62	2	30.62		175		
	Till	258.50	3	38.50			220	
	Till	329.00	4	49.00				280
3/3	Total	1733.12		258.12	800	175	220	280

Payments

Expenditure / Stock (£)

199X Date	Item	Cheque no.	Ref.	Bank	VAT	Stat.	Sundries	Wages	Rent
3/3	ABC Ltd	3459	2	262.50	52.50		300		
3/3	Allson's Sweets	3460	3	235	35.00		200		
8/3	Staff	3461		175				175	
3/3	Landlord	3462		200					200
	Total			962.50	87.50		500	175	200

Note: VAT is not paid on 'wages' or 'rent' but is paid on purchases of sundries.

▲ *Dorset Publications cash book, Hardy Stores, Poole*

Have you made money?

At the end of each week or month, the columns should be totalled. This will show which items have sold the most, and the stock which has been purchased. The cash book is only used to show income and expenditure which passes through the company bank account. The total of the two 'bank' columns shows how much money, if any, there is in the bank. If income is more than expenditure it should mean there is money in the bank.

Look at Dorset Publications cash book. £1,733.12 has been received as income, whereas £962.50 has been paid out. For this day at least, income is greater than expenditure. However, the bank statement might not be the same because:

a)   Cheques the organisation has written might not yet have been put into the bank for payment. The organisation appears to have more money than expected.

b)   Cheques the organisation has received and recorded might not have been paid in. The organisation appears to have less money.

The process of comparing the cash book totals with the bank statement is called **reconciliation** – the organisation has to reconcile the two amounts.

Sales day book

In this book a company will record all the money that it is owed. Once goods are sold to a customer, an invoice will be sent to them. There should be an entry made in the sales day book for every invoiced sale. The customer receives an invoice, the selling company keeps a copy on file.

The sort of information a company would keep in the sales day book is shown in the diagram on page 210. The columns are:

- **Date.**
- **Item**   This could be the customer's name.
- **Price excluding VAT**   This is the net amount, the price without VAT added on.
- **Invoice Number**   Useful for filing and tracing invoices. This number is quoted by customers if they have a query.
- **Invoice amount**   The amount the customer pays, e.g. Chris Chocs pays £352.50 or £300 (price excluding VAT) + VAT at 17½% = £300 + £52.50 = £352.50.
- **VAT**   Value Added Tax calculated at 17½%.
- **Discount**   This is a lower price being offered to a customer in the same trade, or for prompt payment. In this example no discounts have been given.
- **Progress**   Some comment as to whether the invoice has or has not been paid, and whether or not the customer has been contacted.

The columns under which entries are made can vary according to the type of business. The purpose of the columns is to provide information to help the company to:

- Keep records.
- Keep up to date.
- Get paid quickly by chasing up customers.
- Answer customer questions.

ACTIVITY

Make these entries into a sales day book. You will need to calculate VAT and the invoice amount. All entries are for June 199X.

Fiona's Music, £230.00 on invoice no. 00417, 6 June
Sidcup Socks, £190.00 on invoice no. 00419, 7 June
Croydon Eng., £335.00 on invoice no. 00420, 9 June
Aberavon Electrics, £711.00 on invoice no. 00421, 12 June
Redhill Inc. Ltd., £492.00 on invoice no. 00422, 13 June

199X Date	Customer Item	Price Excl. VAT £	Invoice Number	Invoice Amount	VAT £	Discount	Progress
3.5	Chis Chocs	300	00379	352.50	52.50	—	Paid
4.5	ELEANOR 2000	650	00380	763.75	113.75	—	'phoned again 20.5
20.5	Southwark Commodities	220	00381	258.50	38.50	—	Paid

Notes: 1 No discounts have been given.
2 Only the company Eleanor 2000 owes money, the other two invoices have been paid.

▲ Example of sales day book entries

Purchase day book

199X Date	Supplier	Invoice number	Price excluding VAT (£)	VAT (£)	Invoice total (£)	Progress
6·5	R. Patel Ltd	0084C	270	47·25	317·25	sent cheque
7·5	J. Solomon	3712	140	24·50	164·50	
7·5	V. Magyar	XV17	450	78·75	528·75	

Note: Three purchases have been made. Only R Patel Ltd has been paid (£317.25 incuding VAT). Two invoices are outstanding, these still have to be paid.

▲ *Purchase day book entries*

This account book is used to record all the purchases that the company makes. The company will have to pay money to the supplier. It will get an invoice from the supplier. The entries in this ledger will show whether or not the company owes money. Entries should be made as soon as an invoice is received. The company will only enter the information that it needs. The example shown above uses date, name of supplier, supplies invoice number (useful if the organisation has a query or question about a particular order), price excluding VAT, VAT (which it may later claim back), invoice total and progress (whether the invoice has been paid or any action the organisation has undertaken regarding the invoice). Other columns could include the suppliers address, telephone number, a contact name (someone the organisation could ring to answer questions), etc.

─┤ **ACTIVITY** ├────────────────────────────────────

1   You work in the accounts department of Dorset Publications. Please record these purchases in the purchase day book. All entries are for 8 May 199X.
     G Smith supplied £330.00 of items (excl. VAT) on invoice no. GS300. M Lawrence provided £85.00 worth of goods (excl. VAT) on invoice no. M912.
     A Grosch supplied £117.00 of goods on invoice no. AG3111.

2 Please check these invoices. If they are satisfactory, make the entries in the purchase day book.

Fine Cards Ltd

Invoice

To:

Dorset Publications

Date:
Invoice no.:

Dear sirs, we are pleased to submit the following for your consideration

Quantity	Description	Unit cost	Amount
50 boxes	Xmas cards	25p	12.50
10 boxes	Valentine cards	10p	1.00
		Net	13.50
		VAT	2.36
		Total	15.86

Allsort Sweets Ltd

Invoice

To:

Dorset Publications

Invoice no.:   SLA115

Dear sirs, we are pleased to submit the following for your consideration

Quantity	Description	Unit cost	Amount
5 kg	Lemon drops	0.80	4.00
3 kg	Pear drops	0.90	2.70
6 kg	Apple toffee	1.00	6.00
1 kg	Peanut treats	0.70	0.70
		Net	13.40
		VAT	2.34
		Total	15.74

Invoice

To:

Dorset Petroleum

From:

K9 Pet Foods Ltd

Date: Your order no:
Invoice no: VAT registration no:

Quantity	Description	Unit price	Amount
3 doz	Cans Baby Pet Food	0.10	3.60
5 doz	Cans Dog's Dinner	0.08	4.80
9 doz	Cans Cat's Cuisine	0.11	11.88
21 boxes	Wild Bird Food	0.12	2.52
E&OE		Sub-total	22.80
		VAT at 17½%	3.99
		Total	26.79

Operating a computerised accounting package

You already know how to make entries in these manual books of accounts:

- Petty cash book.
- Cash book.
- Sales day book.
- Purchase day book.

In a small business these books will be enough to keep the accountant satisfied and happy. However, it will be necessary to have all the documents on which the book entries are made, permanently filed. If you work in an accounts section you are likely to spend much of your time making and checking entries in books and ledgers. Much of this work can be avoided if a computerised accounting package is used.

A typical computerised accounting package will be able to set up accounting books for you. You will only need to put in the basic data. To do this, first log in to the computer.

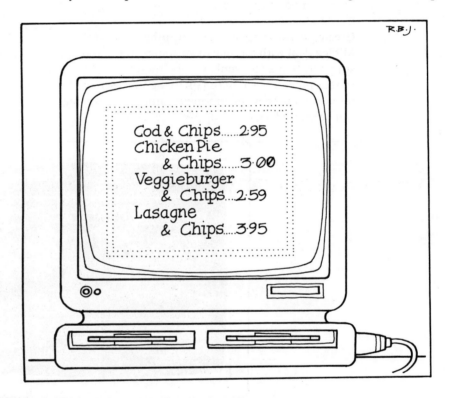

▲ *Computer menu*

A menu screen will appear giving you a series of choices. Make your choice by moving the cursor onto the choice you want. The screen will change and should now look like an invoice or order form. You will be asked to input the same type of data as you did for the manual books, then the computer will do the rest. The various parts of the computer package (the books) are all linked together. When data is entered into one part or area of the program, it will also appear in other areas. Every transaction, whether it is a sale or purchase, is followed through each part of the accounts. For example, if a sale is made and the details of the sales invoice are inputed. The computer program will record the sale in the sales day book and reduce the level of stock by the same amount.

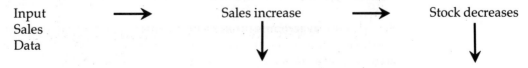

Entering, recording and storing information on computer

We will use a company called Mirage Wholesale Ltd. to show how a typical accounting computer program works. Like all wholesalers, Mirage buy in bulk and sell in smaller quantities. They deal with a large number of suppliers and customers. Almost all of their accounts are computerised, from book-keeping to the printing of delivery notes and invoices.

Mirage have a specially made package which is custom designed to their own needs. However it does all the jobs a typical accounting package does.

With a typical accounts package, three sets of accounts can be made:

1 **Supplier or purchasing accounts** These will give information about suppliers and the purchases which Mirage makes.
2 **Customer or sales accounts** These provide information about customers and sales.
3 **Nominal accounts** This is where items are accounted for, if they do not appear under 1 or 2 above.

Create purchase accounts or supplier accounts

Mirage deal with a range of suppliers in the food and drink industries. They have a new supplier, Ivor's Heavenly Cakes, therefore a new account has to be set up. Details about the supplier can be entered on to the VDU screen. For example, supplier's name, address, reference number, telephone number, contact person, value of business, etc. Accounts can be created for each supplier in this way.

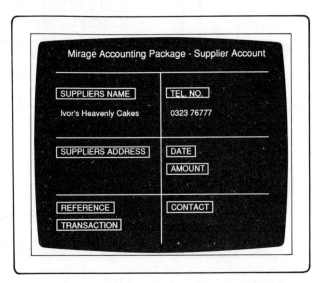

▲ VDU screen showing supplier's details. The data can be inputed by following the prompts, then moving cursor to where you need to input the next piece of information using the keys → ← ↑ ↓

Set up sales accounts or customer accounts

Mirage have many customers. The details for each customer can be entered directly on the screen. Separate accounts can then be created for each customer. Extra details can added as necessary, e.g. further sales. This process of making entries is similar to the o we used to complete manual books.

Whenever an entry is made on the screen, always take care to check it thoroughly as it often be very difficult to find mistakes later.

Set up nominal accounts for non stock items

The nominal accounts are those items that are not included in the customers or suppl accounts, for example:

- Expenses or overheads for administration, selling and distributing goods. These costs often cannot be identified with any one product or department. They have to be divided or shared between them according to experience and company policy.
- Income, which comes from non stock items, such as hiring out the company van or hiring out premises.
- Assets or possessions such as factory buildings, have to have a value put on them. This is a legal requirement.
- Liabilities are amounts owed by the business to its creditors. The creditors are firms which have supplied Mirage with services.

The purpose of purchase accounts, sales accounts and nominal accounts is to keep track of how well the business is doing. The information for them comes from transactions which the Mirage Wholesale Company will have made, the details of which must all be recorded accurately using the original documents. For example:

Type of transaction	Documentary evidence
Sale by cash	Invoices
or	Bills
Sale by credit	Receipts

For every transaction the documentary evidence will need to be collected and filed. Whilst detailed entries are made in the accounts ledgers and day books. Entries into the computer can be made to show:

a) **Payments received**   These are either payments received as cash or at the bank and payments made to run the business. (N.B. Remember to enter your user identity number after each account reference has been keyed in.)

b) **Purchase invoice details (stock bought)**   Mirage have bought stock on credit from their suppliers. This means that they do not pay for the goods immediately. They are given some time to pay. The details of these transactions (purchases) are recorded on purchase invoices sent by the suppliers and entered into the computer at Mirage.

c) **Sales invoice details (stock sold)**   Mirage also sell goods on credit to their customers. Here the customers are given some time to pay. The details of the sales invoices are entered into the computer.

Every time an entry is made into the computer, its store of knowledge is increased, and the program files each bit of information under its own heading in different accounts.

Entering purchase returns
Sometimes Mirage have to return damaged goods to their suppliers. In return they receive a credit note from the suppliers concerned. This credit note has to be accounted for, therefore the details are inputed into the computer. The various account areas can then be updated.

Entering sales returns
When customers of Mirage return unwanted goods, the customers are issued credit notes. Again all the information is fed into the computer so that credit notes can be matched.

Matching credit notes
Credit notes must be matched or paired with the invoices to which they belong, e.g. purchase credit notes with purchase invoices, sales credit notes with sales invoices. Matching credit notes will give the exact money still owed to Mirage:

- Money still owed to Mirage is the original sales invoice total minus the credit note value.
- Money owed by Mirage to its suppliers is found by calculating the purchase invoice total minus the credit note value, e.g. Mirage has purchase invoices for £300.00, £200.00 and £150.00 (total = £650.00) and a credit note for £100.00. Mirage therefore owes £650.00 − £100.00 = £550.00 to its suppliers.

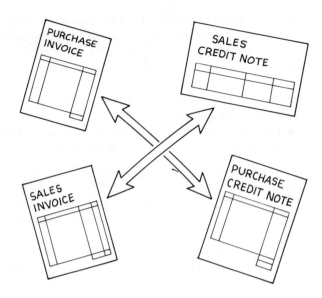

▲ *Matching credit notes*

Reporting, analysing and extracting information

Now that we have put all our information into the computer we need to know how to ge[
information out. We can ask the computer to reproduce the information we have inpu[
We can also ask the computer to analyse and collate data from various parts of th[
accounting package to produce new accounting documents such as trial balance, tradin[
and profit and loss accounts and balance sheets.

The program has a menu which tells us what accounts it has. For example, if we choo[
'Day books', the program will show our entries for:

- Sales invoices – which record all Mirage sales to customers.
- Purchase invoices – which record all Mirage purchases from suppliers.
- Sales credit notes.
- Purchase credit notes.

Alternatively, it can choose 'Account balances' we can either print (or view) a list [
customer account balances which show what each customer still owes to Mirage, o[
list of supplier account balances which show what Mirage owes to its suppliers.

Conclusions

Whether you use a manual or computerised accounting system you should get the sa[
results. The same details are entered or posted and the same sets of accounts are k[
under both methods. You will have to keep all the primary documents, such as b[
receipts, invoices, credit notes, etc. and however you keep the accounts, the same lev[
accuracy is needed whenever you make an entry.

Double-entry book-keeping

It is known that merchants have practised double-entry book-keeping since the thirte[
century. Double-entry book-keeping is a method where every transaction is entered int[
account books twice – first as a debit, and then as a credit.

One of the first known written works on double-entry book-keeping was written by [
Pacioli and published in Venice in 1494. In 1543 Hugh Oldcastle, a school teacher, wro[

first book in English on double-entry book-keeping. This was a translation of the book by Pacioli. Today this method of book-keeping is used everywhere.

Discounts and value added tax

Discounts

A discount is a percentage reduction off the normal cost price. Discounts can be given to customers for:

- Paying the bill quickly, say within 10 days of receiving it.
- Paying by cash.

There are two types of discount, these are:

- Cash discount – when a price reduction is made for prompt payment.
- Trade discount – when firms work in the same industry they will often reduce the price they charge each other for goods and services.

Calculating discounts
You will need to use percentages to calculate discounts.

Example
The total price shown on an invoice is £110.00. There is a discount of 10% for payment within 10 days. (This means that the customer will pay 10% less than £110.00 for prompt payment.) Work out the discounted price.

Method
Stage 1 Find 1% of the total, i.e. 1% of £110.00 $\left(1\% = \dfrac{1}{100} \text{ or } 0.01\right)$. Therefore

$$1\% \text{ of £110.00} = \frac{1}{100} \times £110.00 = 1.1$$

(On a calculator, key in '110 ÷ 100' to find 1%)
Stage 2 Once 1% has been found, you must find 10%, which is 1% × 10.

$$
\begin{aligned}
10\% \text{ of £110.00} &= 10 \times 1\% \text{ of £110.00} \\
&= 10 \times \frac{1}{100} \times £110.00 \\
&= \frac{10}{100} \times £110.00 \\
&= £11.00
\end{aligned}
$$

(On a calculator key in '× 10' to give you 10% of the total so that the full expression for finding 10% of £110.00 is '110 ÷ 100 × 10'.)

The discount is £11.00 so the customer pays £11.00 less than £110.00

Discounted price = £110.00 − £11.00 = £99.00

Example
The marked price of an item is £280 and there is a cash discount of 15%, find the cash price.

Method
On a calculator

15% Discount = 280 ÷ 100 × 15 = £42.00

Cash price = Original price − Discount
= £280.00 − £42.00
= £238.00

Example
The list price is £17.50 and there is a 2.5% discount, find the price paid.

Method
On a calculator
Discount = £17.50 ÷ 100 × 2.5 = £0.4375 (rounded up to £0.44 or 44p)
Price paid = £17.50 − £0.44 = £17.06

Check your calculator to see if you have a % key. Read the instruction booklet for your calculator or ask your supervisor to show you how to use it.

─/ **ACTIVITY** /─────────────────────────

1   C J Enterprises have given I Amrich a 12% discount on the £320.00 balance owing, for prompt payment by cash. If he fulfills the conditions, how much would he pay?

2   Calculate a 15% discount for each entry shown in the sales day book on page 210.

Value Added Tax (VAT)

All businesses, except those which are very small, must register for VAT. They will then put their VAT registration number on their business documents. Businesses put VAT on to the price of the goods they sell – the customer pays the VAT. At the end of each month or every three months the business sends the money collected for VAT to the Customs and Excise tax authority. If the business pays VAT on its own purchases it can claim this back. At the end of each month the business will either:

● Pay the Customs and Excise VAT if it has taken in more VAT than it has paid out; or
● claim back VAT if it has paid out more to other businesses than it has taken in from customers.

Calculating VAT
VAT must be added to the price of an item to show the final selling price. Statements and/or invoices can show:

● Prices exclusive of VAT, i.e. without VAT.
● Prices including VAT, i.e. VAT has already been added.
● VAT separately, item by item.
● Total VAT payable.

To calculate VAT we must use percentages again. This time the amount is added to the price.

Example

Look at the Worldwide Furniture Company statement to the Ramblers Rest. What is the total price of the chairs inclusive of VAT?

Worldwide Furniture Company

STATEMENT

Date_____Your Ref._____

Customer_ **Ramblers Rest** _____

No.	Item	Unit Cost		Amount Exclusive of VAT		VAT	
		£	p	£	p	£	p
10	21st Century	17·40		174	—	30	45
4	Alpine	18·60		74	40	13	02
Vat Registration No.				248	40	43	47
				Total			

Method

Cost of 21st Century chairs at £17.40 each exclusive of VAT

$= 10 \times 17.40 = £174.00$

VAT is currently 17.5%, therefore, on a calculator

$\text{VAT} = 174 \div 100 \times 17.5 = £30.45$

Price of 21st Century chairs inclusive of VAT

$= £174.00 + £30.45 = £204.45$

Cost of four Alpine chairs exclusive of VAT

$= 4 \times £18.60 = £74.40$

VAT of the Alpine chairs is

$74.4 \div 100 \times 17.5 = £13.02$

Cost of Alpine chairs inclusive of VAT

= £74.40 + £13.02 = £87.42

Total cost of chairs = Total cost of 21st Century chairs + Total cost of Alpine chairs

$$= £204.45 + £87.42$$

$$= £291.87$$

ACTIVITY

1 Make out the statement from the Worldwide Furniture Company to be sent to EAL Wholesales Greenwich for:

- 4 Mont Blanc chairs
- 40 Continental chairs
- 100 Alpine chairs
- 15 21st Century chairs
- 200 European chairs

Use the price list on page 59 to calculate the total amount exclusive of VAT and the total amount of VAT payable. Work out the total of the statement and put in today's date and the customer reference which is EAL 374.

Worldwide Furniture Company
STATEMENT

Date_____ Your Ref._____

Customer_____

No.	Item	Unit cost		Amount exclusive of VAT		VAT	
		£	p	£	p	£	p

Vat Registration No.

Total

2

Mirage Wholesale Purchase Accounts

Ref.	Supplier	Ref.	Supplier
MF	Mega Foods Seaford Sussex	CW	Country Wines Ltd. Grebe Court Norwich
SRF	Sun Rich Foods Redhill Surrey	HBW	Home Bakery Worldwide Bolton Lancs.
US	Universal Supplies Walworth Road London	PG	Peoples Grocer Corn Street Wandsworth
CS	The Cheese Shop Green Lane Lambeth	DM	DM Foods Old Kent Road London SE1
PS2	Posh Shop Richmond Surrey	PS3	Pizza Shed Victoria Street London SW1

Purchase invoices received in the month:

Supplier	Date	Invoice no.	Item	Cost (£)
Mega Foods	07039X	M0029	Beans	700.50 + VAT
Mega Foods	07039X	M0029	Fruit	500.00 + VAT
Sun Rich	10039X	S7138	Cakes	650.00 + VAT
Sun Rich	10039X	S7139	Biscuits	1090.00 + VAT
Country Wine	11039X	C8766	Red wine	1200.00 + VAT
Country Wine	11039X	C8766	White wine	1400.00 + VAT
Universal	13039X	U9875	Cheeses	980.00 + VAT
Mega Foods	15039X	M0030	Fruit	£806.00 + VAT
Home Bakery	16039X	H1193	Pies	1700.00 + VAT
Home Bakery	17039X	H1194	Rolls	2300.00 + VAT

a) Enter these purchase invoice details into the purchase day book.
b) Calculate the VAT for each invoice.
c) Make out the cheques ready for payment (including VAT) for all invoices dated up to and including the 13.03.9X.

3

Mirage Wholesale Customer Accounts

Ref.	Customer	Ref.	Customer
AK	A Kahn High Street Deptford	WW	Wonderful Wines Oxford Street London
BP	B Patel Lee Green Lee	BT	B-Tec High Holborn London
AS	A Shah File Road Camberwell	AF	A Felon Reed Avenue Westminster
PS1	The Pastry Shop The Cut Waterloo	RO	Rogues Ltd. Whitehall London

Sales invoices issued in the month:

Customer	Date	Invoice no.	Item	Price
Pizza Shed	03039X	M3931	Pastry	800 + VAT
DM Foods	03039X	M3932	Cheeses	175 + VAT
Cheese Shop	03039X	M3933	Cheeses	190 + VAT
Peoples	04039X	M3934	Pies	200 + VAT
Posh	04039X	M3935	Biscuits	150 + VAT
Wonderful	05039X	M3936	White + Red	320 + VAT
B Patel	05039X	M3937	Biscuits	96 + VAT
A Khan	06039X	M3938	Fruit	140 + VAT
A Shah	07039X	M3939	Fruit	320 + VAT
B-Tec	07039X	M3940	Rolls	70 + VAT
DM Foods	07039X	M3941	Rolls	400 + VAT
Cheese Shop	09039X	M3942	Cheese	228 + VAT
DM Foods	10039X	M3943	Rolls	220 + VAT

a) Fill in an invoice for each transaction.
b) Calculate the VAT for each invoice.
c) Enter the sales invoice details into the sales day book.

4   Mirage have received payments for all transactions up to and including 09.03.9X. Use the information given in the activities above to make up the statement of account for all the business done with DM Foods Ltd., Old Kent Road, London SE1, up to and including invoice number M3943.

MODULE 4

People in Business

13

Personnel

Summary

This chapter looks at the work of the personnel department. You are introduced to personnel work by an assignment which looks at a job you might be doing already at work or work experience. The following topics are covered:

- Personnel: function and role
- Job analysis, job role, job description
- Personnel specifications
- Recruitment procedures
- Records and data protection
- Databases
- Welfare, accidents

This chapter will help you to achieve the following outcomes:

Core Module 2	Administrative Systems and Procedures
Outcome 2.3	Produce documents and material and process data
Outcome 2.4	Understand and follow health and safety procedures

Core Module 3	Business Resources and Procedures
Outcome 3.4	Investigate and apply simple measures of performance

Core Module 4	People in Business
Outcome 4.1	Investigate and analyse the nature and purpose of work
Outcome 4.2	Identify the main rights and responsibilities of employers and employees to one another
Outcome 4.3	Examine and compare the main job roles in different organisations
Outcome 4.4	Contribute to achievement of organisational goals by fulfilling job role

The assignment can be used to cover the following performance criteria:

2.1d	business records managed using a simple database
2.3a	business documents produced using a word processing package
2.3b	information processing equipment used to run standard applications
2.3c	data examined and analysed using a spreadsheet package
2.3d	copies of original documents produced using reprographic equipment
2.4a	potential hazards to the well-being of self and others recognised and reported
2.4b	equipment used in accordance with operating instructions and procedures
2.4c	work area kept free from hazards
3.4a	meaning of performance investigated and explained
3.4b	methods of measurement of performance investigated and described
3.4c	suitable method chosen to gauge performance in identified jobs, tasks of operations

3.4d	methods applied to job/task/operation selected and conclusions drawn from results
4.1a	reasons for working identified
4.1b	the nature of work examined and different types compared
4.1c	different organisational structure examined and compared
4.1d	different work cultures identified and their importance assessed
4.2a	basic contractual requirements identified
4.2b	financial and non-financial benefits identified and assessed
4.2c	health and safety requirements identified and followed
4.2d	commitments and mutual expectations not binding in law recognised
4.3a	functional areas within organisations identified
4.3b	job roles in different functional areas of organisations identified
4.3c	job roles compared
4.4a	relationship between organisational objectives and job role identified
4.4b	given tasks completed to agreed criteria
4.4c	contribution made both as an individual and as a member of a team to the achievement of agreed targets and goals
4.5a	own skills and experience identified
4.5b	career advice and information sought
4.5f	job seeking and selection procedures identified and investigated

The assignment will help with the development of Common Skills, especially the following:

Managing and Developing Self
Outcome 1   Manage own roles and responsibilities
Outcome 2   Manage own time in achieving objectives
Outcome 3   Undertakes personal and career development
Outcome 4   Transfer skills gained to new and changing situations and contexts

Working with and Relating to Others
Outcome 5   Treat others' values, beliefs and opinions with respect

Communicating
Outcome 9   Present information in a variety of visual forms
Outcome 10   Communicate in writing

Managing Tasks and Solving Problems
Outcome 12   Use information sources
Outcome 13   Deal with a combination of routine and non-routine tasks

Applying Technology
Outcome 16   Use a range of technological equipment and systems

Read the following assignment to help you to understand some of the things you should be able to do by the end of the chapter. Normally it will be best to read the chapter and carry out the set activities before you tackle the assignment.

Check whether you can do the assignment on your own or with one or more colleagues. Some assignments will require organising by your tutor. Seek guidance, where needed, from your tutor.

Your job _____

Using the company where you work or are on work experience as a resource complete the following assignment. This may be completed in two parts.

Situation   You have been enjoying your job and have been so helpful to the department that the company have decided that another person should be taken on to help you. This in turn will mean that you will be free to take on extra responsibilities and thus gives you a chance of promotion.

Part A

There are several things that have to be done before the new person is appointed. Firstly, personnel need to know exactly what your duties are and what skills are needed. They also need to know the type of person best suited to the job. This will mean undertaking a job analysis.

Task 1   Make a timetable like that shown below and fill it in meticulously with the work you do for one complete week. You will need to record all the different types of work you do. If your job consists largely of the same type of work (e.g. telephonist) try to put the types of call/visitor into categories, e.g. enquiry, transferring calls, etc.

	Monday	Tuesday	Wednesday	Thursday	Friday
9.00					
9.30					
10.00					
10.30					

Task 2   Once you have completed the timetable you will need to work out what it shows.

Write down the main duties of your job and how long you spent at each during the week. It will make it easier if you round the time you spent up or down to half-hour slots, e.g.

- Filing $1 + 1 + 1\frac{1}{2} + 1 = 4\frac{1}{2}$
- Opening/distributing mail $\frac{1}{2} + \frac{1}{2} + \frac{1}{2} + \frac{1}{2} + \frac{1}{2} = 2\frac{1}{2}$

Telephone calls may need to be recorded separately, e.g. if you take ten telephone messages a week then the total 'message taking' time will be about half an hour.

Task 3   Once you have worked out how much time you spend on each duty, draw a bar chart (see p. 228) to show the percentage of time you spend on each duty over the week.

On the chart you should also try to break down the skills that are used.

You should now have a clear picture of exactly what your job entails. Some of it may surprise you.

Task 4   Your next task is to write a job description explaining the most important duties and the skills that a person will need. You should also say what personal characteristics would help in the job. You may find that your job consists mainly of inputting data and that accuracy rather than speed is important, the type of person suitable for this job may be a careful, patient person who doesn't mind sitting still for a long time. You can write the job description as a narrative (in paragraphs) rather than as a point-by-point check list.

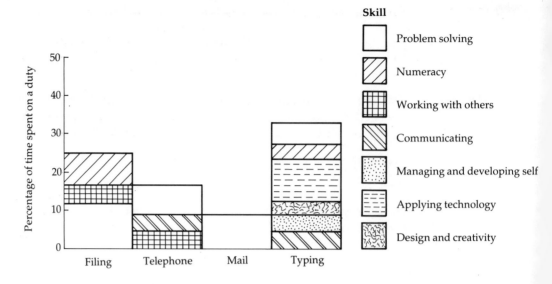

▲ Example of a bar chart showing job skills

Part B

You are now ready to give the details of your job to personnel. The first thing personnel will need to do is draft a job advertisement.

Task 1   Obtain examples of recent adverts for jobs from your company. Following in-house style, draft an advert for the new job. Remember to include all the points made earlier in the chapter and the benefits and training if appropriate, including chances to take qualifications (like your BTEC First Award).

Task 2   An advert will also be displayed internally. Find out where job vacancies are displayed or circulated internally and obtain some examples of old adverts. Highlight any differences between the external adverts and the internal adverts.

Task 3   Obtain an application form from your company. The form asks job applicants to give a lot of personal and work details. Ask the personnel officer why they need these details. Record your answers under headings such as: personnel records, suitability for job, legal requirement.

Task 4   On company headed paper prepare a letter for signature inviting applicants for interview. As you will not yet have their name and address leave these blank and store the letter on disk. Supply one hard copy of the letter for approval together with details of the main transport routes and a map of how to get to your company.

Task 5   Try to find out what your company's norms are and how an interviewee may display these qualities at an interview and then when employed, e.g.

- **Good time keeping**
  Interview – arrive for interview on time.
  Work – arrive back from breaks on time.
- **Neat appearance**
  Interview – wear 'quiet' rather than 'statement' clothes.
  Work – try to dress in keeping with other employees.
- **Willingness to learn**
  Interview – keenness to undertake training.
  Work – ask advice and listen to explanations.

Personnel department

It is very likely that as an employee (or potential employee) your first contact with an organisation will be through the personnel department. As the name implies, personnel deals with all matters relating to the personnel, or employees, of a company.

The diagram below shows some of the main functions and activities of the personnel department.

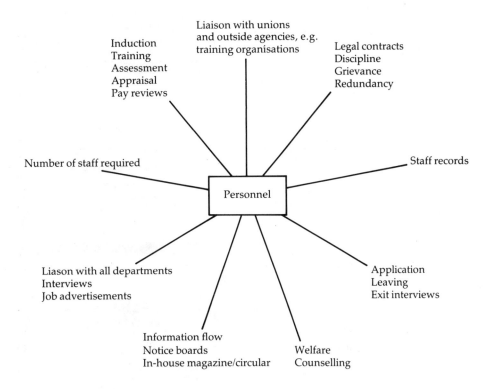

Induction
Training
Assessment
Appraisal
Pay reviews

Liaison with unions
and outside agencies, e.g.
training organisations

Legal contracts
Discipline
Grievance
Redundancy

Number of staff required

Staff records

Personnel

Liason with all departments
Interviews
Job advertisements

Application
Leaving
Exit interviews

Information flow
Notice boards
In-house magazine/circular

Welfare
Counselling

▲ *Functions and activities of the personnel department*

Although not directly involved with the main business activity of the company or the money handling, it can be seen that personnel must have good communication links with all departments to ensure that they get the right people to do the right jobs at the right price in the right way.

Staff recruitment

When employing people there are a number of considerations. Some of these will take the company view, some are legal requirements set up by government to protect employees.

The job advertisement

When a vacancy is identified, obviously it needs to be advertised. Very often the advertisement will be in local or national newspapers, but Job Centres, recruitment agencies and radio stations are also popular methods of advertising vacancies.

NEGOTIATOR REQUIRED

preferably with experience, to
work in our busy High Street office.
Apply for application form to
Stephen Rudkin (0444) 458961.
Agencies need not apply.
Home Property Services.

(38MRX

Garage in Kettering requires

EXHAUST FITTING TECHNICIAN

Good working conditions.
Pay negotiable.
Please contact Derek on
742020.

(388M

SALESPERSON REQUIRED

High earnings.
Must be smart appearance
and over 21 years.
Full training given.
Tel. 642075

(39MRX

ACTIVITY

Collect an assortment of job advertisements. Make a checklist of all the information you
find on them, e.g. company name, company address, job title, salary.

As a group compare your answers and make one large list of all the information that is gi
in the advertisements.

- Why do you think these things are included?
- Which do you think are legal requirements?
- Which say something about the company?
- Which say something about the job/department?

You may have come across the expression 'an equal opportunities employer'. This m
anyone with the ability to do the job will be considered irrespective of sex, religion,
disability, marital status, etc.

Make a list of your ideal work mates. Try to be honest and say whether this would be a balanced work force.

You may have left old people off your list, but would this be sensible? What have they got to offer?

Is there a particular group of people you do not like? Why?

You may feel that you want to keep these thoughts private, but you learn by hearing other people's viewpoints. In a group discussion, try to explain your attitudes. It may be helpful to base the discussion on a news item and see how other people feel.

Once a person has been employed they will be given a job description. This will describe their duties so that both sides know exactly what is expected of the person. A job description may change as we work in an ever changing environment. However a contract of employment on the other hand does not (see Chapter 2, page 24).

Selection of personnel

Although a company will be most interested in the applicant's ability to do the job, there are also other considerations taken into account by the company. These are often called **company norms**. Naturally, they should not contravene the Equal Opportunities Act but they may still be particular to a company as these are what make companies individual. Some examples companies have given of their norms are:

- Willingness to learn
- Time keeping
- Smartness of appearance.
- Attendance.
- Honesty.
- Self-discipline.
- Loyalty.

Hence, on interview it is necessary to create the 'right impression' by showing that you have these qualities. How do you think a potential employee can show that they have these qualities?

Personnel records

Once a person is employed by a company then a file will be opened on them. This file will contain many details which are necessary to the company, e.g. name, address, department, years of service, etc. Much of the information will be obtained from the job application form (see page 232).

Naturally, the details given on an application form are highly confidential and must be kept safe, secure and away from prying eyes. If a company is large and has many employees then it is quite likely that these details will be stored on computer. If this is the case then the company is obliged to protect the data under the Data Protection Act. This Act requires organisations and individuals who hold personal records on computer to register with the Data Protection Registrar (a government watchdog).

Under this Act it is necessary for companies to tell the registrar what they do with the information they hold. For instance, do they sell it to other interested parties? This is not likely in the case of personnel records, but it is fairly common practice for lists of subscribers to specialist magazines to be sold to manufacturers in that area. These manufacturers and services then add the people on the magazine lists to their mailing lists

Gatton Point, Redhill, Surrey RH1 2JX
Telephone: 0737 772611 Fax: 0737 768641

East Surrey College

Principal Richard Latham MSc, BSc (Econ), Cert Ed
Surrey County Council – An Equal Opportunities Employer

1   Post applied for

2   Surname   Forename(s)   Title
    Address

    Tel. No. (inc. code)   (a) home   (b) work
    Date of birth

3   Present post (stating grade of post, College or name of employing organisation)

    Date of appointment (a) to College or organisation   (b) to present post

    Present salary £   p.a. Allowances £   p.a.

    Name of superannuation scheme to which you now contribute

4   Places of education

Secondary School, College, University	Full or part-time	From month	year	To month	year

5   Qualifications: degrees, diplomas, certificates, etc. (excluding professional membership)
    with class of award, main and subsidiary subjects

Qualification, with class	Awarded by	Period of study and date of award

6   Professional membership, with any other qualification not included in (5)
    Dates and details of any published work, research, educational projects, etc.

7   DES teachers reference number (if any)

8   Experience in teaching

Educational Establishment	Employing L.E.A.	Full or part-time	Position held	From month	year	To month	year

9   Appointments held in industry, commerce, etc.

Employer	Full or part-time	Position held	From month	year	To month	year

10 What is the earliest date on which you could take up this appointment?

11 Details of three persons to whom reference may be made. (Referees should be able to speak
    about the applicant's work or career, and at least one must be the candidate's present
    employer). Unless you specifically request otherwise, these references will be taken up
    prior to interview.

	Title & Name	Position	Address	Tel No:
(i)				
(ii)				
(iii)				

12 Statement of application providing other relevant information (eg: details of job
    responsibilities/duties, training and development undertaken, specialist interests/subjects,
    extra mural activities). Please continue on separate sheet if necessary.

13 (a) This post is exempt from the provisions of section 4 (2) of the Rehabilitation
         of Offenders Act 1974 (Exceptions) Order 1975. Applicants are, therefore, not
         entitled to withhold information about convictions including those which for
         other purposes are "spent" under the provisions of the Act, and, in the event
         of employment, any failure to disclose such convictions could result in
         dismissal or disciplinary action by the Authority.
         Any information given will be considered only in relation to an application
         for positions to which the Order applies.
         Please state whether or not you are affected by this by indicating "Yes" if you
         are affected and "No" if you are not affected.
    (b) In accordance with the Department of Education and Science Circular 4/86
         'Protection of Children: Disclosure of Criminal Background of those with
         access to Children' you are asked to sign the declaration below:
         Should I be selected for this post I agree to a check being made into the
         existence and content of any possible criminal record held by the police.

    Signature .... Date ....
    Failure to agree to the above may lead to no further consideration being
    given to your application for this post.
    If you are affected by (a) and/or (b) details should be given in a sealed
    envelope and enclosed with this application.

14 Please state whether in the past you have retired prematurely from the teaching
    profession and received superannuation benefits.

15 Are you registered as a disabled person?

    Are you suffering from any medical condition which would disqualify
    you from teaching?

    If you wish to include any additional information, you may do so on a separate
    sheet or, if of a confidential nature, in a sealed envelope.

17 In applying for a post at EAST SURREY COLLEGE under the SURREY
    EDUCATION AUTHORITY I declare that the particulars given herein are
    correct and complete to the best of my knowledge and belief.

    Signed .... Date ....

This form, duly signed, should be returned by the closing date specified in the relevant adv
to:-
    Personnel Officer, East Surrey College, Gatton Point, Redhill Surrey RH1 2JX.

For Office Use

ND	NQ	NE	NI	NS	NO		
IN	IQ	IE	IC	IP	IA	IJ	IC

▲ *Sample application form*

and send them promotional material. It is this practice that results in much of your 'junk' mail dropping through the door.

The Act also requires the company holding the data to say how they gathered the information and who has access to it. It follows, therefore, that if you have access to personal information you treat it with total respect and do not gossip about any information that you may have found out by this means. The seriousness of this is usually borne out by the company's disciplinary procedures should you contravene this Act.

If you find, as an individual, that you suffer from information passed on by contravening this Act, then you may receive compensation from the guilty party. Exceptions to this are data held for payroll or pension purposes, data given by ourselves and data held for statistical purposes where it is impossible to identify individuals.

ACTIVITY

Set up a data base containing personal details of your group. Include name, date of birth, town of residence, whether working full-time or part-time, chosen career path.

a) Sort on: names alphabetically, town, career path.
b) Delete a record.
c) Amend a career path.
d) Add an additional field.

Welfare

R.B. JACKSON

▲ *Welfare*

ACCIDENT REPORT FORM

FIN 241(REV 3/90)

This form must be completed in Quadruplicate by the Officer-in-Charge and Forwarded within 48 hours of the Accident **IN ACCORDANCE WITH GUIDANCE NOTE No. 12**

Write or Type. No Carbon required.

1 Full Name of injured person (Mr. Mrs. Miss Ms.)	
2 Home Address	
3 Age Sex Precise details of Occupation	

4 STATUS OF PERSON (Please tick relevant box)	Employee	Client	Pupil or Student	Self Employed Person	Member of Public

5 Date and Time of Accident	6 County Dept.
7 Work Base School or Establishment	8 Address where accident occurred
9 Exact location of accident (eg. office, canteen, courtyard, work site, biology lab. general classroom etc.)	10 Injury Type Bodypart

11 FULL DETAILS to be given of how the accident happened and precisely what the injured person was doing eg. if a fall of person or material, plant etc. state height of fall and type of object.

Names, occupations and addresses of witnesses

To whom and on what date was the accident first reported?

12 What do you consider was the cause of the accident? (mention defects or hazards in Machinery or Premises)	13 What action has been taken to prevent a recurrence

14 Has the accident been entered in the Accident Book Form B1 510?   Yes ☐   No ☐

If a notifiable injury have you

1. Phoned the Health and Safety Executive   Yes ☐ No ☐

2. Completed Form F2 508 (Rev 1/86) and sent it to the Health and Safety Executive   Yes ☐ No ☐

ENSURE ALL COPIES ARE LEGIBLE

15 If taken to hospital say which and whether as an "in" or "out" patient

16 The Information contained on this form is correct as far as I am awa

....   Tel No. ....

Signature of Officer-in-Charge   Ext. ....

....

Designation   Date

This copy should be forwarded to the COUNTY TREASURER (Insurance Section) who must also be notified immediately the Employee returns to w

▲ *Accident report form*

234

The personnel function does not end with the selection and employment of staff. Once staff are recruited it is up to personnel to ensure that their welfare is looked after in order that they become part of a happy, well-motivated workforce. The advantage to the company is that if the workforce feel that they are cared for they usually work better.

ACTIVITY

What do you think it is important for a company to provide? Discuss this with your group and check your answers over the next few pages.

Welfare is a term that often conjures up 'tea and sympathy'. Personnel will perform this task, but it also has a wider function.

Canteen facilities, sport and social clubs, cleanliness and staff facilities, preparing people for retirement are all likely to come under the welfare policy of a company. Sickness and sickness benefit, again are matters for personnel and in the case of long term or terminal illness the company may well look into the welfare of the employee's family, advising them on rights, state benefits, etc. especially where the sickness causes hardship in families.

Health and safety is, or should be, taken very seriously by companies and it is personnel's job to ensure Health and Safety laws are strictly carried out. If somebody has an accident at work then personnel will ensure they fill out an accident report form (see page 234). These must be filed in case of any insurance claim and analysed in case the company is in any way liable.

ACTIVITY

Obtain a copy of an accident report form from your company or place of study. Many incidents which require you to fill in an accident report form are, on the surface, quite minor. It is the sum of the incidents or the later, unforseen effects which can give concern to the company.

Imagine that you have cut your hand (but not deeply) on a sharp piece of metal sticking out from a door. On closer investigation you notice that it is part of the door push that has become slightly bent. Fill in the accident report form. You will have to make up the date, time, etc. Why do you think you should report this? What complications could follow? Any complications may take some time to occur – days, weeks or even months.

Holiday can also be the business of welfare. Holiday entitlement will be mentioned in conditions of service, and it is often personnel who will draw up rosters to ensure that not everyone in the company goes away at the same time.

ACTIVITY

Using your group as a resource find out when their holidays are booked for (Christmas, Easter or summer). If you were all working in an office would the office be staffed for the whole year, excluding Public Holidays? Draw up a roster which ensures that it would be. If somebody has to move their holiday how do you think it would be best to approach them? What basis would you use to give someone their choice – seniority, first come first served, etc.?

Staff appraisals and reviews

More and more companies are holding staff appraisals as a means of informing employees where they stand and to give employees an opportunity to discuss how they think they are doing. These appraisals will normally note how well a person is doing and point out any particular skills that the company feel they are developing. They will also note where there is a short fall and goals will be set for the next appraisal. Where necessary, training will normally be arranged. Staff appraisal can reflect the employee's ambitions and get them ready for their next career move or promotion.

---/ **ACTIVITY** /─────────────────────────────────

At your work place or work experience find out what training is available for someone working there.

14

Paying the wages

Summary

This chapter looks at the work of the wages department. You are introduced to this by an assignment and activities which take you through the process of calculating wages and salaries. The following topics are covered:

- Hours of work, time cards
- Gross and nett wages
- Deductions
- Pay slips
- Averages
- Spreadsheets
- Processing expenses

This chapter will help you to achieve the following outcomes:

Core Module 2   Administration Systems and Procedures
   Outcome 2.3   Produce documents and material and process data

Core Module 3   Business Resources and Procedures
   Outcome 3.3   Record financial transactions

Core Module 4   People in Business
   Outcome 4.3   Examine and compare the main job roles in different organisations
   Outcome 4.4   Contribute to achievement of organisational goals by fulfilling job role

The assignment and related activities can be used to cover the following performance criteria.

2.1d	business records managed using a simple database
2.3a	business documents produced using a word processing package
2.3b	information processing equipment used to run standard applications
2.3c	data examined and analysed using a spreadsheet package
2.3d	copies of original documents produced using reprographic equipment
3.3a	flow of money in the organisation charted and explained
3.3b	recording documents and systems identified and their purpose described
3.3c	correct systems and documents or files chosen or accessed
3.3d	information recorded neatly and accurately
3.3e	necessary calculations made accurately
3.3f	recording and calculations checked for accuracy
4.1b	the nature of work examined and different types compared
4.1d	different work cultures identified and their importance assessed
4.3a	functional areas within organisations identified
4.3b	job roles in different functional areas of organisations identified
4.3c	job roles compared
4.4a	relationship between organisational objectives and job role identified
4.4b	given tasks completed to agreed criteria
4.4c	contribution made both as an individual and as a member of a team to the achievement of agreed targets and goals

The assignment will help with the development of Common Skills, especially the following:

Managing and Developing Self
Outcome 1   Manage own roles and responsibilities
Outcome 2   Manage own time in achieving objectives

Applying Numeracy
Outcome 15   Apply numerical skills and techniques

Applying Technology
Outcome 16   Use a range of technological equipment and systems

Read the following assignment to help you to understand some of the things you should be able to do by the end of the chapter. Normally it will be best to read the chapter and carry out the set activities before you tackle the assignment.

Check whether you can do the assignment on your own or with one or more colleagues. Some assignments will require organising by your tutor. Seek guidance, where needed, from your tutor.

Assignment

You work as a wages clerk in the small but busy personnel department of P.T.R. Travel.

▸ At P.T.R. the workers are all aged 18 plus. They pay national insurance at the standard rate.
▸ The standard working week is 35 hours. The hours are 0900–1700 Monday–Friday. One hour per day is allowed for meals – this is not paid.
▸ The overtime rate is time and a half Monday–Friday, with double time for Saturday or Sunday working.
▸ Workers can be up to 10 minutes late in total for the whole week without stoppages being made. If workers are between 11 minutes and 30 minutes late during the week 30 minutes is deducted from wages.
▸ Union dues are 90p per week for all employees.
▸ D. Blott and L. Alonso save £2.50 per week.
  B. Cook and F. Patel save £3.30 per week.

Task 1   Fill in the time cards for each employee.

Task 2   Calculate basic wages, overtime and gross pay for each employee.

Task 3   Transfer this information to the payroll.

Task 4   Calculate the deductions for each employee. Enter the information on the payroll. Your section head will have tax tables you can use and the current rates of national insurance.

Task 5   Calculate net pay for each person.

Task 6   Fill in a P11 for each employee.

Task 7   Complete a note and coin analysis for each employee and show the total weekly requirement.

Task 8   Complete a pay slip for each employee.

Task 9   Complete a P45 for C. Renton who leaves at the end of week 1.

Task 10   Write a memo to your section head explaining why it might be a good idea to pay employees monthly by cheque.

PAY No.:			
NAME:			
Dept:			

DAY	IN	OUT	TOTAL
a.m. MON p.m.			
a.m. TUE p.m.			
a.m. WED p.m.			
a.m. THU p.m.			
a.m. FRI p.m.			
a.m. SAT p.m.			
a.m. SUN p.m.			

▲ Time card front

Week ending	
Hours clocked	
Hourly Rate	
Total	

Shift hours clocked			
Shift rate			
Shift adjustment			

		x 1½	x 2
Overtime clocked			
Overtime rate			
Overtime adjustment			
TOTAL THIS WEEK			

▲ Time card back

Name		Dept.	No.	
Payments				

		Week No.		
Tax code			Week ending	

Hrs. Worked	Hrly. Rate	Basic Wage	Overtime OT x 1½	x 2	GROSS PAY

DEDUCTIONS				
Inc. Tax	Nat. Ins.	Pension	Savings	Loan
Social	Union Subs.	Rent	Total Deds.	NET PAY

▲ Pay slip

Week No. 1

Week ending ....

No.	Name	Monday		Tuesday		Wednesday		Thursday		Friday		Saturday		Sunday		Grade
		IN	OUT	IN	OUT	IN	OUT	IN	OUT	IN	OUT	IN	OUT	IN	OUT	
19	C Renton	0901	1700	0902	1700	0900	1900	0910	1700	0900	1701	0900	1200	—	—	TA
24	B Cook	0900	1700	0900	1701	0905	1701	0900	1730	0900	1800	—	—	—	—	TA
27	M Peters	0900	1700	0900	1700	0902	1700	0907	1730	0900	1700	—	—	0900	1200	TX
36	D Blott	0859	1701	0901	1700	0905	1700	0900	1730	0900	1700	0900	1200	—	—	TY
37	D Ling	0858	1701	0900	1815	0901	1700	0900	1730	0900	1700	0900	1200	—	—	TX
38	F Patel	0901	1702	0900	1830	0903	1700	0900	1730	0900	1800	—	—	0900	1200	TZ
40	L Alonso	0900	1830	0902	1700	0900	1701	0901	1731	0900	1700	—	—	0900	1200	TY
41	J McCross	0903	1800	0901	1700	0901	1701	0902	1730	0901	1700	—	—	—	—	TZ

Notes: Rates per hour depend on staff grades for each job

TA = £2.40
TX = £3.50
TY = £5.10
TZ = £5.50

▲ *P.T.R. Travel clock in and clock out times*

P.T.R. Travel

Week No. ....   Week ending ....

| Payroll | | Payments | | | | | Deductions | | | | | | | | |
No.	Name	Hour rate	Basic pay	OT	SSP SMP	Gross pay	Nat. Ins.	PAYE tax	Save	Union subs	Tax code	Total ded.	Net Pay	E Nat. Ins.

▲ *Payroll*

241

P.T.R. Travel Ltd.
Maine Road – Nottingham
Employee Records

Name	Tax Code	Pay No.	Date of Birth	N.I. No.
C Renton	215L	0019	9.12.72	ZY.15.15.15C
B Cook	330L	0024	8.11.70	JM.12.19.27A
M Peters	175L	0027	3. 6.70	PY.80.80.70C
D Blott	300L	0036	1. 3.69	LZ.12.24.48C
D Ling	150L	0037	11. 4.71	CU.18.16.32A
F Patel	200L	0038	12.11.73	UR.12.09.09C
L Alonso	185L	0040	8. 8.60	PT.12.39.12D
J McCross	280L	0041	1. 5.65	XC.30.59.85C

Extra information for Colin Renton

Private Address   1 Advance Drive
                        LIBANUS
Date of leaving   5/4/92

▲ Employee records

Note/coin analysis sheet

Name	£50	£20	£10	£5	£1	50p	20p	10p	5p	2p	1p	Total
Total												

▲ Note/coin analysis sheet

Wages and the payroll

By working through this chapter you will be able to:

- Process documents for wages and salaries.
- Process direct payment of wages and salaries.

- Process expenses claims for payment.

The difference between wages and salaries

Wages are payments made in return for work. They are paid hourly, daily or weekly in cash, usually to manual workers. Salaries are fixed payments made to non-manual workers, such as professional or office staff. They are often paid monthly.

A typical working week in the payroll section

The **payroll** is either the list of employees, showing the gross and net wage to be paid, or it can be the total amount of money to be paid to workers.

Wages are paid traditionally on a Friday – payday – one week after the work was done. For example, the wage paid on 13.11.92 is for the week ending 6.11.92. A typical working week in the payroll section of a company is as follows:

- **Monday**
  Correct any mistakes made the previous Friday.
  Record any weekend overtime.
  Enter clock on times on to payroll sheets.
- **Tuesday**
  Enter clock on and clock off times for each employee.
- **Wednesday**
  Complete calculations for gross and net wages for each employee.
  Do cash analysis and inform bank.
- **Thursday**
  Obtain cash and make up pay packets.
- **Friday**
  Pay staff.
  Correct mistakes where possible.

Wages and salaries

Every new employee will receive a wage or payment for the work they do. The money may be paid as cash or by cheque. It could be paid directly into a bank or building society account. This process is called credit transfer. Wages may be paid weekly or monthly.

/ **ACTIVITY** /──────────────────────────────

Carry out a small survey of how people are paid. Each person in the group must ask five people (not in their group) how they are paid. What can you say about your results?

In Britain, most people still prefer to be paid in cash. Can you say why? Do your figures show this? Can you say why or why not?

Work – arrival and departure

Most employees, when they start work each day, must 'clock-in' or 'clock-on'. That is, they must record or show their time of arrival. This can be done in several ways, for example:

- By putting a card into a machine which stamps or prints on the time. Each worker has their own time card with their name and pay number.
- By signing a book and noting the time of arrival.
- By keying in or inputing a personal pay number directly into a computer when you are ready for work. This is done by pressing 'in' or 'enter' on the machine, then keying in the personal pay number. The information will be used later to work out the employees pay.

Employees must also record when they leave work. This is called 'clocking-off' or 'clocking-out'.

Once this is done, the organisation will have a permanent record of the number of hours an employee worked that day. An employee must do this every day. The company will use this information to calculate the weekly hours worked. From these figures the weekly wage can be determined.

Never clock-in or clock-out for anyone else. This is a very serious offence.

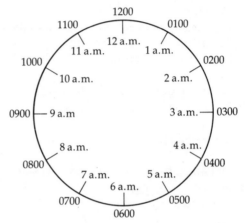

Getting to work on time – up to 12 noon (midday)

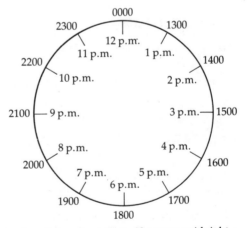

Leaving work on time – 12 noon to midnight

▲ *The 24-hour clock*

/ **ACTIVITY** /

1 Find out from your friends and/or relatives whether they have to clock-in and clock-out their employment each day. Make a group list of jobs where this is not done, e.g. teach Suggest reasons for the differences.

2 What time do workers arrive and leave? Fill in the missing times.

12 hour clock	24 hour clock
6.30 p.m.	1830
9.00 a.m.	0900
4.15 p.m.	1615
?	1921
?	0806
?	1310
11.16 p.m.	?
11.06 a.m.	?
12.20 p.m.	?
?	2015
?	0327

Working in the wages department

If you work in the wages section of a company, these are the types of task you could do:

- Keep details of employees holiday leave.
- Keep a record of sickness and absence.
- Calculate and check hours worked and any overtime.
- Make up pay packets.
- Calculate gross and net pay.

Interpretation of pay slips

The pay slip given to employees is the document which records how much money they are paid. It shows how the wage is calculated and what deductions or 'stoppages' are made. It will be either inside the pay packet or printed on the front cover of the pay packet.

Wage earners can be paid weekly or monthly. They can be paid either:

1 A rate per hour for a set number of hours, with higher rates for overtime (hours worked above an agreed minimum).
2 A basic wage each week, e.g. £120.00 with a bonus or extra pay for producing more goods or completing a job quickly.
3 A basic wage plus a commission, or extra money which can be earned, e.g. for selling more than a set amount.

What the terms on a pay slip mean

Payments
Basic Wage The minimum amount of money. It does not include overtime. No deductions have been made. Nothing has yet been taken away or added.

OT at 1½ or OT × 1½ Overtime at time-and-a-half. Overtime is extra hours worked at a higher rate of pay. Here the pay is the normal hourly rate plus one half of the hourly rate. For example, if the rate per hour was £3.00, then OT at 1½ would be £3.00 + £1.50 (the half) = £4.50 per hour.

OT at 2 or OT × 2 Overtime at twice the hourly rate, that is 'double time'. If the hourly rate is £3.00 then double time would be £3.00 + £3.00 = £6 per hour. Overtime is only paid if employees work more than their normal hours, e.g. if daytime workers work an

Name			Dept.		Clock No.	
Payments						
Tax code			Week No.			
					Week ending	
Hrs. Worked	Hrly. Rate		Basic Wage	Overtime OT x 1½	x 2	GROSS PAY
DEDUCTIONS						
Inc. Tax	Nat. Ins.		Pension	Savings		Loan
Social	Union Subs.		Rent	Total Deds.		NET PAY

▲ Pay slip

evening. People who work shifts such as 2 p.m.–10 p.m. (afternoon shift), 10 p.m.–6 a.m. (night shift), 6 a.m.–2 p.m. (morning shift), get overtime if, for example, they work an extra shift.

Gross wage or gross pay   The total of the basic wage plus any overtime, bonus or commission.

Gross wage = Basic wage + Overtime + Bonuses + Commission

Statutory or compulsory deductions

Nat. Ins. or NI   National insurance is the employee's contribution to the government This will help pay for any future benefits an employee may get such as unemploymen benefit.

TAX or PAYE pay as you earn   This is the employee's payment to the Inland Revenue o tax collecting authority. Everyone in a regular job is liable to pay income tax. The amoun someone pays depends on their tax code.

Total deductions   The sum of all deductions.

Net wage   The 'take home' pay. This is the amount of money received by the employee

Net wage = Gross wage − Total Deductions

Voluntary deductions

Voluntary deductions are deductions or stoppages which are decided by the employe They are not required by law, that is they are not statutory deductions. Tax and insuran are statutory, they are required by law. The employer must make the statuto deductions.

Examples of voluntary deductions from pay:

1 **Trade union subs**   Employees who belong to a trade union can pay the yearly su scription or amount by regular deductions from their wages. 'Sub' is short for s scription.

2 **Pension**   All employees aged 18 and over have to make contributions to a pension scheme. Three types are available, which are run by the government, the employer (sometimes called an occupational pension scheme), or a private pension company chosen by the employee.

3 **Social activities**   A deduction which pays for sports and social clubs often run by larger organisations.

4 **Savings**   Where the employee's pay is deducted to enable them to save.

5 **Board and lodging**   A deduction made when the employer provides accommodation for employees. Rent can also be deducted in this way.

6 **Loan repayments**   Companies often provide loans to their employees with repayments being made through direct deductions from pay, e.g. loans may be made to purchase annual season tickets for travel.

National insurance contributions

Employers pay national insurance for all employees aged 16 and over who earn more than the lower earnings limit which is currently £52.00 per week gross (Sept. 1991).

Table 14.1   National insurance contributions

| | Employee Contribution | | Table B | Table C | Employer Contribution Tables A, B, C |
	Table A On first £52 a week or £226 a month	On earnings over £52 a week or £226 a month			
£52 to £84.99 weekly or £226 to £368.99 monthly	2%	9%	3.85%	Nil	4.6%
£85 to £129.99 weekly or £369 to £563.99 monthly	2%	9%	3.85%	Nil	6.6%
£130 to £184.99 weekly or £564 to £801.99 monthly	2%	9%	3.85%	Nil	8.6%
£185 to £390 weekly or £802 to £1690 monthly	2%	9%	3.85%	Nil	10.4%
Over £390 weekly **or** over £1690 monthly	2%	9% Up to £390 a week or £1690 a month	3.85% Up to £390 a week or £1690 a month	Nil	10.4%
Column 1	**Column 2**	**Column 3**	**Column 4**	**Column 5**	**Column 6**

All the figures in Columns 2–6 of Table 14.1 above are percentages of an employee's gross earnings.

Tables A, B and C are the amounts employees pay.

▸ Table A (Columns 2 and 3) shows the standard rate for workers aged 16 plus and below pension age (currently 60 for women and 65 for men).
▸ Table B (Column 4) is the reduced rate payable by married women and widows.
▸ Table C (Column 5) is either for those employees over pension age, or those who pay elsewhere (that is who do not pay).

The employer's contribution is shown in Column 6 of Table 14.1.

The national insurance payable is based on the employees gross pay which includes basic wages plus overtime.

Example – How national insurance is worked out

An employee earns £1300 a month gross pay, and pays NI at the standard rate. This is shown in Row 4 of Column 1 of Table 14.1 between £802–£1690 monthly.

The employee pays 2% on the first £226 per month (Column 2)

$$2\% \text{ of } £226 = £4.52$$

... then pays 9% (Column 3) on the remainder which is £1300 − £226 = £1074

$$9\% \text{ of } £1074 = £96.66$$

Therefore total NI payable = £4.52 + £96.66 = £101.18

The employer pays 10.4% (Column 6) on earnings of £1300

10.4% of £1300 = £135.20

Form P11

National insurance contribution information is recorded on a form P11, the Deductions Working Sheet. It is used for weekly or monthly records. One of these forms must be completed for every employee.

Deductions Working Sheet P11	Year to 5 April 19

Employer's name *PTR Travel* Tax District and reference	Complete only for occupational pension schemes newly contracted-out since1 January 1986. Scheme contracted-out number S 4

National Insurance Contributions *

Earnings on which employee's contributions payable 1a	Total of employee's and employer's contributions payable 1b	Employee's contributions payable 1c	Earnings on which employee's contributions at contracted-out rate payable included in column 1a 1d	Employee's contributions at contracted-out rate included in column 1c 1e	Statutory Sick Pay in the week or month included in column 2 1f	Statutory Maternity Pay in the week or month included in column 2 1g	Month no
£ *1300*	£ *236* | *38*	£ *101* | *18*	£	£	£	£	6 April to 5 May **1**
							6 May to 5 June **2**

▲ *Form P11*

- Column 1a shows the gross pay or total earnings per month, for our example this is £130⬚
- Column 1b is for recording the total contribution made by the employee (£101.18) a⬚ employer (£135.20). This is £101.18 + £135.20 = £236.38.
- Column 1c records the employees' payment (£101.18).
- Column 1f shows SSP or statutory sick pay. Employers must pay SSP to the majority ⬚ employees aged 16 plus, providing they have been off sick for a minimum of f⬚ consecutive days.
- Column 1g is for recording SMP or statutory maternity pay. The employer will send ⬚ national insurance and income tax due from employees on maternity leave to the Inl⬚ Revenue accounts office each month using Inland Revenue paying-in slips.

Form P14

Form P14 is completed by the employer at the end of the year. It shows the gross pay, National Insurance and income tax deductions for each employee for a year.

(**Source:** Social Security Quick Guide to National Insurance, Statutory Sick Pay, Statutory Maternity Pay, from 6th April 1991.)

Statutory forms

P60

An employer must send all employees the form P60 at the end of each financial year. The financial year runs from April 6th 199X to April 5th of the following calendar year. The P60 shows the amount of tax which the employer has deducted from the employees gross pay.

Form P45

This form is issued by an employer when an employee changes jobs. It shows the employee's:

- PAYE reference.
- National Insurance number.
- Surname and forenames.
- Date of leaving.
- Tax code.
- Last entries on deductions working sheet.
- Pay number.
- Employee's private address.
- Name and address of employer.
- Instructions to deal with the form.

Prompt completion of this form will help the new employer fix the level of tax which needs to be paid by a new employee.

Calculating gross wages

The time card below shows the hours worked during a week by A Meeson.

A Meeson has one hour for lunch on Monday to Friday. This is unpaid. Any overtime between Monday and Friday is paid at time-and-a-half. Any overtime on Saturday or Sunday is paid at double time. The normal working week is 0830–1730 Monday to Friday. Employees are deducted 15 minutes worth of pay if they are late during the week, e.g. 0–14 minutes late – 15 minutes is deducted, 16–30 minutes late – 30 minutes is deducted.

Steps in calculating gross pay.

1 Find the standard hours worked.
2 Find the overtime hours worked.
3 Multiply the hours worked by the appropriate rate per hour.

Example
Calculate the hours worked from the time card.

Hours worked at normal rate
= Mon. 7 hours + Tues. 7 hours + Wed. 7 hours + Thur. 7 hours + Fri. 7 hours
= 35 hours

<table>
<tr><td colspan="4">Clock No.: **3789**
Dept: **SALES**</td></tr>
<tr><td>DAY</td><td>IN</td><td>OUT</td><td>TOTAL</td></tr>
<tr><td>a.m.
MON</td><td>0830</td><td></td><td></td></tr>
<tr><td>p.m.</td><td></td><td>1730</td><td>7</td></tr>
<tr><td>a.m.
TUE</td><td>0830</td><td></td><td></td></tr>
<tr><td>p.m.</td><td></td><td>17·30</td><td>7</td></tr>
<tr><td>a.m.
WED</td><td>0832</td><td></td><td></td></tr>
<tr><td>p.m.</td><td></td><td>1731</td><td>7</td></tr>
<tr><td>a.m.
THU</td><td>0830</td><td></td><td></td></tr>
<tr><td>p.m.</td><td></td><td>1750</td><td>7</td></tr>
<tr><td>a.m.
FRI</td><td>0831</td><td></td><td></td></tr>
<tr><td>p.m.</td><td></td><td>1900</td><td>8½</td></tr>
<tr><td>a.m.
SAT</td><td>0830</td><td></td><td></td></tr>
<tr><td>p.m.</td><td></td><td>1300</td><td>4½</td></tr>
<tr><td>a.m.
SUN</td><td>0831</td><td></td><td></td></tr>
<tr><td>p.m.</td><td></td><td>1200</td><td>3½</td></tr>
</table>

Week ending **3.10.9X**
Hours clocked **35**
Hourly Rate **£4**
Total **£140**

Shift hours clocked
Shift rate
Shift adjustment

	×1½	×2
Overtime clocked	1½	8
Overtime rate	£6	£8
Overtime adjustment	£9	£64
Total this week **£213**		

▲ Pay slip for A Meeson

Overtime hours worked at time-plus-a-half (these are overtime hours worked betwee
Monday–Friday).
Looking at the time card, A Meeson worked 1½ hours extra on Friday evening, i.e. h
worked 1½ hours at OT × 1½.

Overtime hours worked at double time (these are only hours worked on Saturday
Sunday). A Meeson worked: 4½ hours on Saturday and 3½ hours on Sunday, i.e.
worked a total of 8 hours at OT × 2.

Total hours worked by A Meeson:
35 hours at normal rate of pay
1½ hours at OT × 1½
8 hours at OT × 2

A Meeson earns £4.00 per hour as the standard/normal/basic rate of pay. Therefore
overtime rates are:

- Time-and-a-half = £4.00 + £2.00 = £6.00
- Double time = £4.00 × 2 = £8.00

Therefore A Meeson's gross wage is

35 hours at £4.00 per hour	= 35 × £4.00	= £140.00
1½ hours at £6.00 per hour	= 1½ × £6.00	= £ 9.00
8 hours at £8.00 per hour	= 8 × £8.00	= £ 64.00
	Total	= £213.00

The time cards for three employees are shown below.

a) Find the overtime at × 1½ (time and a half) and ×2 (double time). The rate per hour is £3.92.
b) Enter the times details on to the overtime sheet.
c) A further four employees were called in on Saturday and Sunday only, to repair the Central Heating system. Enter their details on the overtime sheet.

	Saturday		Sunday	
	In	Out	In	Out
N Southern	0700	1530	0700	1300
P Field	0700	1615	0700	1245
F Grimaldou	0700	1600	0700	1315
J Krakov	0700	1545	0700	1300

Clock No.: **0459**
NAME: **Z. GROLSCH**
Dept: **ENG.**

DAY	IN	OUT	TOTAL
a.m. MON	0500		
p.m.		1600	
a.m. TUE	0800		
p.m.		1700	
a.m. WED	0800		
p.m.		1600	
a.m. THU	0800		
p.m.		2115	
a.m. FRI	0800		
p.m.		2100	
a.m. SAT	0800	1200	
p.m.			
a.m. SUN	0800	1200	
p.m.			

Clock No.: **0786**
NAME: **M. OLUBO**
Dept: **ENG.**

DAY	IN	OUT	TOTAL
a.m. MON	0500		
p.m.		1615	
a.m. TUE	0800		
p.m.		1730	
a.m. WED	0800		
p.m.		1745	
a.m. THU	0800		
p.m.		1815	
a.m. FRI	0800		
p.m.		1600	
a.m. SAT	0830	1030	
p.m.			
a.m. SUN	0830	1130	
p.m.			

Clock No.: **0016**
NAME: **P. HONG**
Dept: **ENG.**

DAY	IN	OUT	TOTAL
a.m. MON	0500		
p.m.		1630	
a.m. TUE	0800		
p.m.		1600	
a.m. WED	0800		
p.m.		2130	
a.m. THU	0800		
p.m.		1600	
a.m. FRI	0800		
p.m.		1630	
a.m. SAT			
p.m.			
a.m. SUN	1130		
p.m.		1930	

Overtime Sheet

Maintenance
Section Head Signature

Name	Reason for overtime	Dates Worked	Hours @ 1½	Hours @ 2	1½ Rate	1½ Total	X2 Rate	X2 Total	Total to pay

1½ (time and half) payable for hours between 6.00a.m. Monday and 12 midday Saturday.
2 (double time) payable for hours between midday Saturday and 6 a.m. Monday and public holidays.
Overtime is only paid for hours worked outside normal hours 0800–1600 Mon–Fri.

Approved

Date

Direct payment of wages and salaries

Wages are paid in cash; salaries by cheque. This is the last part of an administrative process which began with:

- Workers clocking in and out each day.
- Daily and weekly hours being totalled.
- Gross and net wages being calculated.

The final stage is to obtain the cash from the bank and to make up the wage packets. The amount of coins and notes needed each week depends on the net wages to be paid to the employees. For example, in a small firm, four employees are to receive these wages:

A North	£173.26
B South	£142.33
C East	£215.15
D West	£72.67

What coins and notes are needed to make up their four wage packets? To find this out we need to do a note and coin analysis for each employee. These analyses can then be totalled to find the amount of notes and coins needed to pay all four workers.

The total wages = £603.41, but if you collected 12 × £50 notes, 3 × £1 coins, 2 × 20p coins and 1 × 1p coin from the bank you would not be able to make up the four separate wage packets. For example to make up A North's wage packet you need:

$$
\begin{aligned}
3 \times £50 \text{ notes} &= £150 \\
1 \times £20 \text{ notes} &= £20 \\
3 \times £1 \text{ coins} &= £3 \\
1 \times 20\text{p coins} &= £0.20 \\
1 \times 5\text{p coins} &= £0.05 \\
1 \times 1\text{p coins} &= \underline{£0.01} \\
& \ 173.26
\end{aligned}
$$

These are the notes and coins that would be put into A North's pay packet and hence would need collecting from the bank along with the other coins and notes needed to make up the remaining three pay packets.

Note/coin analysis sheet												
Name	£50	£20	£10	£5	£1	50p	20p	10p	5p	2p	1p	Total
A. North	3	1			3				1		1	173.26
B. South	2	2			2		1	1		1	1	142.33
C. East	4		1	1				1	1			215.15
D. West	1	1			2	1		1	1	1		72.67
Total	10	4	1	1	7	1	2	3	3	2	2	603.41

▲ Note/coin analysis sheet

Once the total cash needs have been worked out, the money can be collected from the bank. This could be done by someone from the organisation, however, there are risks. Whenever you carry money there is always a danger of theft. If you collect or move money regularly, always vary the time, day, route, method, etc. Many companies today hire security firms to move money if large sums are involved.

──/ **ACTIVITY** /──────────────────────────────────────

Name	Week 1(£)	Week 2(£)	Week 3(£)	Week 4(£)	Pay No.
G Parkhouse	156.23	165.32	161.14	161.14	013
R Lindwall	175.29	157.21	170.21	157.21	015
A Barrelto	186.50	188.60	187.70	188.60	016
S Badawi	202.13	198.20	200.02	198.20	020
L White	85.15	170.16	170.16	175.25	021
J Bishop	193.20	180.20	185.42	193.20	027
M Tyson	210.33	202.33	202.30	210.33	028
P Valentine	250.74	248.60	248.60	248.60	030
K Omar	178.20	176.20	176.20	176.20	035
L Jones	178.20	190.30	188.33	189.00	036
F Da Silva	201.00	201.00	201.00	201.00	037
Z Newbould	152.21	152.21	152.21	159.00	040
M McKenzie	161.90	165.04	164.29	165.04	046
F Sawyer	185.84	180.84	182.72	182.72	047
P Francis	130.13	140.21	145.52	145.00	050
A Minor	200.76	202.70	201.60	201.60	051
F Parks	179.99	181.90	180.00	179.99	057
L Olufi	120.20	130.42	130.42	130.42	058
N Ng	150.31	155.20	154.75	180.88	059
P Ling	176.29	176.29	176.29	195.00	060

You work in the wages department of a small company employing 20 people, who are paid weekly in cash. Their wages are shown over a four week period. Work out the notes and coins needed each week to pay each employee. Show these on a note/coin analysis sheet. Also show the total weekly requirement for each week.

Three kinds of average

An average is a typical or normal amount, e.g. average contents of matchbox = 40 matches.

The mean or arithmetic mean

To find the mean, work out the total or sum of the values of all the items and then divide by the number of items.

$$\text{Mean} = \frac{\text{Total of items}}{\text{number of items}}$$

For example, what is the mean value of orders if a salesperson obtained these orders over seven days:

£157.00   £167.00   £157.00   £149.00   £152.00   £154.00   £135.00

$$\therefore \text{Mean value of orders} = \frac{157.00 + 167.00 + 157.00 + 149.00 + 152.00 + 154.00 + 135.00}{7 \text{ (number of items or days)}}$$

$$= \frac{1071.00}{7}$$

$$= £153.00$$

To calculate the mean, all the values have to be included, so it can be affected by extreme high or low values (work out what would happen if sales were £969.00 on the eighth day. Notice that the salesperson did not obtain £153.00 of orders on any of the seven days – the figure is an approximation.

The median

When all the items are placed in ascending or descending order (from the highest to the lowest or from the lowest to the highest) the middle value is called the median.

£135.00   £149.00   £152.00   £154.00   £157.00   £157.00   £167.00

Lowest value   Median (middle) value   Highest value

The median is £154.00 in this example. As it is the middle value it tells us that as many of the order values are greater than £154.00 as are less.

The mode

This is the most fashionable or popular value. The mode is the value which occurs most frequently.

£135.00   £149.00   £152.00   £154.00   £157.00   £157.00   £167.00

In our example the mode is £157 because it appears most frequently.

To summarise for our example:

▸ Mean order value = £153.00
▸ Median order value = £154.00
▸ Mode order value = £157.00

All the answers are averages and they are all correct. Because using a different average in a calculation can give you a different answer it is very important to say which average you are using.

—⟋ ACTIVITY ⟍**Averages** **Averages** ————————————

Find the arithmetic mean and the median of the wages shown for weeks 1, 2, 3, and 4 in the activity on p. 255.

Note
When there are an even number of items, use this formula to find when the median value occurs:

$$\text{Median occurs at } \frac{\text{Number of items} + 1}{2}$$

So, if the number of items is 20, median occurs at:

$$\frac{20 + 1}{2} = \frac{21}{2} = 10\frac{1}{2} \text{ items}$$

This means that the median is the value that falls between the 10th and 11th items, i.e. it is the arithmetic mean of the 10th and 11th items and again for eight items:

$$\frac{8 + 1}{2} = \frac{9}{2} = 4\frac{1}{2} \text{ items}$$

Therefore the median is the average of the 4th and 5th items.

Using a computer program to calculate wages

How a spreadsheet works

Spreadsheets are computer software packages. On the computer screen they appear as a series of columns and rows. You will only see and can only use a small number of rows and columns at any one time. This is what you can see on the screen. It is called a window of the whole spreadsheet.

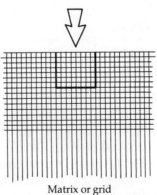

Matrix or grid

	Col 1 A	Col 2 B	Col 3 C	Col 4 D	Col 5 E	Col 6 F
Either or						
Row 1				N		
Row 2		X				
Row 3			CELL.			Y
Row 4	M					

▲ *The spreadsheet is a series of rows and columns*

The square or block where a row meets a column is called a **cell**. Each of these cells can be pinpointed or located by using the row and column numbers. For example in the diagram above, the cell 'X' can be identified as Column 2, Row 2 and the cell 'Y' by Column 6, Row 3. If the columns are headed with letters rather than numbers, then cell 'M' would be identified by Column A, Row 4 which is written as A4. Using the same method the cell 'N' would be identified as D1.

Any of the cells can be called up and viewed on the screen. Information can be put into each cell separately. A cell can have three types of information in it:

● Written words or letters.
● Numbers.
● A formula or instruction.

An example of a spreadsheet for wages

R1	Col	Col	Col	Col	Col	Col	Col
R2	1	2	3	4	5	6	7
R3		Number	Basic	Total	OT at	Ot at	Total
R4		of	hourly		x1 ½	x2	
R5	Name	hours	rate				
R6							
R7	C Abel						
R8	M Bull						
R 9	L Calne						
R10	C Davies						
R11	F Dawes						

Steps

1 Load the spreadsheet software.
2 Once it is loaded there should be a matrix or grid of rows and columns on screen.
3 A cell is identified by its row and column numbers, so R10C3 is Row 10 Column. This is the **address** of the cell. (The cell address can consist of a combination of letters and numbers as described above, e.g. A9 is Column A, Row 9.)

4 Move the cursor – the highlighted cell or white square – to the cell you want. You can move the cursor using the keys with arrows on the computer or by using a mouse or electronic pad linked to the computer. For this example we want the cell R5C2. Key in HOURS. Press ENTER. This command transfers the information which has been keyed in to the computer memory. (On some spreadsheets you will need to put inverted commas or quotes before and after the word you want to enter. Check in the manual for your spreadsheet to see if you have to do this.)

5 Move the cursor to R5C3. Key in RATE. Press ENTER.

6 Move the cursor to R5C4. Key in TOTAL. Press ENTER.

7 Move the cursor to R6C4. This time we need to put in a formula which will give us the total wage. We know how to find this figure, Total basic wage = Hours × Rate. Enter R5C2 × R5C3. This means that the figure for hours will be multiplied by the figure for the rate.

8 The position so far:

	C1	C2	C3	C4
Row 1				
Row 2				
Row 3				
Row 4				
Row 5		Hours	Rate	Total
Row 6				R5C2 x R5C3

9 Move the cursor to R6C3 and put in a number figure for the hourly rate, e.g. use 3 for a rate of pay of £3.00 per hour. Press ENTER.

10 Move the cursor to R6C2 and put in a figure for the number of hours, e.g. 40. Press ENTER.

11 You should get an answer for the total basic wage in R6C4. (If you have used the same figures as above the answer should be 120.)

This is a straightforward example of how a spreadsheet package might work. What could be done next?

● Further rows could be added for other employees. It is always easier to input data by working down the columns.

● Extra columns could be added to show the overtime hours and rate. Formulae will have to be put in to make the calculations.

● It could now be made more attractive by using the format command.

Advantages of using a spreadsheet

Using a spreadsheet program to calculate wages has many advantages:

1 Once the data has been put in, employees' wages can be calculated very quickly.

2 Considerable time is saved.

3 It is efficient and accurate. This of course depends on the data input being correct. If it is correct, the computer should not make any mistakes. (There is a saying about computers: garbage in, garbage out.)

4 Very large amounts of information can be stored.

5 It can be updated quickly.

6 The same program can also deal with deductions from the gross wage – Net pay can then be calculated.

Processing expense claims for payment

An expense is money which is spent by an employee while doing a job for the employer. Managers in an organisation sometimes have an expense account. This is a system by which the employees expenses are paid for by the employer. Here are some examples of expenses which could be paid for by the employer:

- Entertaining customers.
- Travelling to meet customers or sell goods.
- Petrol for a car used on company business.
- Clothing used for doing a job.

All organisations will have rules about expenses. These will deal with:

- What types of expenses are allowed.
- Who can claim expenses.
- How much can be claimed in expenses.
- Who can agree the expenses.

Below is the list of rules applied by BTEC, the Business and Technician Education Council to its moderators' expense claims. (The moderator is the person who looks after your course for BTEC. Moderators can only claim expenses whilst working for BTEC.)

1 All expenses claims must be signed.
2 Claims must be sent in no later than two weeks after a visit is made to a centre. (You should see your moderator at least once.)
3 Receipts must be attached to any claim (this is to prove that a payment has been made e.g. hotel bills, rail tickets, meals costing more than £10.
4 Please remember the need for economy in the interest of students.
5 Car mileage can be claimed at current rates.
6 Travel by taxi is only allowed when no other method is available – receipts must be attached.
7 Saver tickets should be bought whenever British Rail is used.
8 Actual postage and telephone costs will be refunded.

Rules such as these will be found in any organisation. The need for economy and the provision of receipts is very important.

ACTIVITY

1 Find out what expenses are allowed in your organisation. Compare these with those allowed to other members of your group. What are the similarities? What are the differences? Can you say why the differences exist?
2 What are the rules about claiming expenses in your organisation? Are they the same BTEC or different?

Expenses claims forms

Every organisation will have its own expenses claim form. The design and content of the will depend upon the type and needs of the organisation. However, they will all contain some or all of these basic elements.

Section 1 – personal

The personal details needed on the form are: name, department, pay number, address, date of claim, signature, etc. The section often includes a sentence to say that everything is true and that money has only been spent on company business.

Section 2 – expenses and payments made

Includes date, details and amount under each heading, e.g. fares, car mileage, subsistence (meals), accommodation, entertaining by type of customer (UK, overseas, etc.), VAT details.

Section 3 – bank information

Includes the bank details of the person making the claim, e.g. name and address of bank, account name and number. This information enables the employer to make payments directly into the employee's bank account.

Section 4 – 'for office use only'

This is the section you, as an office worker, would have to complete:

1 **Receipts attached**   Are all receipts attached? Are they correct? Do they match the claim? Are the dates the same?
2 **Authorised by**   You should sign if you agree that the claim is correct.
3 **Date**
4 **Account code**   Decide which account the expenses should be paid from and write down its account code. This account will be debited.
5 **Amount paid**   Confirm how much you are paying in expenses.
6 **Date paid**   Confirm when the money was transferred to the claimee's account.

Distance chart

Cardiff				
302	Carlisle			
68	289	Carmarthen		
230	312	293	Colchester	
130	364	192	209	Dorchester

259

The distance chart shows how far one town is from another. For example, the distance from Cardiff to Colchester is written in the square where the column under Cardiff meets the row along from Colchester. The chart below gives this distance as 230 miles.

▸ Carlisle to Colchester is 312 miles.
▸ Carmarthen to Colchester is 293 miles.
▸ Carlisle to Dorchester is 364 miles.

─┤ ACTIVITY ├ Travel expenses ─────────

1   Nationwide Wholesale Distributors Ltd. sells its products to the brewery trade in England, Wales and Belgium. It has seven salespeople who cover the three countries on a regular basis. They do this by travelling by car from one town to another, stopping on the route to meet various clients. The expenses they are allowed to claim are:

● £35 per night for bed and breakfast.
● £6.50 for lunch.
● £10.50 for an evening meal.
● 35p per mile.

Each salesperson will usually claim the maximum they are allowed. This is an accepted practice in the company. They are not allowed to claim for breakfast on the first morning, or an evening meal when they arrive back at the end of a trip (this is normally about 6 p.m.).

You have the job of checking the expenses claims.

a) Mark the towns visited by the salespeople on an outline map that shows England, Wales and Belgium (the towns and routes they travelled are listed at the end of the activity).
b) Check each expenses claim at the end of the activity and authorise it for payment if it is correct.
c) If any of the expenses claims are incorrect, write a memo to the person concerned pointing out the errors and asking for an explanation.

Example – checking the expenses claim of M Abel
Use a map and a distance chart to find the distance between the towns M Abel visited.

Barnstaple_____	Taunton	51 miles
Taunton_____	Exeter	34 miles
Exeter_____	Plymouth	45 miles
Plymouth_____	Barnstaple	59 miles
		Total 189 miles

The mileage cost should be 189 miles × 35p = £66.15. This is correct – it is the amount Abel has claimed. Put a tick on the expenses sheet to confirm this.

Lunch expenses, days 1, 2, 3 and 4 = 4 × £6.50 = £26.00

Evening meals expenses, days 1, 2, and 3 = 3 × £10.50 = £31.50

Hotel costs, 3 nights 1, 2, and 3 = 3 × £35 = £105.00

Is the total correct?

M Abel's claim is correct for that section. Check the total and if that is correct too, sign your name to authorize the claim.

For this activity you should assume that all claims are supported by receipts. In practice a claim is not accompanied by a receipt it should be returned to the salesperson.

Now check the other six expenses claims.

Salespersons' Routes

Region 1 – M Abel
Barnstaple_____Taunton
Taunton_____Exeter
Exeter_____Plymouth
Plymouth_____Barnstaple

Region 2 – J Barnes
Bristol_____Guildford
Guildford_____Southampton
Southampton_____Dorchester
Dorchester_____Bristol

Region 3 – D Cox
Sheffield_____Manchester
Manchester_____Leeds
Leeds_____Kendal
Kendal_____Liverpool
Liverpool_____Sheffield

Region 4 M Utrillo
York_____Middlesbrough
Middlesbrough_____Hull
Hull_____Lincoln
Lincoln_____York

Region 5 – I Brunel
London_____Brussels
Brussels_____Antwerp
Antwerp_____London

Region 6 – N Gresley
Cardiff_____Carmarthen
Carmarthen_____Aberystwyth
Aberystwyth_____Gloucester
Gloucester_____Cardiff

Region 7 – D Gooch
Oxford_____Birmingham
Birmingham_____Nottingham
Nottingham_____Cambridge
Cambridge_____Oxford

Summary of expenses

Date	Name	Mileage	Lunch	Evening meal	Hotel costs	Total	
		✓	✓	✓	✓		
4.4.9X	M Abel	66.15	26.00	31.50	105.00	228.65	h.g.
4.4.9X	J Barnes	94.85	26.00	31.50	105.00	257.35	
5.4.9X	D Cox	143.50	32.50	42.00	140.00	358.00	
5.4.9X	M Utrillo	93.10	32.50	31.50	115.00	272.10	
5.4.9X	I Brunel	280.00	19.50	21.00	70.00	390.50	
5.4.9X	N Gresley	102.20	35.00	31.50	105.00	273.70	
5.4.9X	D Gooch	108.15	26.00	31.50	105.00	270.65	

* M Abel has been done for you.

2   While you were out, one of your colleagues took this phone message from F McCullum, one of the directors of Nationwide Wholesale Distributors Ltd.

Memorandum

Telephone Message
To: M. George
From: F. McCullum

Date: 19.10.9X
Time: 1.40 p.m.

Can you fill in a claim form for Ms McCullum. Here are the details of her business trip last weekend.

Monday 11 Oct.	London to Kendal Lunch, evening meal B & B at two star hotel
Tuesday 12 Oct.	Kendal to Nottingham lunch, evening meal B & B in hotel in Derby Rd.
Wednesday 13 Oct.	Nottingham to London

15

Meetings and travel arrangements

Summary

This chapter through its assignment gives you an opportunity to practise a number of work tasks and administrative procedures through organising meetings which also involve making travel arrangements. The following topics are covered:

- Purpose of meetings
- Organising a meeting
- Job roles and duties
- Routine administrative tasks
- Telephoning
- Written communications
- Budgeting
- Travel information and timetables
- Documentation
- Business image

This chapter will help you to achieve the following outcomes:

Core Module 2 Administrative Systems and Procedures
Outcome 2.1 Understand and be able to use established information storage and retrieval systems
Outcome 2.2 Identify and use different communication systems and methods of a selected organisation
Outcome 2.3 Produce documents and material and process data
Outcome 2.4 Understand the following health and safety procedures
Outcome 2.5 Understand the importance of maintaining and developing good business relationships with callers, customers/clients and colleagues

Core Module 3 Business Resources and Procedures
Outcome 3.4 Investigate and apply simple measures of performance

Core Module 4 People in Business
Outcome 4.4 Contribute to achievement of organisational goals by fulfilling job role

The assignment can be used to cover the following performance criteria:

2.1a documents filed in correct location and sequence
2.1b different methods for filing and storage compared and contrasted
2.1c explanation of importance of effective storage, control and retrieval of information given
2.2a oral and written messages received and acted upon
2.2b information obtained from appropriate sources
2.2c routine business communications produced
2.2d channels of communication identified and used
2.2e incoming and outgoing mail processed
2.2f electronic telecommunications used to receive and send information
2.3a business documents produced using a word processing package
2.3b information processing equipment used to run standard applications
2.3d copies of original documents produced using reprographic equipment
2.4a potential hazards to the well-being of self and others recognised and reported
2.4b equipment used in accordance with operating instructions and procedures
2.4c work area kept free from hazards

2.5a	callers greeted promptly and courteously and dealt with appropriately
2.5b	polite and effective responses made to a range of customer/client situations
2.5c	liaison and communication with peers and senior colleagues conducted effectively
2.5d	rapport and mutual respect between colleagues and customers/clients established
3.2b	resources used and cost effectively and safely
3.2c	own performance measured and recorded
3.2d	suggestions made or implemented to improve the use of physical resources
3.4a	meaning of performance investigated and explained
3.4b	methods of measurement of performance investigated and described
3.4c	suitable method chosen to gauge performance in identified jobs, tasks of operations
3.4d	methods applied to job/task/operation selected and conclusions drawn from results
4.3b	job roles in different functional areas of organisations identified
4.3c	job roles compared
4.4a	relationship between organisational objectives and job role identified
4.4b	given tasks completed to agreed criteria
4.4c	contribution made both as an individual and as a member of a team to the achievement of agreed targets and goals

This assignment will help with the development of Common Skills, especially the following:

Managing and Developing Self
Outcome 1   Manage own roles and responsibilities
Outcome 2   Manage own time in achieving objectives
Outcome 3   Undertakes personal and career development
Outcome 4   Transfer skills gained to new and changing situations and contexts

Working with and Relating to Others
Outcome 5   Treat others' values, beliefs and opinions with respect
Outcome 6   Relate to and interact effectively with individuals and groups
Outcome 7   Work effectively as a member of a team

Communicating
Outcome 8   Receive and respond to a variety of information
Outcome 9   Present information in a variety of visual forms
Outcome 10   Communicate in writing
Outcome 11   Participate in oral and non-verbal communication

Managing Tasks and Solving Problems
Outcome 12   Use information sources
Outcome 13   Deal with a combination of routine and non-routine tasks
Outcome 14   Identify and solve routine and non-routine problems

Applying Numeracy
Outcome 15   Apply numerical skills and techniques

Applying Technology
Outcome 16   Use a range of technological equipment and systems

Applying Design and Creativity
Outcome 17   Apply a range of skills and techniques to develop a variety of idea the creation of new/modified products, services or situations
Outcome 18   Use a range of thought processes

Read the following assignment to help you to understand some of the things you should be able to do by the end of this chapter. Normally it will be best for you to read the chapter and carry out the set activities before you tackle the assignment.

Check whether you can do the assignment on your own or with one or more colleagues. Some assignments will require organising by your tutor. Seek guidance, where needed, from your tutor.

▲ *The meeting*

You work for Worldwide Furniture Company as an assistant in the Director of Sales Office. Your boss's name is Ross Savage, Sales Director.

Due to the environmental pressure to preserve rainforest wood your chairs which use traditional hard woods from Brazil are declining in sales and new designs using more acceptable materials are being planned. To discuss these and other matters it is necessary to hold an executive meeting. The items to be discussed will affect the Brazilian production team – updating of the factory machinery in Brazil will be required – so it has been decided to call this meeting in Brazil.

Ross Savage is away attending The 20th Annual Wood Convention and his secretary is also attending with him. He phones you from the convention to ask you to arrange and set up the meeting and prepare all the papers for him, ' . . . in return,' he concludes, 'you can join us – so don't forget to book yourself a place. Hope you've got a passport and had all the necessary injections.'

His secretary faxes you a helpful list of details and instructions.

Fax Message

12 May 199X 13:24 Birmingham Conference Centre 021 432320

From: Holly Ilex

For the attention of: Assistant – Director of Sales Office Worldwide Furniture Company 0253 91623

Great news that you can come with us this time. Sorry I'm not in the office to help you organise everything but I have great confidence in your abilities, so I know you can handle it.

You need to:

1 Set up the meeting room and accommodation.

 a) Choose a suitable five star hotel that offers conference or business suites. It should be in Recife. Our travel agent will supply a list of the hotels.

 b) Book the hotel for three nights' stay commencing two months from now. The names of the people attending this meeting are:

> Ross Savage
> Don Pager
> Seamus Fitzpatrick
> Holly Ilex
> Harry Rosenthal
> Yourself (of course)

 Where possible book twin-bedded rooms, but Ross must have his own room. We should need four rooms in all.

 c) Book us a smallish room for our meeting with flipchart and overhead projector. The chairs and table should be set up in a round. We won't need a wordprocessor as we can take the lap-top. We will need this room for the evening we arrive and the next two days.

 d) We need orange, tea and coffee in the morning at about 10.30 and in the afternoon at about 3.30. Time will be tight so we would like them to bring a cold buffet to the meeting room at 1.00 so that we can have a working lunch.

 e) They should supply pens, etc. and mineral water and juice for use during the meeting but you had better mention it.

 We use a travel agent to make all the final bookings, etc. so get the form and fill it in. There's one in the filing cabinet filed under 'Travel'.

2 Prepare meeting

 Contact the relevant people with a notice of meeting. They also need copies of the following papers some of which need to be prepared. (They've already received minutes of the last meeting.)

 a) Agenda – notes for this are in my in-tray.

 b) Research and Development Report. You will need to contact the R and D department on ex 300 for this.

3 Travel arrangements.

 Send all the delegates details of hotel and their travel arrangements. They will have all expenses paid including a call home and an English newspaper. Tell them if there is a sports suite and swimming pool, some of them will want to do fitness training – we will pay their membership.

Can you take £70.00 equivalent in currency to pay for taxi, etc. You can claim this back of course. The day before we leave we will visit the factory but you can have a free morning if you like so take some travellers cheques in case you want to buy something. You can't of course claim this back!

Sorry this is rather a long list. Any problems please contact me at the Wood Convention.

Holly Ilex

This is a major task for you but you are determined to make a success of it.

These are the notes you find in Holly's in-tray. They need to be put into a proper agenda. You may like to tidy-up the subject headings.

Notes for agenda for meeting in Brazil

* Report by Ross Savage on 20th Annual Wood Convention.

* Report on sales figures for last year by Regional Sales Manager.

* Proposal for new designs by Research and Development.

* Changes needed for production team.

Task 1 Action the fax

Write down a checklist in order of priority, first.

Task 2 You discover that your passport is out of date so obtain a form from the Post Office and fill it in as a matter of some urgency.

Task 3 Role play the telephone call to the Research and Development Department.

Note that whilst you are talking to them they tell you their paper will not be ready until the day before you go. What are you going to do about this?

Task 4 Find out the currency used in Brazil and the exchange rate. Work out how much you will get for £70.00 sterling.

Task 5 Once all the papers are prepared make copies for all the delegates. Make a pack for them informing them of all the arrangements and enclose an expense claim form. Obtain this from your place of work or college, or design one.

The Brazilian contingent will also have to know all the arrangements and the agenda. Work out the best way of informing them and prepare the communication.

Meetings

Whenever a group of people have a common aim or purpose it is inevitable that before long they will have a meeting. This applies to life as well as business – residents' meetings, parents' meetings, social club committee meetings, executive meetings are a few examples.

Meetings are popular because they provide a forum where views can be expressed and exchanged with immediate feedback from others involved. However, if meetings are to be effective and not just opportunities for chat, then a few rules and a procedure are necessary.

People and roles

However informal the meeting may be, people still need to know the role they are expected to perform and the duties they are to undertake.

It is necessary to have a leader to ensure that there is an equal exchange of ideas and that the agenda is covered. In formal meetings the leader is called the chairperson.

Chairperson

The job of a chairperson is to:

1 Ensure that all the paperwork has been dealt with (but not necessarily to actually do The chairperson will set the agenda and sign the minutes of the last meeting.
2 Ensure that all the rules governing the meeting are kept to.
3 Ensure everyone has the opportunity to express their views.
4 Keep order.
5 Move the discussion on to the next item of the agenda after a fair hearing, or a resolut has been passed. In some instances the chairperson will have to call and oversee a v The chairperson can only vote in the event of a tie where a casting vote is needed to decide the matter.
6 It follows, therefore, that the chairperson should remain as neutral as possible on issues, and may well have to sum up all sides of an argument in preparation for a v
7 Arrange the date of the next meeting.

The role of chairperson is a responsible role which requires many skills. The larger ar more formal the meeting, the more difficult the role will become.

Secretary

This role may vary depending on the nature of the group or reason for the meeting. It is, however, always a responsible role.

If it is a manager calling a departmental meeting then the secretary is likely to be the manager's secretary. If it is a committee meeting then the secretary would need to act rather more like a company secretary and have legal and administrative training.

As a minimum it is the responsibility of the secretary to:

1 Deal with all the paperwork, i.e. send out notices of meeting, agenda, minutes and to ensure that they are typed and reproduced.
2 Accept the replies and inform the chairperson of apologies for absence.
3 Arrange and set up the room.

The secretary may also:

- Deal with all correspondence.
- Deal with or prepare 'matters arising' for the agenda.
- Take the 'Minutes' (sometimes there is a special Minuting Secretary).
- Discuss the agenda with the chairperson.
- Prepare a chairperson's agenda.

To sum up, much of the administration and planning leading to the smooth running of the meeting is the responsibility of the secretary. The secretary is the chairperson's 'right hand' but does not have the public face of the chairperson.

Treasurer

The role of the treasurer also depends on the type of meeting. In a business meeting the treasurer may not be given that title but someone with 'money sense' will almost certainly be there. It may be someone from Finance or Accounts Department, etc. On a committee, however, a treasurer is essential to:

1 Advise on all money matters.
2 Keep the books.
3 Handle all the money, income and
   expenditure.
4 Arrange an audit and prepare an
   annual report.

Members

The three roles mentioned above are likely to be necessary at any type of meeting, b[...]
course there will be other people or members who are just as important and who will [...]
the largest part of the meeting. The reason their job titles are not mentioned he[...]
because they will differ depending on the type of meeting being held. For a comm[...]

meeting they will be known as committee members but may also have other titles such as Fixtures Secretary, Publicity Co-ordinator, etc. The role of such people is to:

1 Attend meetings.
2 Participate.
3 Learn.
4 Express their views.
5 Express the views of others they may represent.
6 Help to solve problems and plan action.
7 Prepare information for the meeting.
8 Put into practice what has been decided.

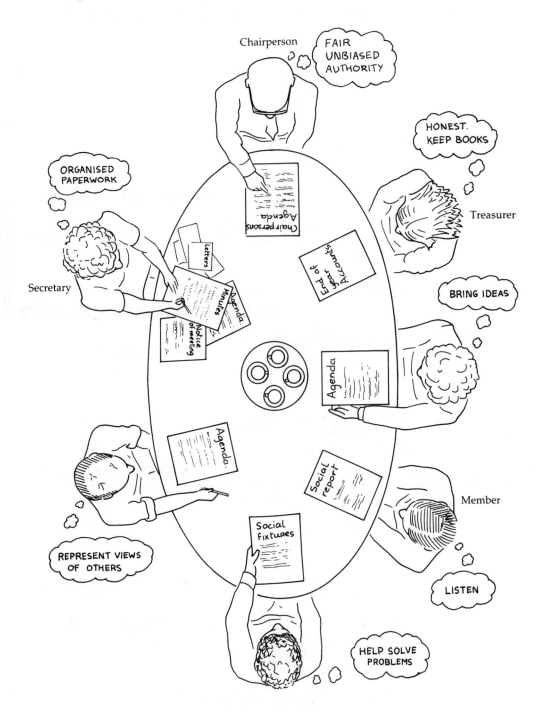

▲ *The committee*

It should be emphasised that meetings are not the place for a snooze or for the attitude of 'this won't affect me'. All meetings are important, if they are not they should not be called.

/ ACTIVITY /

Make a list of the skills and personal qualities you think are needed for each role taken by the main people in the meeting. Explain why these are necessary and what parts of the duties they apply to. Discuss your lists with the group or your tutor.

Here are a few to start you off:

▸ Chairperson – communication, organisational, interpersonal, . . .
▸ Secretary – organisational, administrative, . . .
▸ Treasurer – honest, . . .

Match your qualities to those of each role played at a meeting. What roles could you play? What role would you be best suited to? If you are in a group go round the whole group.

Paperwork

Notice of meeting

EASTSIDE STUDENT UNION

A committee meeting is to be held at 6.00 p.m. on Wednesday 10 October in Student Union Lounge.

Secretary

Memorandum

To: All booking staff   *Ref:* CD/CM

From: Booking manager   *Date:* 12 June

Subject: – Staff Meeting

There will be a meeting of all staff in the 'Bookings' dept at 9.30 on Thursday 14 June in Seminar Room 302.

▲ *Notices of meeting*

Whatever the type of meeting, the people involved need to have information about They need to know:

a) Who is holding the meeting, e.g. Regional Sales Managers, Anytown Reside Association.
b) When the meeting is to be held.
c) Where the meeting is to be held.
d) At what time the meeting is to start.
e) Who the notice of meeting is from.
f) Sometimes the type of meeting is mentioned, e.g. annual general meeting.

The format of the notice may vary from a poster to a memo. If it is a company meeting then a memo is usual, but notice of a committee meeting may be given on a blank post card.

If a person is unable to attend they should reply to the secretary with their 'apologies for absence'.

Items to be discussed

In order to keep the meeting within limits it is helpful to have a list of topics you wish to discuss prepared in advance. There are several reasons for this and you may be able to think up some more:

a) It allows people to prepare for the meeting in advance.
b) It provides a running order for the meeting.
c) It prevents people from introducing 'red herrings'.
d) It ensures that you really need a meeting.

This list of topics is called the **agenda.** An agenda is usually sent out in advance, sometimes with the notice of meeting or later if the chairperson wishes to invite the people attending to suggest items to be discussed.

Eastside College YT

Programme Review Team Meeting to be held at 3.00 p.m. on Wednesday 22 September 1992 in Room 46 Youth Training Scheme Suite, Ranmore House, Hillgate.

Agenda

1 Apologies for absence
2 Minutes of last meeting
3 Matters arising
4 Course Supervisors' reports
5 1991/92 BTEC First results
6 Company/trainee feedback
7 Integration on/off the job
8 Any other business
9 Date of next meeting

Above is an example of an agenda. You should note the format carefully for some items never change whoever is calling the meeting.

The format is as follows:

- Name of group holding the meeting.
- Repeat of the Notice of meeting.
- Agenda.

1 **Apologies for absence**   At the meeting these will be read out so that the meeting can start on time without having to wait for somebody who cannot come. Usually it is just stated, 'Apologies have been received from (say) Mr Baggins and Miss Everdene'.

2 **Minutes of the last meeting**   Minutes are explained more fully later on in this chapter, but briefly they are a record of what happened at the meeting. They are sent to all the people who were invited to the meeting. These people may then comment on their accuracy or if they were unable to attend, find out what was said. If everyone agrees they are accurate they are signed at the next meeting by the chairperson as 'a true and accurate record'.

3 **Matters arising**   These are not new matters to be discussed but any development that may have taken place since the last meeting. For example, if at the last meeting it was decided that someone was to book a venue for a publicity launch which has yet to

happen, they or the secretary would report at this point whether or not they were successful in doing so.

4 **Correspondence**   This is not always included (as the agenda on p. 273 shows) as it depends on the type of meeting. At business meetings correspondence relating to the meeting would be mentioned. Committees find correspondence a useful item for the agenda but sometimes it is dealt with under 'matters arising'

5 **Item to be discussed**   e.g. sales report.

6 **Item to be discussed**   e.g. new products.

7 **Other items to be discussed**   It is a good idea to keep the items to be discussed as limited as possible. Including too many items will mean that no item can have a fair discussion and will probably make the meeting too long.

8 **Any other business**   This is a chance for people to introduce their own items for discussion. They should be short points for clarification but if someone introduces a big topic then generally the chairperson will put it on the agenda for discussion next time.

9 **Date of next meeting**

ACTIVITY

Make up an agenda with items suitable for your group to discuss. Some ideas for these items are: provision of sports or social activities, canteen facilities, a group outing. Try to make these items genuine and of actual concern or relevance to your group.

Minutes of meeting

Minutes of the Business Studies Programme Review Team Meeting held on 22 September 1992.

PRESENT   Gill Salter – (Chairperson)
Marian Clarke – (minutes secretary) ESTC
Judith Alman – ESTC
Joanna Burke – Trainee
Oscar Duncan – Trainee
Mrs Filberg – Lanzotic Travel
Mr Wix – Royd and Jones
Helen Parr ⎫
Liz Hamley ⎭ Cruise Travel
Pam Sayers – ESTC
Colin Sales – Training Agency
Avarine Wilson – Careers Service
Emma Hicking – Trainee
Peter Davies – ESC

1 APOLOGIES FOR ABSENCE

Apologies for absence were received from Louise Sneeth of American International Underwriters and Mr Muirhead of Legal and General.

2 MINUTES OF THE LAST MEETING
The chairperson explained that the meeting was the first Programme Review Team Meeting this year and, therefore, there were no minutes of the last meeting

3 MATTERS ARISING
None

4 COURSE SUPERVISORS' REPORTS

The chairperson explained the meeting was to be an open forum to discuss the Business Studies YT course. However, before discussion began she pointed out that:

a) The section had recently transferred from Nutfield Point to Gatton Centre.

b) There had been some changes in staff. Pam Sayers had left the Business Studies team to join East Surrey Training Consortium and Peter Davies had joined the department. It has, therefore, been a time of many changes but is more settled now.

The chairperson then went on to explain how the course was broken down:

a) The first term was largely a settling in period for the students, both at work and college, and assignments were geared to that end.

b) The second term concentrated on work-related skills used in clerical and administrative duties.

c) The third term concentrated on linking these skills more specifically to the option subjects and final assessment.

5 1991/92 BTEC FIRST RESULTS

60 students took the BTEC First Certificate, 49 passed and six obtained a Certificate of Achievement. Five failed completely.

Pam Sayers said that the Certificate was awarded on a continuous assessment basis. One core area and eight skill areas were assessed. Final grading took in all these aspects.

6 COMPANY/TRAINEE FEEDBACK

Copies of the work programme were distributed for discussion/interpretation.

Mr Wix said that although he wanted his trainees to gain a BTEC Certificate, he thought that the course should relate to the specific work place, as for him, that was the point of YT, whereas Mrs Filberg felt that the college course was more a general introduction to work and good work practices and that the workplace would provide specific skills.

Mr Wix felt that the trainees should be told why they are studying a particular topic. He felt that they would be better able to relate a topic to their work place if they brought real forms and tasks into College to use in those assignments.

The chairperson said that all areas of work are explained to trainees and some employers would not allow the trainees to bring work documents into college due to confidentiality.

Mrs Filberg went on to say that trainees needed to have guidance and clear instruction in the early part of the course on the correct way to answer the telephone and take messages.

7 INTEGRATION ON/OFF THE JOB

Emma Hicking said there was confusion when the college and the company had conflicting ideas in the layout of memos, letters, etc. Lecturers explained that the course policy was to follow the company in-house style but a 'correct' way is taught if there is no set company style.

Avarine Wilson suggested the company ran an induction course to familiarise trainees with company styles.

Pam Sayers supported this by emphasising that the course consisted of transfer of skills in both on-the-job training as well as off-the-job training and companies perhaps should devote, at a specific time, some in-house training. This could occur when the company closed at the end of the day, or first thing in the morning on a regular weekly basis.

Mr Wix suggested that each project should be related to the specific workplace and it was confirmed that the course plan was to incorporate some set time for this.

Copies of the NVQ (Competency Objectives) were circulated. These had received approval from the NCVQ and Mr Sales explained that it had been handed out by the Training Agency.

Mr Sales confirmed that at the end of the day as far as the Training Agency was concerned, the trainees counted most and that one should not get 'bogged down' with the paperwork. It was agreed that one copy of the competency objectives would be left at the workplace, one at college and updated on monitoring visits.

Mr Wix said he was satisfied with the quality and level of training given. Pam Sayers confirmed that Dave Spicer as manager cared about training and YT and this, coupled with the dedication of the business studies team, proved a successful formula in the training of young people.

8 ANY OTHER BUSINESS

French exchange trip – sponsored by the Training Agency, with a view to 1992. 12 trainees have an opportunity to exchange with French students and visit their workplace and college for five days. They will stay with the families. This exchange was being offered to Business Studies, Catering and Motor Vehicle trainees. The chairperson asked the employers to think about whether they would like to send their trainees.

9 DATE OF NEXT MEETING

The date of the next meeting was arranged for Wednesday 15 October at 3.00 p.m. at Eastside College.

Date ....Signed ....
                                         Chairperson

These are taken at a meeting by the secretary or minuting secretary. They sum up wh was said and what action if any was agreed to be taken. They are then typed and circulat to those present for comment. At the next meeting they are amended if required a signed as an accurate record. In this way there can be no arguments over what was sa and agreed. These minutes are filed and kept. Minutes of this nature are called narrati minutes. If the meeting was at a very high level or highly confidential then only resoluti minutes may be kept. These simply state what was agreed.

All this paperwork is generally sent out in advance of the meeting together with a 'special papers' which relate to the items to be discussed. If for any reason special pap cannot be sent out then they may be 'tabled' at the meeting. The obvious disadvantag this is that people will have to be given reading time during the meeting.

Preparing the room

There is little point in preparing for a meeting if the venue is unsuitable. Although it need not be elaborate, it must be adequate.

Check List
- Size.
- Equipment such as flip charts, video recorders, etc.
- Adequate tables and chairs.
- Layout of seating.
- Refreshments if required.
- Spare copies of all paperwork. You should have copies of:

  a) Notice of meeting sent.
  b) Minutes circulated.
  c) Minutes of last meeting.
  d) Correspondence/matters arising.
  e) Special papers circulated or tabled.
  f) Minutes of meeting taken.

Booking rooms and travel arrangements

If the meeting is departmental then there will be no travel to arrange and booking the room may be a simple task of filling in your company's internal booking form.

ACTIVITY

Find out the procedure for booking a room at your company or college and acquire a form. Fill in the form to book a room for a meeting to be held between your group. It would be a good idea to use a study time when you know you can all meet together. You may like to order refreshment, but be prepared for the group to have to pay for it.

Run the meeting for which you have prepared the agenda and booked the room. Before you start choose people to take up the key roles based on the discussion you held earlier on people's suitability for each role.

Ensure that the secretary makes adequate notes for producing minutes. For this exercise, the secretary should photocopy the notes so that everyone can practise producing minutes. It is not advisable for each member to take full notes during the meeting as this will interfere with any discussion. If you do not feel confident that your secretary will produce notes everyone can understand then you could tape the meeting.

If you are holding a regional meeting or meeting overseas then the procedure is likely to become more complicated. Ideally, there will be plenty of time and notice to arrange everything beforehand, and then to contact the delegates. Unfortunately life is not always so straightforward, and the people attending do need as much advance warning as possible if they are to travel and spend time away. This is where a secretary will need organising and problem-solving skills. It may be better to send a notice of meeting, stating that a meeting is planned for a certain date in France, with details and travel arrangements to follow, than wait until everything is settled and only give the delegates a few days' warning.

Booking and arranging travel for business is in many ways similar to booking a holiday as you will still need to:

1 Keep to a budget.
2 Choose a suitable hotel.
3 Book the hotel.
4 Make the travel arrangements.
5 Find out about surcharges, taxes, etc.
6 Find out about innoculations, visa requirements, etc.
7 Find out the currency used, the exchange rate, and whether it is better to take travellers cheques in local currency or sterling.

ACTIVITY

Using a travel agent, Prestel and other suitable sources find out:

a) If there are any innoculations or visa requirements for USA.
b) Whether it is better to take dollars or sterling traveller cheques to USA.
c) How much local currency you would get for £50.00 in Italy.
d) How long the flight takes from Heathrow to Recife, Brazil. What is the time difference between the UK and Brazil?
e) If you left from London, Heathrow at 0800 hrs at what time would you arrive in Recife, Brazil? Find out both the local time and the British time.
f) Do you need a passport if you are a British citizen travelling to France?

The main difference between business travel and a holiday is that for business the trip will have to be tailor-made each time and not come in a 'package'. However, many travel agents specialise in arranging business travel and conferences and will offer advice. Many companies have arrangements with particular travel agents. You do, however, still need to brief the agent so you need to have a careful and detailed plan of the necessary requirements Embassies can also give help and advice on any special requirements for a country and will also offer lists of hotels, tourist information, etc.

Passports and visas invariably take two months to process. Although there are ways round this, it is better to find out what documents are needed and deal with these as quickly as possible.

Budget
You may or may not be given an actual figure to work to, but you should certainly be given some guidelines on the class of hotel and class of travel expected.

ACTIVITY

How many classes of air travel are there? List them and state for whom they are most suitable e.g. private traveller, tourist, business.

If you are working, find out the policy of your company for travel class. Often MDs and executives will get 1st class, long haul will be club class, etc.

Worldwide Furniture Company

HOGG ROBINSON BUSINESS TRAVEL

Name(s) of traveller(s)	Date(s) of travel	Class of travel	Travel details

Accommodation details	Other details

Purpose:

Cost code:

Requisitioned by:

Date:

Authorised by:

Once correctly authorised, please pass this form to the Property Services Department, so that an order may be placed with Hogg Robinson.

▲ *Form used for arranging business travel*

Once everything is settled delegates need to be informed of the exact arrangements. A letter with all the information including what the company will pay for – normally no bar bills but often one telephone call home, etc. – will then be sent to them.

ACTIVITY

Make a list of all the things you think should go in the letter informing delegates of travel arrangements, not forgetting, of course, where they will pick up their tickets.

Itineraries

When you are confirming travel arrangements it is very helpful to people to receive an itinerary. This becomes even more important if people are meeting up from various parts of the country (or world). An itinerary gives the times and dates of any arrangements starting from the earliest point.

Itinerary for BTEC First students — European Trip October 199X

Please note the following times and travel arrangements.

Day 1, 12 October 199X

0700	Meet Eastside College car park
0730	Depart Eastside College
0830	Students from Westside College join coach at Westside College car park
1000	Board ferry at Dover
1230	(local time) Arrive Calais
1330	Stop for lunch
1830	Arrive Hotel du Lac for overnight stop etc.

▲ Itinerary

ACTIVITY

Using timetables, maps and other suitable sources, work out a realistic itinerary for the BTEC First students for a 10-day tour taking in Brussels, Germany and Luxembourg. Hotel du Lac is a fictional hotel, but which country, given the times on the itinerary, do you think it could realistically be in? The students will need to stop for a few days in one or other of the countries. Which towns do you think would provide places or sites of interest to business studies students?

Work out a costing for such a trip. Include the cost of the ferry, the coach and two hotel stops. You will need to discuss together a maximum cost and then decide what star rating hotel you could afford and whether you want full board, half board or bed and breakfast.

If you had decided not to book through a travel agency, what would be the best way to book the hotels? The chapter Communication and Reception should help you to decide. Draft the necessary communication basing any information required on your group.

The times given in the itinerary above are not accurate. Find out the actual times of sailing (your local library should have a ferry timetable) and prepare a revised itinerary for your group, meeting at a suitable venue. You can of course change the ports if you so wish.

16

Pastures new

Summary

This chapter looks ahead to what you can do after you finish your BTEC first course. The future is yours. The following topics are covered:

▸ Further education
▸ Finding a job
▸ Job applications
▸ Interview skills
▸ Curriculum vitae
▸ Action plans and the future

This chapter will help you to achieve the following outcomes:

Core Module 4   People in Business
Outcome 4.5   Develop a career plan based on potential employment and training opportunities and personal career paths

The chapter activities can be used to cover the following performance criteria:

4.5a   own skills and experience identified
4.5b   career advice and information sought
4.5c   information on requirements of jobs/careers obtained
4.5d   career path selected
4.5e   plans for achievement devised
4.5f   job seeking and selection procedures identified and investigated

The assignment will help with the development of Common Skills, especially the following:

Managing and Developing Self
Outcome 2   Manage own time in achieving objectives
Outcome 3   Undertakes personal and career development
Outcome 4   Transfer skills gained to new and changing situations and contexts

Working with and Relating to Others
Outcome 5   Treat others' values, beliefs and opinions with respect
Outcome 6   Relate to and interact effectively with individuals and groups

Communicating
Outcome 8   Receive and respond to a variety of information
Outcome 9   Present information in a variety of visual forms
Outcome 10   Communicate in writing
Outcome 11   Participate in oral and non-verbal communication

Managing Tasks and Solving Problems
Outcome 12   Use information sources
Outcome 13   Deal with a combination of routine and non-routine tasks
Outcome 14   Identify and solve routine and non-routine problems

Applying Technology
Outcome 16   Use a range of technological equipment and systems

Applying Design and Creativity
    Outcome 17   Apply a range of skills and techniques to develop a variety of ideas in the creation of new/modified products, services or situations
    Outcome 18   Use a range of thought processes

Read the following assignment to help you to understand some of the things you should be able to do by the end of the chapter. Normally it will be best to read the chapter and carry out the set activities before you tackle the assignment.

Check whether you can do the assignment on your own or with one or more colleagues. Some assignments will require organising by your tutor. Seek guidance, where needed, from your tutor.

Assignment

If you are nearing the end of your course, or planning to apply for a job, this is a good time to review your achievements and write a new action plan.

Task 1   Consider:

> ‣ Where you are now
> > Full time college
> > Full time work
> > College and work

> ‣ What you have achieved
> > BTEC First Award
> > Units towards BTEC First
> > NVQ level 1
> > NVQ level 2

Look back to the first induction exercises where you stated 'Where I need help/improve';

‣ Which two things have you improved upon and now feel confident doing?
‣ Which two things have you improved upon and feel you can now get by with in a workin situation?

Add these to the areas which you know you find easy and enjoy.

‣ Are there any areas which you still find difficult? List these.
‣ List the areas you do not enjoy (competent or not).
‣ Finally add any further achievements you have made over the course: e.g. passed driving te obtained mainly Merits or distinctions, gained confidence with dealing with people, gaine promotion or position of responsibility such as year/group rep for College Review Team.

You should now have a good profile of yourself and be able to match up your qualifications a skills to the type of job you would like, and be suitable, to do.

‣ What type of job do you think would suit you best
  – indoor, outdoor, dealing with people, problem solving, working under pressure, etc.?

You should have some idea of what type of work or business you want to work in: e.g. banki insurance, accounts department, office services, start your own business, etc. If you do not, t your profile to a careers counsellor and research the types of job for which you would suitable.

Task 2 If you know the job or area of business you want to work in (or gain promotion if you are already working) answer the following:

1 What is preventing you from starting straight away?
- ☐ No position available in company yet.
- ☐ Too young i.e. need to be over 18.
- ☐ Finding the right opening.
- ☐ Need to move to a different part of the country, etc.

2 In order to help you to achieve your goal you should now carry out some research and take a positive action. This will differ depending on your personal circumstances and the answers you gave to question 1.

If in work

a) If you have a job and are hoping for promotion this may well depend on your knowledge of the business and related systems.

b) Take an area of knowledge you know is important to your job or the person above you and undertake a project. You could ask your manager for advice. One of the following may be suitable:

▸ Where does the paperwork you deal with come from and go to?
What happens if mistakes are made?
Which people and which departments may be affected by mistakes on the paper work?
▸ Do you need product knowledge? Research your companies products/services and market areas.
▸ There may be special legal requirements. Research a legal aspect or the regulating body.

c) Apply for an appraisal interview.

If you are starting work or changing occupational area

a) What openings there are for a person with your qualifications and abilities.
b) The career route open to employees. This may apply to an area of work rather than a particular company.
c) Whether you will have to take professional qualifications to proceed further up the ladder, e.g. AAT.
d) What are the professional qualifications and what you can be doing before you take them, e.g. BTEC National Award exempts you from units of many professional qualifications.
e) Can you join a management training course? What do you need to do this, e.g. be over 18, a BTEC National Award, A levels, work experience.
f) Any further information which would be useful.

If starting your own business

a) Research how to draw up a business plan.
b) Produce one.

3 When you have completed this project state your course of action, e.g. study for a BTEC National Award, apply for a job and study part time for a BTEC National Certificate or a professional qualification.

4 Start work and gain work experience.

When you have carried out Tasks 1 and 2 it would be a good idea to summarise all your thoughts on a form. Either design one or use the one below as a basis.

```
Action plan
Name                          Date
_____
Review
1
2
3
Confident and enjoy           Not confident or do not enjoy

_____
Goal/aim
1
2

_____
Planning
Area researched (attached)
 1
2

_____
Action
1
2
```

Introduction

We looked earlier at some of the tasks of personnel and recruiting, but, of course, in order to be employed you will have had to have been through this process yourself.

Finding a job

Nearly anyone can find any job to do, but to find a job that you will enjoy, that will satisfy you and will give you a chance to develop, needs a good deal of planning.

Job vacancies

You will find pages and pages of advertisements in various sources such as newspapers, journals, job centres, etc. such that you may wonder how it is there is any unemployment. The problem, of course, is have you got the right skills for the types of job on offer?

You may have heard the expression 'skills shortage'. It does not mean that the people in that part of the country do not have skills to offer, but that a particular area of business or industry has a shortage of trained staff or potential employees. This can have as much to do with government policy as anything else, hence the campaign for training to get people with the right skills to do the right job.

If you live in an area of high unemployment, look through the job advertisements and see what exactly is on offer. There will be jobs: the high unemployment figure will most likely be caused by the area changing its traditional role. Many of the people unemployed, tragically, will be the skilled and semi-skilled people who were involved in the traditional area of industry, e.g. steel workers, coal miners, etc. As tradition goes deep, it is likely that younger members of the community will also have expected to join the same industry; they find that there are no openings and similarly join the job queue.

Of course, this is simplifying a rather more complicated issue, but the message to any young person today entering the job market has to be maximise your chances of employment by gaining the right skills.

The right skills in today's frequently changing environment are likely to be the transferable skills. These are the skills that can be used or transferred to any job. The BTEC Common Skills are transferable, so if you are on a BTEC course you can be sure that you are already maximising your chances. The NVQs are another way of trying to ensure that people entering a vocational area have relevant training to do the job.

/ **ACTIVITY** /

Make a collection of newspapers and magazines with job vacancies in your area and make a list of the vocational areas of work and the number of jobs offered. It is particularly important to note the type of work on offer and the skills required, e.g. the job may be in a manufacturing company but do they want shop floor workers or computer operators? Draw a graph to show this visually. Split these vocational areas further and chart the progression of jobs, e.g. how many of the jobs are for juniors, supervisors, managers? Can you work out the skills shortage for your area? Your local Job Centre will give you more information on this, visit them to see if your analysis was right.

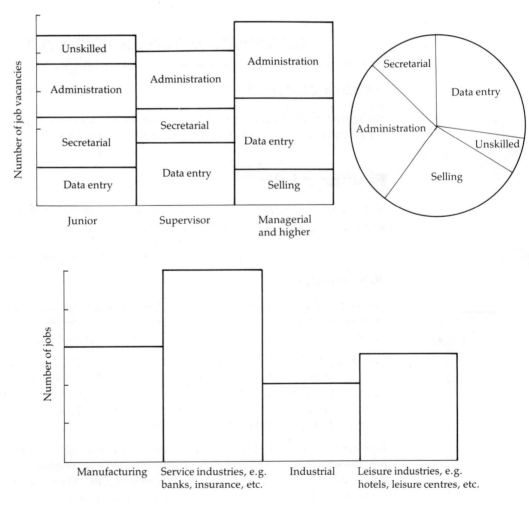

▲ Jobs and vacancies

When you are looking at adverts keep an open mind. You may think they are asking for specialists but remember your transferable skills and you may well find that you could in fact do the job, especially if the company are offering training or day release.

---/ **ACTIVITY** /--

Look at several job adverts and see if you can paint a picture of the type of company, type of job and type of person they are looking for. If the advert asks for a 'self starter' what do you think that means? Are you a self starter? How do you think you could show this in a letter of application? Use your personal activities to help as well, e.g. 'I suggested we raise money to paint the youth centre. Organised a Boot sale . . .'

Applying for a job

Once you are satisfied that a job is a possibility for you, the next step is to apply for it. Note carefully the instructions they give you at the bottom of the advert, e.g.:

> Phone personnel for further details and an application form.

> or
> Apply in writing with CV.

If you have to phone, you may find that there is an answering machine, so be prepared. Have ready:

● Job no. or reference.
● Job title.
● Where and when the job was advertised.
● Your name, address and telephone number.

Application form

We have looked at application forms in Chapter 13. As you now know they are kept for company records, you should realise how important it is for you to fill them in correctly.

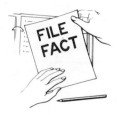

It is an offence to falsify or lie on an application form.

An application form is your first foot in the door so

1 Write in black ink (this photocopies better than any other colour).
2 Write neatly and use BLOCK CAPITALS where requested.
3 Do not use crossings out, so fill the form in lightly in pencil first and then go over in black ink. When the ink is quite dry (even the ink from ballpoint pens need time to dry completely) rub out any pencil marks that show. If you can, it is a good idea to photocopy the application form and have a practice run first.
4 Remember to sign and date it.

Collect some application forms as a group and practise filling them out. You will probably need quite a lot of information that you may have forgotten, such as dates of examinations, examination grades, when you commenced or left jobs.

Curriculum vitae

Through the application form the company will begin to form a picture of you, but as application forms are uniform they do restrict the information you can give. For this reason it is better to also send in a curriculum vitae or CV for short.

A CV is a history of your working life and can also give other details about you. If you have not worked before it may be quite short but it can still give some vital information. As you build up your business experience so you should update your CV. A good, neatly presented CV can mean the difference between an interview or not, so it is worth working at it to make sure you do as good a job as possible. Over the page is a model of a CV. You will see others that differ but this does have the vital information and has been tried and tested.

1 Start with personal details, e.g. your full name, address, date of birth, etc.
2 Education, e.g. where and when you were educated.
3 Qualifications.
4 Vocational qualifications.
5 Work experience. Some people start with their first job and end on their current job, but as this is usually the one most relevant, it is often considered better to go the other way and work backwards.

Note, it is a good idea to state your duties or special responsibilities as job titles can be misleading as they differ from company to company. Consider the man who signs our bank notes 'Chief Cashier'. What mental image do you have of a cashier's job? Do you think this is what the Chief Cashier does?

Letter of application

In addition to your CV you will have to send a letter of application or a supporting statement. There is usually a space on the application form for you to write this additional information.

This should not just go over what you have told them in your CV but try to give them the idea of your personal qualities which make you right for the job, e.g. I enjoy working under pressure, I am very organised so feel this would help me in the job, etc. As the interview team will read this they are bound to ask some questions about it, so this is an opportunity for you to control at least part of the interview.

CURRICULUM VITAE

NAME: Angela Woodhouse

ADDRESS: 19 Shrivenor Road
Colchester
Essex
CO4 9TT

TELEPHONE: 0321 90421

DATE OF BIRTH: 4 April 1973

MARITAL STATUS: Single

EDUCATION: Colchester Comprehensive School (1984–1989)
Colchester College of Further Education (1990–1991)

QUALIFICATIONS:

GCSE	Art	grade C	(1989)
	PE	C	
	Childcare	C	
	English	D	
	Maths	D	
	Scripture	D	
	Geography	D	
	French	D	
	History	E	

EXAMINATIONS TO BE TAKEN:

GCSE:	English – Projected grade	C	(1991)
	Maths	C	
	French	C	
	History	C	
	Psychology	C	

WORK EXPERIENCE:
Part-time assistant Sainsbury's Supermarket, Colchester 1989–present

Main responsibilities: Operating a till
Shelf-filling
Stock-taking
Ordering stock
Quality control

I have taken and passed the training courses provided by Sainsbury's in Till Operation and Stock-Taking

Voluntary Helper. St Mary's Children's Home, Colchester 1989–1990

Main responsibilities: Washing and dressing the children
Playing with the children
Helping the permanent staff on trips out
Helping to prepare the children's meals

Unpaid assistant Hall's Department Store, Colchester (one week) 1989 (school work experience)

Main responsibilities: Serving on the perfumery counter
Helping with stock-taking
Working in the warehouse
Gift wrapping presents
Invoicing

Other work experience includes babysitting (from 1987 until the present) and a newspaper round (1987–1989)

INTERESTS: Reading, swimming and meeting people

REFEREES: D Harwood Esq (Manager)
Sainsbury's Store
High Street
Colchester
Essex CO6 9HG
Tel: 0321 96387

Mrs J Hill (Course Tutor)
Colchester College of Further Education
Brownton Square
Colchester
Essex
CO5 3FD

```
                                                    19 Shrivenor Road
                                                           Colchester
                                                               Essex
                                                             CO4 9TT

                                                      5 January 1991

Mrs T James
Director of Personnel
Thompson's Ltd
Black Road
Colchester
Essex
CO5 8VW

Dear Mrs James

Further to your advertisement in today's Colchester Gazette for trainee
supervisors commencing next July, I enclose my curriculum vitae and
would like to be considered for the position.

As can be seen from my curriculum vitae, I possess the requisite three
GCSE passes, and I am taking five more (which I am expected to pass) this
summer.

I have had some experience of retailing, both during school work
experience and in my current part-time employment at Sainsbury's
Supermarket; a post I have held for some two years.

On a personal level, I am loyal, enthusiastic and hard working. Although I
enjoy working on my own initiative, I have always worked successfully as
part of a team.

Yours sincerely,

Angela Woodhouse
```

▲ *Letter of application*

Interviews

These are a fact of working life. You will find that there are many types of interview, the most obvious being the job interview, but appraisals are another form which you are likely to come across. Beware of the term 'informal interview', there is no such thing really, it is just a way for people to see you as you really are, so prepare just as hard for them! The key to a successful interview is, as is so often the way in business, to plan and prepare thoroughly.

Preparing for an interview

Before you go to an interview:

1 **Plan your journey**   Look up the times of buses, etc. Make sure that you know which route you've got to take and leave plenty of time to allow for delays. If at all possible, make a dummy run first; although interviewers are becoming more sympathetic to our chaotic traffic system, it won't do you any good to arrive in a rush and a panic.

2 **Dress appropriately**   Work out in advance what you are going to wear. Get it out of the cupboard and try it on. Does it still fit? Are there buttons missing, tears, catches, etc? Does it need washing or cleaning. Try to keep your dress simple for business, a two piece or suit is the best idea for both men and women, but if you do not possess such a thing then keep your dress simple. Clean your shoes and ensure you have socks or tights of a suitable colour without holes. It is a good idea for women wearing tights to have a spare pair in case of disaster as these always seem to have a habit of developing a run at the most inconvenient time.

▲ *Work out in advance what you are going to wear*

3 **Prepare a few notes** Notes on why you want the job, why you think you are suitabl[e] for the job and a couple of questions to ask them about the job or company are alway[s] useful. Good questions to ask your interviewers are, 'Do you give training or da[y] release?' 'Are there opportunities for advancement?', or perhaps, 'Is the compan[y] expanding?'

You want as little to think and worry about on the day of an interview as possible, so don['t] think these are exaggerated preparations: they really do help.

Nerves

'Nerves' are actually quite helpful. They are caused by the adrenalin hormone, a hormo[ne] that prepares the body for 'fight or flight'. Many experienced performers will admi[t to] nerves, but they need to be harnessed so that you do not end up in a panic, whereupo[n a] common effect is for your mind to go completely blank. Routine on the day of an interv[iew] will help, as will a bath the night before to relax you and help get a good night's sle[ep]. Deep breathing is a well known antidote to nerves – take a deep but slow breath thro[ugh] your nose, hold for a count of three, and then breathe out through your mouth to ten.

Keep your hands in your lap or read to stop you fidgeting.

Think positive.

The interview itself

It is said that many interviewers make up their mind in the first two minutes. First impressions therefore can count for a lot. Although you do not want to appear over confident or cocky, you do want to appear confident.

When the moment arrives that you are called, walk into the room and make eye contact with your interviewer. Walk towards them with a smile and offer your hand to shake.

Much can be told about a person through their handshake. A weak, 'dead-fish' handshake will not inspire people, neither will a vice like 'hand-crusher' handshake. Daft though it sounds, it is quite a good idea to actually practise your handshake. A firm grip and brief shake is all that is required.

Practice handshakes with your group and give and accept feedback.

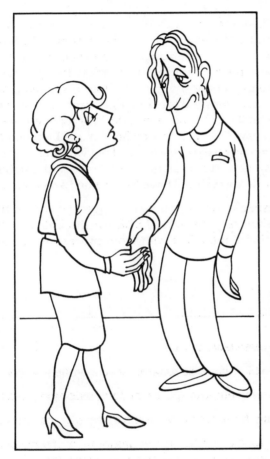

▲ *The 'dead-fish' handshake*

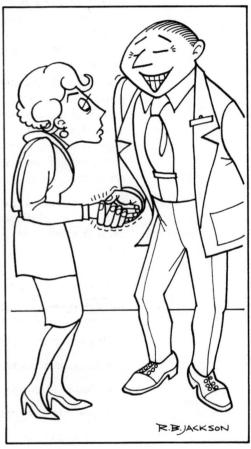

▲ *The 'hand-crusher' handshake*

You will most likely be shown where to sit. Interviewers can be very crafty with the type and positioning of the chair they offer. With a school leaver or first time interviewee they tend to be quite helpful and genuinely want you to relax but:

a) If you are given a deep armchair do not lean back and lounge as you would at home.
b) If offered a hard, straight back chair do not swing on the back legs. If you do this in class or the office you may do this unconsciously at the interview so stop the habit now.

Do not smoke in an interview. Even if your interviewer were to offer you a cigarette (which is increasingly unlikely), you would do better to decline.

Do:

- Sit on the chair – not the very edge or corner.
- Sit straight backed without looking like a ramrod.
- Try not to cross your legs or arms. This body language can be interpreted to mean that you are 'closed' or worse, lying.

ACTIVITY

Can you suggest some reasons why you should not smoke in an interview? Discuss some other habits that it may be better to avoid, but be clear about your reasons why.

Interview questions

Answer the questions in as straightforward a manner as you can, but it is better to avoid just 'Yes' or 'No' answers. Hopefully you will have prepared answers for some of the questions, although they rarely come in quite the form you expect. Always remember that an interview is a two-way process. The interviewers are trying to find out whether or not you could do the job and you are trying to find out if the job is what you want. It is perfectly all right to ask questions and to ask for clarification as you go along, but generally you are given an opportunity at the end of the interview for questions. It is best not to start with 'How much will I earn?' or 'How much holiday am I entitled to?' as this gives the impression you are more interested in money and not working than doing a good job. It is usual for the interviewers to run over the basic terms and conditions of the job, but remember you will not start work until have have signed a contract with these stated.

If you are asked a question to which you do not know the answer try to avoid saying, 'I don't know'. More positive responses are, 'I'll have to think about that', 'I haven't actually used that programme but I'm familiar with word-processing so I'm sure I could easily learn'.

ACTIVITY

As a group set up an interview situation.

▶ Choose an advert which would be suitable for your group to apply for.

▶ 'Apply' for the job complete with application form, supporting statement or letter and C

▶ Split into two groups, those for interview and those to be interviewers.

Either as a whole group or in your smaller groups think of some of the skills and qualit
you would want the applicant to have and make a checklist.

If you are an interviewer draw up a list of questions which would help you to find out if t
application is suitable.

If you are an interviewee think of some answers which present you in the best light.

▶ Run the interview.

It is better to have an audience. Although this may make you nervous they can offer feedb
on the performance on both sides. If you have a video camera available it is useful to use
as it can be most revealing about your mannerisms.

When you have had some practice and are beginning to feel more confident it would be n
helpful if you could ask tutors and employers to set up an interview panel for you. M
certain that you receive feedback from them on your performance at the 'interview'.

Index